MULTIPLE LENSES, MULTIPLE IMAGES

Green College Thematic Lecture Series

The Green College Thematic Lecture Series provides leading-edge theory and research in new fields of interdisciplinary scholarship. Based on a lecture program and conferences held at Green College, University of British Columbia, each book brings together scholars from several disciplines to achieve a new synthesis in knowledge around an important theme. The series provides a unique opportunity for collaboration between outstanding Canadian scholars and their counterparts internationally, as they grapple with the most important issues facing the world today.

PREVIOUSLY PUBLISHED TITLES

Governing Modern Societies, edited by Richard V. Ericson and Nico Stehr (2000)

Re-alignments of Belonging: The Shifting Foundations of Modern Nation States, edited by Sima Godfrey and Frank Unger (2004)

Love, Hate, and Fear in Canada's Cold War, edited by Richard Cavell (2004)

Multiple Lenses, Multiple Images: Perspectives on the Child across Time, Space, and Disciplines, edited by Hillel Goelman, Sheila K. Marshall, and Sally Ross (2004)

Green College Thematic Lecture Series

Multiple Lenses, Multiple Images: Perspectives on the Child across Time, Space, and Disciplines

Edited by
Hillel Goelman, Sheila K. Marshall, and Sally Ross

UNIVERSITY OF TORONTO PRESS
Toronto Buffalo London

© University of Toronto Press Incorporated 2004
Toronto Buffalo London
Printed in Canada

ISBN 0-8020-8931-3

Printed on acid-free paper

Library and Archives Canada Cataloguing in Publication

Multiple lenses, multiple images : perspectives on the child across
time, space and disciplines / edited by Hillel Goelman, Sheila K.
Marshall, and Sally Ross.

(Green College thematic lecture series)
ISBN 0-8020-8931-3

1. Children.   2. Children – Research.   I. Goelman, Hillel, 1951–
II. Marshall, Sheila, 1956–   III. Ross, Sally   IV. Series.

HQ767.9.M84 2005   305.23   C2004-904370-6

This book has been published with the assistance of Green College,
The Human Early Learning Partnership, and the School of Social Work
and Family Studies, University of British Columbia.

University of Toronto Press acknowledges the financial assistance
to its publishing program of the Canada Council for the Arts and the
Ontario Arts Council.

University of Toronto Press acknowledges the financial support for
its publishing activities of the Government of Canada through the
Book Publishing Industry Development Program (BPIDP).

Contents

MULTIPLE LENSES, MULTIPLE IMAGES

Multiple Lenses, Multiple Images:
An Introduction

HILLEL GOELMAN, SHEILA K. MARSHALL,
AND SALLY ROSS

Many North American drivers post a little yellow sign in their automobiles to alert other drivers that there is a 'Child on Board.' Recently, we observed a new variation on this sign informing us that while an actual child may not be in the car, the adult driver of the car was carrying his or her own *'Inner* Child on Board.' This play on words points to the different interpretations that are assigned to the terms 'child' and 'childhood' from colloquial, academic, and disciplinary perspectives. In the example above, we have one image of the child as young and vulnerable and another image of the child as metaphor. In the latter image, the adult, far removed from the chronological age of childhood, experiences the social and emotional needs of that stage of life as very much present. The many different meanings of the word 'child' are social constructions that are imparted and reified through the lenses of family, community, institutional, and political cultures. The major thrust of this book – and the original lecture series upon which it is based – is to learn more about childhood and about some of the lenses that are responsible for the construction of the images of children from different professional, academic, and artistic perspectives.

Since the 1960s, there has been a significant increase in the attention paid to multidisciplinary and interdisciplinary perspectives on childhood. The works of Ariès (1962) and de Mause (1976) are two major reference points in the modern study of the history of childhood and have led, directly or indirectly, to research on childhood from broader disciplinary perspectives. The study of children, which incorporates scholarship from multiple disciplines, is exemplified by collaboration between historians, sociologists, and developmental psychologists employing the life-course perspective (e.g., Elder, Modell, & Parke, 1993).

The results of such inquiry generate a greater understanding of the importance of considering historical time and social context while challenging assumptions about the universality of child development.

These assumptions are also being contested on a number of disciplinary fronts including developmental psychology (e.g., Rogoff, 1990; Valsiner, 1987) and cultural anthropology (e.g., Harkness & Super, 1996; Harkness, Raeff, & Super, 2000) and are supported by cross-disciplinary research comparing conceptualizations of children. Hwang, Lamb, and Sigel's edited volume (1996) offers an excellent overview of the various 'images' of childhood that are revealed in anthropology, psychology, religion, history, and other disciplines. Other investigations (e.g., Kuczynski, Harach, & Bernardini, 1999) compare disciplinary depictions of children as starting points for interdisciplinary collaboration in developing new areas of inquiry. The discourse on childhood is interrogating long-held assumptions and beliefs about childhood and integrating multiple disciplines and methodologies to advance child development research. Increasingly, researchers in the social sciences, medical sciences, natural sciences, health professions, and the arts have turned their attention to the ways in which their own disciplines understand the phenomenon of childhood and to the areas where the boundaries of their own knowledge can be expanded upon by the perspectives of other disciplines (e.g., Shonkoff & Phillips, 2000).

This book is intended to deepen and expand the collaborative, interdisciplinary discourse on children and childhood in various ways. The contributors were asked to reflect not just on *what* they have learned about children by peering through their respective disciplinary lenses, but *how* they came to learn what they know. That is, they were asked to carefully examine the ontological, epistemological, and methodological properties of the lenses that they use in their respective inquiries into the worlds of children and childhood. We hoped these contributions would go beyond a comprehensive description of the current state of research on childhood and offer readers the opportunity to embark on a journey of discovery in which scholars would be able to explain, compare, and contrast their respective maps of the topography of childhood. Maps are representations of a perceived reality, and this book is very much about the construction of these representations.

Three Lenses: Time, Space, and Discipline

We adopted three specific lenses to study childhood in this volume. The first is the lens of *discipline*, through which different fields of study perceive childhood. It is our view that while the viewpoints of various disciplines can provide a theoretical framework for the study of childhood, the concepts of *time* and *space* are also valuable tools for analysis. For this volume, we decided to go beyond the study of children *in* historical time and social context. The concept of *time* is addressed in these essays from two perspectives. First, we consider time as specific segments of the lifespan where *chronological* time serves to define the period (or ages or boundaries) of that temporal period in the lifespan defined as 'childhood' (or 'infancy' or 'adolescence'). Precise chronological definitions vary across legal, medical, political, and cultural perspectives, and in many ways childhood is often defined simply as that period of life when one is 'not an adult.' This volume explores the tensions within and across disciplines in regard to 'age-appropriate' norms, behaviours, and expectations for children of different ages and stages of individual development.

The second perspective on time involves the study of childhood across different historical *time* periods. Some of the contributions in this volume consider how conceptions of childhood link the evolution of ideas about child development to alterations in children's education, treatment, and the rights and responsibilities conferred upon them by the state. The lens of *time* that is employed in this book refers both to a period of growth and development and to the particular historical epoch in which individuals are embedded.

In addition to considering the disciplinary and temporal influences on childhood, the essays in this book also attend to the *spaces* children inhabit. The construction of spaces shapes both children's lives and their perceptions of themselves. For example, much research is conducted on children in the immediate *family spaces* in which they live. These spaces are considered to be major determinants of children's health and welfare as well as among the primary sources of socialization for children (Collins, Maccoby, Steinberg, Hetherington, & Bornstein, 2000; Maccoby, 1992). Other spaces that are used to frame the study of children and childhood include the wide range of formal and informal settings, or *institutional spaces*, in which children participate, such as childcare centres, hospitals, schools, and community centres. Families and institutional spaces are embedded within broader *cultural spaces* that contribute to the shaping of values, beliefs, and behaviour. Cultural spaces often do not have physical boundaries in the same way as the home or the school, but they emerge as representations in law, literature, television, and other written or visual media. Within these spaces, children are normally characterized through adult forms of expression that attempt to portray the lived experience of childhood. The images and voices of the children that are captured and then re-released in these cultural spaces can also reflect emergent views of childhood within political and policy discourse. The *political spaces* reflect basic societal values and establish official parameters regarding children's rights and the state's involvement in those rights. During periods of political change, images of children may offer critical information about ongoing processes of cultural transformation.

The Lenses, Authors, and Chapters in this Volume

This volume brings together the views of writers and researchers in a range of disciplines including law, cultural studies, history, psychology, family studies, developmental disabilities, literature, public policy, landscape architecture, and education. Yet, while the 'lenses' heuristic offers certain advantages in discussing and deconstructing traditional disciplinary perspectives used in the study of children and childhood, it also has limitations. The image of a lens seems in some ways too inert and too mechanistic to capture the processes of reflection and representation that are involved in meaningful inquiry. Modes of perception do not simply detect signals from an observable reality but organize them into meaningful patterns and relationships based on past history and future expectations. In our experience, a lens does not simply allow a phenomenon to be observed; it also shapes our perception and understanding of the observed. Artificially teasing apart the lens from the construct might appear to be a route to simplifying the study of the construct. We believe that it provides an opportunity to study both the lens and the phenomenon as well as highlighting the complexity of studying children.

No single chapter in this book can be taken as typical or representative of any one discipline, as differences within disciplines are as sharp as they are across disciplines. Additionally, each chapter studies children within a setting and/or time that shapes the orientation to, and construction of, the phenomenon of childhood. Taken together, then, the multiple lenses of the various disciplines, contextualized in time and space, contribute to valuable insights for studying childhood. To give the reader a sense of the depth of analysis provided in this collection of essays, below we highlight a number of critical features that thread the chapters into a complete work.

In an effort to contextualize our current perceptions of children and childhood, we begin with chapters that introduce us to the children of previous eras and to the lenses through which they were perceived. Historian Adriana Benzaquén's essay 'Childhood, History, and the Sciences of Childhood' argues that during the eighteenth century 'the child' first became an object of scientific exploration. She cites the research program of the Société des observateurs de l'homme (Society of Observers of Man) along with the work of Locke, Rousseau, Voltaire, Montesquieu, and Diderot, through which the study of childhood was objectified and seen as central to an understanding of the development of civilizations. Benzaquén describes the movement to formulate a scientific understanding of children created by an 'adult-as-expert' approach to the nature of childhood.

Questions about the inherent nature of the child and a society's medical and judicial treatment of children in different historical times are raised in legal scholar Anne McGillivray's 'Childhood in the Shadow of Parens Patriae.' McGillivray uses the lenses of legal and historical scholarship to discuss changes in perceptions of the nature of the child, the role of the family, and the responsibility of the state in different time periods. She traces to ancient Rome the perception that the child was essentially seen as property, a view that continued until the period of early common law. In post-eighteenth-century statutory regimes, legal systems upheld the child as a vehicle of state interests, and it was only after the Second World War that Canadian law began to see children as having inherent rights of their own.

Taken together, the chapters by Benzaquén and McGillivray demonstrate how law, social science, and natural science all contributed to the construction of images of 'the child' in order to fit into and to justify the creation of each of these adult-created 'expert' disciplines.

Naomi Sokoloff poses an important question about the extent to which literature can provide insight into the interior landscapes of the worlds of children. Sokoloff in 'The Voices of Children in Literature' explores the ways in which adults represent children in literature by attempting to read, intuit and describe the inner reality of the mind of a child. The imaginary child in the novel she has selected to discuss, Momik, carries on internal dialogues with himself that we are privy to only because an adult author has created them for us. Sokoloff's chapter points us in the direction of a set of very fundamental and, indeed, troubling questions. What, precisely, is going on inside the heads of children? How do children construct reality from their experiences? And can we trust adults to accurately or adequately represent these inner experiences? In short, what is it that we are hearing when we listen to adults' representations of children's voices through literature? Sokoloff emphasizes the importance and the ultimate mystery of children's lived and imagined lives. Gaining an understanding about these realms requires careful observation of the world of childhood informed by sensitivity, empathy, and, ultimately, a sense of awe and wonder.

These initial three chapters introduce the reader to adultified projections of children in history, law, and literature; they are followed by three chapters that focus on the minds and bodies of contemporary children and the spaces where these children play, learn, and grow. The chapter by a professor of landscape architecture, Susan Herrington's 'Muscle Memory: Reflections on the North American Schoolyard,' provides a bridge to the earlier chapters by reviewing the history and development of outdoor play spaces in schoolyards. According to Herrington, industrialization has exerted a different kind of influence in the public-school setting, reflected in the regimented exercise 'training' that children began to receive early in the twentieth century as well as in the construction of schoolyards. Herrington demonstrates the ways in which adult understandings of children's learning and the role that children fill in the 'natural' order of the world were manifested in public-school curricula and the physical structure of play spaces. Schools 'were assigned the task of shaping and aligning the idea of childhood' as part of North American cities' role 'as critical armatures to the capitalistic system, employing, processing and reproducing vast quantities of human and "natural" resources.' This approach stands in stark contrast to early kindergartens, established in Germany in the nineteenth century by Friedrich Fröbel, which maintained a focus on the natural world as a basis from which the child could observe, explore, and relate with nature's cycles. Later, the ascent of industrial life contributed to the transformation of children's outdoor play spaces into mechanisms for regulation and control. Herrington argues persuasively that the cognitive and physical development of children and youth are shaped by programs of ideology based on productive economic activity, the accumulation of wealth, and the consumption of resources.

Similar to Herrington's description of how adult understandings of children serve to shape the regulation of children's bodies, special educator Marci Hanson's 'Disability in Childhood: Views within the Context of Society' further underscores how a given lens on child development can determine the ways in which adults perceive and treat children. The chapter opens with a description of Annie, an eight-week-old child diagnosed with Down's syndrome and a heart condition when Hanson first met her. Annie's parents were advised by the 'adults-as-experts' of that particular historical time period to place their daughter into an institution that was designated as appropriate for a child with her condition. The 'adults-as-experts' of the day were disproved nineteen years later when Annie graduated from community college. Hanson argues that concepts of 'development' and 'disability' are deeply embedded in historical and cultural perceptions. Wide variations in culture and context can produce 'constructs of disability' that largely determine the extent to which an individual's behaviour is seen as typical or atypical for that age, gender, and social environment. Echoing McGillivray and Benzaquén, Hanson draws on historical perceptions of disability to show the evolution from vilification to pity, to tolerance, and, hopefully, to inclusion. Hanson argues that the creation of 'normal' or 'acceptable' patterns of child development and behaviour depend largely upon the historical and sociocultural contexts in which the child and family are immersed.

Michael Lamb's 'Developmental Theory and Public Policy: A Cross-National Perspective,' Jayanthi Mistry and Virginia Diez's 'Multiple Constructions of Childhood,' and Daniel Scott's 'Spirituality and Children: Paying Attention to Experience' all challenge assumptions inherent in the developmental psychology lens. These assumptions tend to ignore the effects of cultural values on child-rearing practices and subsequent outcomes in child development. Lamb addresses the research on mother-infant attachment as observed through the 'Strange Situation' paradigm, examining how infants interpret and react to a situation where their primary caregiver leaves them and then rejoins them after a brief separation. He documents the wide range of infant responses between cultures and then illustrates the ways in which the adult world of developmental psychology interprets behaviours as 'secure' or 'insecure' attachment patterns. Lamb concludes that 'an inclusive and successful science of child development is unattainable unless careful attention is paid to societies with widely divergent goals and patterns of social organization.'

The chapter by Mistry and Diez parallels Lamb's analysis with the assertion that developmental psychology is highly limited by its reliance on Western definitions of the self that emphasize a person as 'an independent, self-contained entity.' The authors draw on studies from a variety of cultures to demonstrate the value of a sociocultural approach to understanding childhood. For example, they cite the extensive research of LeVine et al. (1994), which compares the child-rearing practices of urban, middle-class communities in the northeastern United States with those of the northeast African Gusii people. The evidence presented by Lamb and by Mistry and Diez indicates that approaches to parental caregiving and the learning and development of children have adaptive value within a particular cultural context. Respective differences between cultures, then, underscore variations in the extent to which emphasis is placed, for example, on the autonomy and independence of an individual or on the cooperative relationships among families and communities. The uniqueness of these sociocultural values is to be accounted for in the assessment of children's health and development, the benchmarking of normative criteria for child outcomes, and the enactment of public policy.

Like Lamb as well as Mistry and Diez, Daniel Scott from the field of child and youth care highlights how child development is influenced by sociocultural values. He extends this argument to the issue of children's spirituality in industrialized countries. Scott suggests that the broader culture and, in turn, research and theory tend to disregard children's spiritual development. In his chapter on children's spirituality, Scott points out how childhood has been viewed as an unlikely period during which divine or mystical experiences might occur. However, such views are challenged by the United Nations Convention on the Rights of the Child (1989), which describes opportunities for spiritual development as a fundamental right for children. Scott advocates an acknowledgment of accounts of early spiritual encounters, independent of religious practices or experiences. Rather than viewing children as incapable of spiritual life, Scott suggests that attention to their own spiritual development will recognize children's rights to access this aspect of their life and contribute to understanding spiritual development across the lifespan. Attention to children's spiritual experiences requires theoreticians and researchers who do not dismiss spirituality or the capacity of children to contribute to their own development. With regard to this last point on children's contributions to their own development, Scott alludes to a view of children that is articulated more specifically by Kuczynski and Lollis.

Leon Kuczynski and Susan Lollis in 'The Child as Agent in Family Life' point out that much of the discourse around childhood in all disciplines is characterized by the construction of the passive child, whose role is largely defined and determined by the adult world. This view of the child as a 'passive object' rather than as an 'active subject' has also been reported and critiqued in the essays on law (McGillivray), public policy (Lamb), history (Benzaquén), developmental psychology (Mistry and Diez), and spirituality (Scott). Kuczynski and Lollis endorse an explicit shift in this understanding by arguing that children are active participants in shaping their environments and highlight the reasons for the emergence of this tendency to construct a passive view of children.

Focusing on relationships between parents and children, at the core of their argument is the notion that agency is a characteristic of both children and adults, a view that becomes acceptable when the concept of 'agency' is separated from the concept of 'power.' Natural imbalances of power between children and adults tend to conceal the real agentic capabilities of children. Additionally, expert knowledge, a form of power (French & Raven, 1959), yields a language that enhances the view of children as passive recipients of agentic parental socialization. Common expert terminology applied to the processes of 'parenting' such as 'teaching,' 'disciplining,' and 'child management' strongly suggests that parents have agency in the relationship. In coordination with the terms applied to adults are references to children such as 'learning,' 'non-compliance,' 'obedience,' and 'misbehaviour' that assign children to the 'proper role' of conforming to parental expectations. Understanding the distinction between power and agency opens up new territory for exploring child development and children's interpersonal relationships. Kuczynski and Lollis document how their interest in seeing children's agency as part of the socialization process has resulted in trading one set of distinctive images for another.

The book concludes with John Willinsky's 'Childhood's Ends.' This chapter is based upon the excellent and well-thought-out response he wrote and presented following Sokoloff's original lecture. Willinsky questions whether literature is indeed a 'lens' on childhood and whether it should be included in a volume along with disciplines such as history, psychology, law, and sociology that serve as the lenses for the other chapters in this book. Willinsky draws cautions and opens possibilities at the same time. He points to the possibility of understanding language (and literature) as both a lens through which the child is perceived and as the subject that is perceived through the lens, as childhood is experienced and expressed through and with language. In writing about literature, Willinsky also complements and extends the historical perspectives to which we were introduced in McGillivray's and

Benzaquén's essays by presenting the work of authors such as Wordsworth, Dickens, and Rousseau. Willinsky asks if it is bad or deceptive to use childhood to understand our own adult lives. He responds to this question by stating that 'It is a reminder that literature, no less than our other intellectual efforts, contributes to the very sense and sensibility of the world that we construct. It is a reminder that we have always to study the lens that we would fabricate ... as ... a source of clarity not otherwise available to us.'

The authors contributing to this volume accepted the challenge of going beyond descriptions of the current state of research in their respective fields. The chapters in this collection challenge a number of taken-for-granted notions about children and the way in which they are studied. More importantly, this collection highlights assumptions that distract attention from, or focus attention on, various characteristics associated with childhood or the spaces that children inhabit and then demonstrates how interest or inattention shapes conceptions and treatment of children. Taken together, the chapters demonstrate the plasticity of images and how the representations of children shape, and are shaped by, a range of social institutions.

We hope the various maps of the topography of childhood offered in this volume provide readers with opportunities to explore new or unfamiliar regions of childhood, appreciate familiar territory, and imagine uncharted terrains. Reading any one chapter or a combination of chapters will, we hope, generate a process of 'seeing' images of children in research and practice that is engaging, not easily exhausted, and of practical significance.

References

Ariès, P. (1962). *Centuries of childhood: A social history of family life*. New York: Vintage.

Collins, W.A., Maccoby, E.E., Steinberg, L., Hetherington, E.M., & Bornstein, M.H. (2000). Contemporary research on parenting: The case for nature and nurture. *American Psychologist, 55*, 218–232.

de Mause, L. (1976). *The history of childhood*. London: Souvenir Press.

Elder, G.H., Modell, J., & Parke, R.D. (1993). *Children in time and place: Developmental and historical insights*. Cambridge: Cambridge University Press.

French, J.R. P., Jr., & Raven, B. (1959). The bases of social power. In D.

Cartwright (Ed.), *Studies in social power* (pp. 150–167). Ann Arbor: University of Michigan Press.

Harkness, S., Raeff, C., & Super, C.M. (Eds.). (2000). Variability in the social construction of the child. *New Directions for Child and Adolescent Development 87*, Spring.

Harkness, S., & Super, C.M. (Eds.). (1996). *Parents' cultural belief systems: Their origins, expressions, and consequences.* New York: Guilford Press.

Hwang, C. Philip, Lamb, Michael E., and Sigel, Irving E. (Eds.) (1996). *Images of childhood.* NJ: Lawrence Erlbaum.

Kuczynski, L., Harach, L., & Bernardini, S.C. (1999). Psychology's child meets sociology's child: Agency, influence and power in parent-child relationships. In C.L. Shehan (Ed.), *Through the eyes of the child: Revisioning children as active agents of family life* (pp. 21–52). Stamford, CT: JAI Press.

LeVine, R.A., Dixon, S. LeVine, S., Richman, A., Leiderman, P.H., Keefer, C., & Brazelton, T.B. (1994). *Child care and culture: Lessons from Africa.* Cambridge: Cambridge University Press.

Maccoby, E.E. (1992). The role of parents in the socialization of children: An historical overview. *Developmental Psychology, 28,* 1006–1017.

Rogoff, B. (1990). *Apprenticeship in thinking.* New York: Oxford University Press.

Shonkoff, J., & Phillips, D.A. (Eds.). (2000). *From neurons to neighborhoods: The science of early child development.* Washington, DC: National Academy Press.

Valsiner, J. (1987). *Culture and the development of children's action.* Chichester, UK: Wiley.

1

Childhood, History, and the Sciences of Childhood

ADRIANA S. BENZAQUÉN

What do we know about children and where does this knowledge come from? What is the relation between the concept and category of childhood and the lives and experiences of children? How does what we (adults) know about 'the child' inform what we do to and with children? Any serious attempt to engage with these questions about the relation between childhood and knowledge must first confront, and necessarily challenge, two issues. The first is the long-standing view of childhood as a natural or biological phenomenon falling outside the reach of historical and philosophical inquiry. The second is the disciplinary division of labour according to which 'the child' belongs exclusively to experts and professionals of childhood or to marginalized specializations within the humanities and social sciences (sociology of childhood, anthropology of childhood, history of childhood, philosophy of childhood, and so forth). My opening questions are indebted to recent critical analyses of gender and sexuality, racism, colonialism, and psychiatric expertise showing that certain categories – woman, the homosexual, the savage, the native, the mad – were socially and discursively constructed in particular historical contexts in ways that contributed to the oppression and disqualification of the people who fell (or were made to fall) under those categories. To what extent can these critical analyses shed light on the contemporary positioning of childhood and children, its presuppositions, and its implications?

Two conceptions of childhood dominate the many discourses on childhood and children in the contemporary world. The first one is the *scientific conception of childhood*. The depth knowledge about children postulates that children develop, that this development takes them through a series of stages which may be scientifically mapped, and that in each stage they have needs that must be appropriately met to avoid long-term undesirable effects. (I borrow the notions of 'depth' and 'surface' knowledge from Ian Hacking, who in turn derives them from Michel Foucault's *savoir* and *connaissance*. 'Depth knowledge' is the underlying set of assumptions on the basis of which many types of 'surface knowledge' may be formulated.)[1] The sciences of childhood are grounded on this depth knowledge.

Since their inception in the early nineteenth century, and with renewed assiduity and authority since the turn of the twentieth century – with the rise of the two powerful forces of Child Study and psychoanalysis – the sciences of childhood have put forward a variety of models and specific contents to flesh out the notions of development, stages, needs, and long-term effects, but beyond (or underneath) countless surface debates, these very notions and this general view of the child have rarely been questioned. The knowledge produced by the specialized child disciplines is tied to institutional sites (school, family, hospital, child clinic, welfare agency) and practical applications (education, social work, therapy). The 'developing child' grounds commonsense and expert views of education, good parenting, health and welfare provisions, social policy, and advertising and marketing campaigns.

In principle, the sciences of childhood purport to uphold an understanding of the 'normal child' clearly distinguished from pathological childhoods in need of varying degrees of normalizing intervention. These sciences, however, also conceive *all children* as somehow abnormal or pathological in relation to the (adult) human standard (children are seen as not-yet-fully-human, not-yet-developed, adults-to-be). This is one of the reasons why, in the historical emergence and elaboration of scientific knowledge about childhood, 'abnormal' or extraordinary children were often privileged as objects of knowledge presumed to reveal something about all children.[2]

The scientific view of the developing child (or, in other words, the 'developmental paradigm') originated in Europe and North America, yet lately it has been exported and enforced throughout the world by means of international child aid programs. Written into the 1989 UN Convention on the Rights of the Child, it now gives universal shape to the normal and desirable childhood.[3] In addition, the formulation of a scientific understanding of childhood and of children's needs has had as a historical correlate a narrowing of socially sanctioned relations between adults and children. Ever more exclusive and proprietary parent-child relations are complemented or, when parents are found wanting, supplanted by relations between children and professionals of childhood (educators, social workers, doctors, counsellors, and so on). The tendency is towards allowing and accepting relations between children and adults only when they are based on shared blood (or, in more current parlance, shared genes) or on the adults' expertise.

I noted that there is a second, very different, but equally dominant conception of childhood. In modern Western societies, 'the child' is not only an object known by various disciplines and made to participate in social and cultural institutions, but also a pervasive image or figure in the social and individual adult imagination. Since at least the Romantic movement, marked by Rousseau's pedagogical musings and Blake's and Wordsworth's poetry of childhood, the image of the child has offered one of the most vigorous embodiments for adult attitudes, desires, and beliefs. 'The child' stands for the prelapsarian (or pre-modern) vision of innocence, purity, and unity with nature. In turn, the remembered, imagined, and desired child encapsulates the modern idea (and lived experience) of the adult self as a self *within*, the product of a personal history.[4] Because the child is construed as an internalized memory of the adult's past, childhood is seen as central to the forma-tion and expression of adult identity (the adult self). The twentieth century's foremost theory of subjectivity, psychoanalysis, granted child-hood a position of privilege as a means to explain adult origins, to account for how *we* got to be who we are. In psychoanalysis, childhood is what has been forgotten or repressed and for this very reason affects the adult in the present and must be remembered, reconstructed, or recovered through the work of analysis. This positioning of childhood continues in the many theories and therapies that directly or indirectly evolved from psychoanalysis. The uses of childhood in the modern adult imagination are many, for instance, inner child therapies, the memoir boom, and in general the notion that childhood explains the adult in the present.

For more than two hundred years, children have been at the receiving end of a project of knowledge-production in which the positions of subject and object of knowledge – adult and child – are painstakingly distinguished and hierarchically fixed. The same type of positioning was once common in the dominant forms of knowledge about other kinds of marginalized and subordinate people (women, homosexuals, the primitive, the mad) which are in the process of being contested, giving rise to political movements (like feminism) and academic disci-plines (like gay and lesbian studies) that question definitions imposed from outside and inaugurate collective spaces for self-definition. Still, no major discourse, discipline, or political movement has yet surfaced in which the *subject* is the (self-defining, self-knowing) child.

The Problem

The scientific approach to the child relies on the authority of science in modern societies. Science claims to know children and what they need, how they develop, how adults must intervene in their lives, based on its discovery of true knowledge by using scientific research methods. The imaginary and psychological uses of childhood rely on a different kind of powerful authority: the authority of experience, that is, the adult's past experience of childhood, preserved in memory or recovered through therapy. In both cases, knowledge about 'the child' is produced not by children but by adults.

In this chapter I propose to explore some aspects of the first, scientific conception of childhood. In the last few years, significant (but still peripheral) challenges to the universal legitimacy of developmental knowledge of the child have been posed. Recent critics of the developmental view of the child argue that developmental psychology construes child development as a natural process of unfolding, and as a consequence historically, culturally, and socially variable processes are naturalized; that it assumes a notion of progress from an undeveloped to a developed state (from lower to higher, immature to mature, inferior to superior) that devalues the child and the childish; that it isolates the child (and the child-mother dyad) as the object of study and ignores the child's enmeshment in a social world; that it forgets the work required to bring up children; and that it pathologizes different forms and outcomes of growing up (developmental stages cannot be skipped, only reached by different children at different paces).[5]

In their efforts to understand the developmental paradigm and question its universalist aspirations, critical psychologists and sociologists have had recourse to historical and anthropological evidence showing significant variations in cultural concepts of childhood and in children's experiences. A few historians of psychology and the social sciences, inspired by Foucault's archaeology and genealogy of the human sciences, have historicized developmental knowledge and portrayed the political and social struggles that accompanied its emergence. They argue that the combined action of medicine, psychology, schooling, and different incarnations of philanthropy, social reformism, and social work permitted the creation both of a body of knowledge about children articulated in terms of normality and pathology and of a set of normalizing strategies to deal with the variously perceived problems of poverty and pauperism, moral degeneration, mental defectiveness, and delinquency.[6] In brief, the critics of the developmental paradigm question the view of childhood as a natural, biological, universal, and transhistorical state. They historicize the developmental knowledge of childhood (which, in John Morss's terms, has 'biologized' childhood), and in so doing they show how childhood is reproduced *as* a natural, biological, universal, and transhistorical state. Moreover, these critics emphasize the entanglement of childhood and scientific knowledge, suggesting that in many ways the recent history of childhood is the history of knowledge about 'the child.'

From a historical perspective, two observations remain to be made. First, the scientific view of the child is a relatively recent phenomenon. If we consider European and North American societies and cultures 250 (or more) years ago, we do not find anything even remotely resembling the contemporary sciences of childhood – no developmental depth knowledge, no research methods or experiments especially designed to study children, and (except for a few notable exceptions) no statements expressing the desire to study children or the conviction that this study would be interesting or yield useful results. Second, we do not know the history of the scientific view of the child. We do not know exactly when, why, and how the study of childhood came to be seen as interesting and useful. I find it utterly puzzling that although the developmental paradigm is one of the most established scientific paradigms of the contemporary world, with vast consequences for all children and all the adults who are involved with children in any capacity, for the most part we ignore its history. To grasp this incongruity, think of the number of scholarly studies devoted to the history of the theory of evolution or quantum mechanics. No comparable scholarship exists for the sciences of childhood. It would appear that once interest in studying children became widespread and the 'developing child' established as the dominant understanding of childhood, they both seemed so obvious, so *natural*, that an examination of how they came into being was not deemed necessary.

This then is the problem: When, why, and how did Western societies make the study of children such a central and consequential endeavour? The few published works touching on the history of scientific knowledge of children focus almost exclusively on the late nineteenth century, the period when developmental psychology emerged as a full-fledged science. However, I want to suggest that we cannot understand the emergence of developmental psychology without a parallel investigation of the history of the developmental *paradigm* – that is to say, we need to probe the *pre*history of full-fledged developmental psychology and the conditions of possibility for the rise of the 'developing child.'

The history of the sciences of childhood and the scientific study of children is significantly related both to the history of childhood and to the history of science. In 1960, Philippe Ariès's *L'enfant et la vie familiale sous l'Ancien Régime* (translated into English in 1962 as *Centuries of Childhood*) inaugurated the field of history of childhood with the simple but provocative claim that childhood has a history.[7] Ariès's argument that the idea of childhood did not exist in the Middle Ages and the Renaissance and was 'discovered' in Western societies during the sixteenth and seventeenth centuries opened up a heated scholarly controversy and was challenged by subsequent historians of childhood in the Middle Ages. But Ariès's linked conclusion that from the late eighteenth century onward childhood increasingly became an object of social and scientific concern proved much less controversial.

The field of history of childhood has been steadily growing since the publication of Ariès's work. Historians of Europe and North America have produced cultural histories of childhood (studies of concepts, images, or representations of childhood and attitudes and feelings towards childhood and children), social histories of children (attempts to recapture or recreate the experiences of children in the past), as well as histories of parents and children, child rearing, children in the family, and child abuse.[8] Because most children in the past did not leave written traces (they either did not write or wrote texts that were little valued and seldom preserved), the majority of historical sources on childhood and children are documents written by adults. Historians of childhood have had to be creative in their search for relevant sources and innovative in their reading and interpretation of them.

The history of the scientific study of childhood stands at the intersection of the history of childhood and the history of science – principally the small but growing field of history of the human sciences, which, as I noted above, has been heavily influenced by Foucault's historico-philosophical inquiry into the historical production of knowledge about people and the role of this knowledge in producing and reproducing unequal and oppressive relations of power.[9] The history of the 'science of childhood' is neither a cultural history of childhood nor a social history of children but a history of the manifold relations between childhood and the knowledge produced about it by theorists, experimenters, and experts, the methods used to produce this knowledge; the institutions that sponsored, facilitated, and funded it; the audiences (including parents and educators) that received and regularly acted on it; and, most importantly, the children who were studied, observed, experimented on, and directly or indirectly shaped by the applications of scientific knowledge of 'the child.' The aim of this history is to explain how and why the progress of childhood from non-existence or relative obscurity in the early modern period to the cultural obsession childhood has become in the present was largely effected through an ongoing project of knowledge-production leading to the formation of sciences of childhood and to the very particular ways in which adults now know and relate to children.[10]

I use quotation marks in my references to 'the child' in this chapter not as a concession to much maligned (and often misinterpreted) postmodernist theories according to which discourse constructs reality, or there is nothing outside the text, but in keeping with analytic models recently developed in the history and philosophy of science. The investigation of the scientific study of 'the child' is a case study in what historian of science Lorraine Daston calls 'applied ontology' and philosopher of science Ian Hacking calls 'historical epistemology.'[11] Ontology is the branch of philosophy that deals with the nature of being. *Applied* ontology, Daston proposes, must be concerned with how scientific objects 'come into being' *as* scientific objects in definite historical and social contexts. Some scientific objects, like DNA or quarks, come into being only as scientific objects, while others, like dreams or children, are 'quotidian objects' (objects from everyday life) that at a certain point become scientific objects as well.[12] The history of the scientific study of childhood seeks to trace the emergence of 'the child' as an object of interest for scientists and an object of knowledge for science. The child of science is not merely a true distillation, representation, understanding, or explanation of a hypothetical 'real child' out there, but a scientific object with specific properties that need to be analysed, together with the impact the scientific child has had and has on quotidian (real-life) children since its emergence. Epistemology is the branch of philosophy that deals with the nature of knowledge. *Historical* epistemology, Hacking claims, must be concerned with how scientific concepts and methods (ways of finding out) come into being. One of the main tasks the history of the scientific knowledge of 'the child' must accomplish is to adequately account for why and how the three organizing concepts of *educability, normality,* and *development* were attached to childhood in the early nineteenth century and have since become the major tools we use to think about, understand, raise, educate, and intervene in the lives of children.

Stemming from the powerful Enlightenment idea of perfectibility (first introduced by Rousseau in the *Discourse on the Origins of Inequality*),[13] educability is the notion that children are inherently educable. It not only came to be seen as an essential attribute of childhood (i.e., of *all* children) but also led in the nineteenth century to the conceptualization of a continuum of ability (i.e., not all children are educable to the same degree). The concept of development also appeared in the eighteenth century, but we do not know precisely when (and why) interest in the development of the (child's) faculties gave way to monitoring of the child's development within a framework of normality and abnormality. Through the concepts of educability, normality, and development, the sciences of childhood would in turn form two crucial connections. The first one is the idea that education is inseparable from health. Educability was tied to normality with the result that from a certain point in time it became a conceptual and practical impossibility for a child to be simultaneously normal and 'ineducable' (an educational failure to whatever extent, in the opinion of educational authorities and experts or according to accepted standards or measures of assessment). Failure to learn or perform satisfactorily in school came to indicate abnormality and warrant corrective (normalizing) intervention.[14] The second one is the idea that children's education must be grounded on knowledge about children themselves – what they are, what they are capable of, how they develop, how they learn. The history of the sciences of childhood must explore how these concepts, ideas, and connections between concepts and ideas did not simply spring from great minds or exist exclusively in texts but were forged and moulded in practices and in relations involving adults and children, researchers and experimental subjects, physicians and patients, educators and pupils, reformers and objects to be reformed, professionals and their clients, sporting a variety of interests, motivations, and goals.

The history of the 'science of childhood' must be more than a disciplinary history of developmental psychology.[15] Histories of a discipline written by contemporary professionals or practitioners of the discipline generally suffer from two limitations: first, they tend to look in the past for antecedents of present theories and practices, assessing earlier science in terms of whether it contributed to the progressive accumulation of knowledge in the discipline; second, they approach the past through the lens of present disciplinary boundaries. But to understand the rise of interest in studying children as a historical phenomenon it is necessary first to reconstruct the early manifestations of this interest and the early studies of childhood in their own terms. Only then will we be in a position to ascertain to what extent they provided a basis for the later establishment of developmental psychology, and also to determine whether the pre-developmental study of childhood contained other modes of knowing children no longer available to us. Moreover, even at this initial stage in the research it may be safely argued that 'the child' came into being as a scientific object in the eighteenth and early nineteenth centuries in the context of a very different, and shifting, disciplinary configuration. Because many fields of inquiry participated in the rise of the science of childhood – philosophy, metaphysics, and epistemology; medicine and hygiene; the natural history of man (or anthropology); moral science, pedagogy, and psychology – a history of this science must examine a wide range of texts, investigators, institutions, and approaches.

Two Examples

Historians of developmental and child psychology have generally focused on the late nineteenth century, either not paying much attention to the eighteenth century or limiting their treatment of the period to perfunctory references to the influence of Locke and Rousseau and the widespread change in attitudes toward childhood and child rearing their works both contributed to and exemplify. It was during the eighteenth century, however, and especially in its second half, that 'the child' became an object of scientific concern. In what follows I present two examples of this concern as suggestive markers of all that remains to be investigated. The research program of the Société des Observateurs de l'Homme (Society of Observers of Man) makes visible the uncertain but increasingly important role of children as scientific objects at the end of the eighteenth century, while the treatment of childhood and children in Buffon's natural history constitutes a striking instance of pre-developmental scientific study of children which has so far received scant attention from historians of childhood or science.[16]

The Society of Observers of Man, founded in Paris in December 1799 and counting among its members many of the great figures in French sciences and letters of the time, was part, together with the ideologues and the second class of the Institut National (the class of Moral and Political Sciences), of that institutionally short-lived but historically influential movement which in the aftermath of the French Revolution lay the foundations for the social and behavioural sciences.[17] The program of the Observers of Man was a comprehensive and interdisciplinary 'science of man' encompassing the study of the physical, moral, and intellectual aspects of human individuals and societies.

In its public meeting of 7 July 1801, its permanent secretary, Louis-François Jauffret, read a paper summarizing the Society's principles and projects.[18] Jauffret maintained that the science of man, the most noble of all, was also the most neglected. The Observers of Man were determined to rectify this situation by undertaking an ambitious research program, embracing, among other things, the differences between man and the animals, the varieties of the human species and the variations between individuals, the origin of languages and ideas, and the faculties of the soul. In this same paper, Jauffret proposed that the scientific, empirical study of children was worthy of being pursued by serious investigators. The Observers of Man, he explained, attached enormous importance to the collection of well-made observations on the first developments of the human faculties:

> This task, as new as it is interesting, indicated by the Society to the true friends of philosophy, is no doubt surrounded by numerous difficulties. But these difficulties are not insurmountable; and why, besides, would one not find a certain appeal in the pleasure and the honour of overcoming them? Why would one not find the same charm in considering with an attentive eye the first glimmer of the developing mind, in keeping a detailed journal of the progress of intelligence in a child, in seeing the birth of his faculties one from the other, than one finds in watching closely the habits and industry of an insect, in observing the blooming of some foreign plant?[19]

Living in an age in which scientific research on children does not need any special justification, readers may be taken aback, as I was when I first encountered this document, by the lengths to which Jauffret had to go to entice his listeners to apply themselves to the study of children. As added enticement, the Observers of Man offered a prize, to be given in the year XI of the Republic (1802–3), for the best essay that would 'determine, by daily observation of one or several newborn children, the order in which the physical, intellectual, and moral faculties develop, and to what extent this development is assisted or opposed by the influence of the objects surrounding the child, and by the influence, even greater, of the persons who communicate with him.'[20]

The history of the scientific study of children that I am proposing needs to inquire into the preconditions and assess the import of these two statements. On the one hand, the fact that children were included in the anthropological program of the Observers of Man indicates that the Observers realized the scientific and practical importance of the study of childhood. On the other hand, in his injunction to study children Jauffret acknowledged both that this study was 'surrounded by numerous difficulties' and that, unlike insects or plants, children were not then seen as particularly attractive objects of observation. The Observers' attempt to constitute a science of childhood thus faced the need to neutralize the prevalent view that the study of children was beset with practical and epistemological difficulties and uninteresting to boot.[21]

The Observers' efforts must be situated in relation to earlier expressions of interest in studying children. Throughout the eighteenth century, some philosophers, natural historians, and physicians began to discern in the study of children a means to find answers to questions – about human nature, the progress towards civilization, the development of the faculties and morality – that had long preoccupied them. Beginning in the late seventeenth century, with John Locke's empiricist philosophy, childhood began to be understood and interrogated as a figure of origins.[22] Locke evinced a pronounced interest in children, whom he viewed as key evidence for his claim that ideas and knowledge are not innate but have their origin in experience. He also believed that no reliable method for studying children was then available, suspecting perhaps that this study might be altogether impossible. Because adults neither recall the origin of their own ideas and knowledge nor have access to the contents of young children's minds, Locke restricted his study of childhood to observation of young children's limited behaviour while speculating on what might be going on in their minds. By positing the need to study children if one hoped to understand the origin of ideas and language yet simultaneously casting doubt on the empirical possibility of this study, Locke raised a problem that would run through eighteenth-century human science and whose echoes may still be detected in Jauffret's 1801 paper. In this sense it is possible to construe the famous 'statue' imagined by mid-eighteenth-century sensationist epistemologists Condillac and Bonnet as a speculative 'substitute' for the child.[23]

My second example is the work of the naturalist Georges-Louis Leclerc, count of Buffon, director of the Jardin du Roi (Royal Botanical Garden), who during his lifetime (1707–88) enjoyed fame and honours rivalled only by those of his Swedish counterpart Linnaeus and other celebrated philosophes such as Voltaire, Montesquieu, Diderot, and Rousseau. In his multi-volume, hugely successful *Histoire naturelle, générale et particulière* (1749–67), Buffon covered all aspects of nature but placed 'man' at the centre, as the knowing subject seeking to understand the natural world around him and as an object of knowledge. Buffon first approached childhood in his *Natural History of Man* (1749), a treatise which took up almost two of the first three volumes of the *Natural History* and contained chapters on the dual nature of man (soul and body), on the ages (childhood, puberty, adulthood, old age), on the senses, and on variations within the human species.[24]

The chapter 'On Childhood' combined three kinds of information: anatomical, physiological, and psychological description of the child; description of child-rearing customs in Europe and elsewhere; and hygienic advice and prescription. Buffon began with the newborn child, urging readers to suspend 'the disgust that the details of the care this state requires may arouse in us' (49) and acknowledge the fragile state in which we all entered life. Weaker than any animal, unable to move or make use of his organs and senses, in need of all kinds of care, the child (Buffon does not use the word 'baby') is 'an image of misery and pain' (49). Buffon gave a detailed physical description of the child at birth, considering size, weight, hair and eye colour, the proportion between head and body, the condition of the skin, and the rate of growth. Much of the chapter was taken up by a recital of the child's sensory awakening. Although we do not remember our first sensations, in the newborn child's weeping Buffon saw a sign that the first sensation is pain.

Because for Buffon the weak, helpless human child demands constant care, the description of the child was inextricable from the description of the child-rearing practices of adults. Buffon used the method of comparison to criticize practices he deemed unhealthy or harmful. His impassioned condemnation of swaddling as an infringement of the child's freedom that moreover delays growth and diminishes the strength of the body was supported by examples of the opposite (and harmless) customs of the Siamese, Japanese, and Indian peoples and North and South American 'savages.' In his view, only maternal tenderness could sustain the continuous and strenuous care so necessary to the child, whereas mercenary nurses were prone to neglect or harm the children in their care. Insisting on the importance of breast milk, he offered advice on the choice of a wet nurse, with the caveat that the mother's milk was to be preferred. Buffon inserted hygienic advice in a work of natural history because he was deeply concerned about the high rate of infant mortality. His analysis of mortality tables led to the 'very sad observation' (65) that half the human species died in the first few years of life (before the age of three in London, seven or eight years after birth in France). To prevent 'the loss of an infinity of men, who ... are the true wealth of a state' (67), Buffon suggested that an end be put to the dangerous practice of placing foundlings in large urban institutions and that these children be raised instead in individual homes in the city or, better yet, in the country. The chapter ended with a review of the beginnings of speech and reading. Granting that some children begin to read at three and read perfectly by four, Buffon nevertheless doubted that this was useful in the long run. Young prodigies often grew up to be fools or very ordinary adults. The 'best of all educations,' he wrote, was 'the most ordinary,' the one that did not force nature, 'the less severe,' indeed 'the most proportional' not 'to the strength, but to the weakness of the child' (69).

Buffon returned to childhood and children in later volumes of the *Natural History*. In the 'Discourse on the Nature of Animal' (1753), a text in which he sought to distinguish humans and animals and ascertain the natural basis of human superiority, Buffon addressed the significance of childhood and education. In the child, as in the animal, only the 'material principle' is active. The 'spiritual principle,' the principle of all knowledge, is developed and perfected through education. For Buffon, education, by which he meant adult intervention, 'set[s] the soul to work' and in so doing humanizes the child: 'it is through the communication of the thoughts of others that the child acquires [the spiritual principle] and becomes in turn thinking and rational.'[25] In his 1758 treatise on carnivorous animals, Buffon responded to Rousseau's conception of 'natural man' and the state of nature.[26] He first argued from facts, holding that Rousseau's solitary savages were nowhere to be found, as all known human beings, including the savages met by travellers in remote corners of the world, lived in organized communities. He also argued from necessity. Unlike newborn animals, who 'do not need their mother for more than a few months,' children 'perish' unless 'assisted and cared for during many years.' This 'physical need' demonstrates that 'the human species has only been able to last and multiply thanks to society' and that the union of parents and children 'is natural, because it is necessary.' The prolonged association between parents and child 'cannot fail to produce a respective and lasting attachment' from which result 'all the expressions of feeling and need' – gestures, signs, speech.[27]

Almost ten years later, in 1766, Buffon returned to the relation between childhood and human nature in the section of the *Natural History* where he tried to pin down the difference between humans and the animals that most resemble humans: the apes. He introduced a distinction between two kinds of education: the education of the individual (common to humans and animals) and the education of the species (unique to humans). The child's individual education is much slower than the young animal's. Whereas the latter learns how to do all the things its parents do in a very short time, the child, at birth 'much less advanced, less strong and less formed,' needs years to achieve the same outcome. Yet it is due to this state of weakness and need that the child 'becomes susceptible to [the education] of the species,' the kind of intervention that develops the soul and cultivates the mind (390). If children were physically stronger their education would be as short as that of animals and their mental functions would not be awakened. For Buffon the education of the species was as necessary in the state of nature as in the civilized state, 'because in both [states] the child is equally weak, equally slow to grow' and 'in consequence ... needs help during an equally long time.' The formation of a human being takes a long time and continuous effort by others. What is remarkable is that in Buffon's conception humanization works in two directions. Not only is the child humanized through the intervention of adults but the necessary, long, continuous association between adults and children, whose cause is the weakness of childhood, *humanizes* adults as well, that is, creates the conditions for the invention of language and culture. The education of children by adults is not an individual affair but 'an institution in which the entire species participates, and whose result is the basis and bond of society.' Buffon concluded categorically that 'all the actions that we must call *human* are connected with society' and depend 'first on the soul and then on education, of which the physical [natural] principle is the necessity of the long association of parents and child' (391).

Despite the many pages he devoted to it in his monumental work, Buffon's evaluation of childhood was ambiguous, and it may be fruitfully contrasted with Rousseau's. As I mentioned at the beginning of this chapter, Rousseau's writings on childhood, which highlight the formative significance of childhood experiences, were instrumental in establishing and making attractive the figure of 'the child' in the modern adult imagination. In contrast, Buffon minimized the importance of childhood in the biography of the individual. '[A] man must look at the first fifteen years of his life as being nothing,' he wrote in 1749, 'everything that happened to him, everything that occurred in this long interval of time is erased from his memory, or at least has so little relation to the goals and the things that have occupied him since, that he is no longer at all interested in it; it is not the same succession of ideas or, as it were, the same life' (*De l'homme*, 164). Buffon did not claim that all that happens in childhood is insignificant, and indeed he observed that some childhood experiences, notably the first sense impressions, may have lasting effects on the development of taste and mental operations.

What is missing from Buffon's account is the idea that childhood shapes the adult's identity. For this very reason, Buffon's claims make little sense to us. A powerful, poignant sign of how unthinkable Buffon's child has become is that Jacques Roger, Buffon's biographer and one of the most serious and respectful students of his work, reads the passage where Buffon proclaims the first fifteen years of life to be nothing as a conscious or unconscious attempt 'to repress all memories of his childhood.' Buffon's view of childhood is thus read as a symptom, evidence that something must have happened to him *as a child* that would explain his identity and convictions as a man (Roger laments that 'we will never know what was behind [Buffon's] desire to erase his childhood').[28] But the historian seeking to trace the emergence of a science of childhood will not simply dismiss Buffon's descriptions of children as incomplete or pre-scientific, nor interpret his denial of any significant relation between childhood and adult identity as a sign of his own repressed childhood. On the contrary, I prefer to think that Buffon's puzzling discourse might incite us to look for other early treatments of childhood and children in unlikely places and invite us to reflect on the limits and implications of the developmental paradigm.

Inconclusive Remarks

My examples, far from amounting to a history of the scientific study of childhood, point to an area that must be investigated and open up many new questions. In tracing the early history of scientific interest in children, we may need to pay as much attention to the *absence* of children from discussions and debates where (from our historical viewpoint) we would expect them to appear, as to those texts where children are explicitly mentioned. Indeed, what demands explanation is the shift from silence regarding childhood, through the use of children as evidence that does not itself require investigation (for instance, evidence that human beings do not stand upright or speak at the beginning of their lives), to the *problematization* of childhood and development (how *is* it that children become able to stand and walk and acquire language?). Besides, it is necessary to scrutinize how the rising science of childhood was connected to the Enlightenment science of man, how much the early study of children contributed to the later emergence of developmental psychology, and to what extent the escalating scientific, pedagogical, and medical attention devoted to childhood since the end of the eighteenth century was related to parallel changes in the formation of people and the administration of the population, mainly the politico-administrative goals of reducing infant mortality and homogenizing the nation through public instruction.

What would be the relevance of this history? The many disciplines and professions that make scientific knowledge about children their ground and source of legitimation often lack a historical perspective on this knowledge and its implications. Yet knowledge is not a transparent window onto the world but a tool for doing things. Knowledge does things, both to the producer of knowledge and to the object known. I am troubled by the fact that in our dealings with children we rely so heavily on a knowledge about whose history and conditions of possibility we know so little. No matter how accurate or important, scientific findings do not directly translate into solutions to questions about the care, education, needs and rights, and position of children in a world constructed and reproduced by adults. Awareness of how the sciences of childhood came into being may make us better able to understand, validate or complicate, legitimize or criticize the knowledge they produce for our use in the present.

Notes

The research for this paper was conducted during my tenure as a postdoctoral fellow in the history department at the University of British Columbia. I thank the Killam Trusts and the Social Sciences and Humanities Research Council of

Canada for funding this research, Mark Phillips for being a stimulating and generous host at UBC as well as for his helpful comments and criticisms, and Hillel Goelman for inviting me to collaborate with the UBC Child and Family Project and to participate in the Green College lecture series 'Multiple Lenses, Multiple Images.' Like other activities organized and sponsored by the UBC Child and Family Project, this series was a thoughtful and much-needed step towards an interdisciplinary engagement with the questions I pose at the beginning of this chapter.

1 See Ian Hacking, *Rewriting the Soul*, and Michel Foucault, *The Archaeology of Knowledge*. Hacking writes: 'Depth knowledge [*savoir*] may not be known to anyone; it is more like a grammar, an underlying set of rules that determine, in this case, not what is grammatical, but what is up for grabs as true-or-false. Particular items counted as true, or as false, are *connaissance*, or what I call surface knowledge' (*Rewriting the Soul*, 198–199). The opening section of this chapter revisits concerns I first formulated in 'On Childhood, Wildness, and Freedom.'
2 For a historical account and analysis of the idea of 'the normal,' see Georges Canguilhem, *The Normal and the Pathological*; Michel Foucault, *The History of Sexuality: Vol. 1. An Introduction*; and Ian Hacking, *The Taming of Chance*. On the role of extraordinary or 'abnormal' children in the constitution of knowledge about 'the child,' see Adriana S. Benzaquén, 'Encounters with Wild Children.'
3 See Jo Boyden, 'Childhood and the Policy Makers'; Sharon Stephens, ed., *Children and the Politics of Culture*; and Nancy Scheper-Hughes and Carolyn Sargent, eds., *Small Wars*.
4 See Carolyn Steedman, *Strange Dislocations*, and Marilyn Ivy, 'Have You Seen Me?' See also Jean-Jacques Rousseau, *Émile*; William Blake, *Songs of Innocence*, and William Wordsworth, *The Poems*.
5 See Valerie Walkerdine, 'Developmental Psychology and the Child-Centred Pedagogy'; Nikolas Rose, *The Psychological Complex*; John R. Morss, *The Biologising of Childhood* and *Growing Critical*, and Erica Burman, *Deconstructing Developmental Psychology*.
6 Besides the works mentioned in note 5, see Jacques Donzelot, *The Policing of Families*; Harry Hendrick, 'Constructions and Reconstructions of British Childhood'; James Wong, 'On the Very Idea of the Normal Child'; and Mona Gleason, *Normalizing the Ideal*.
7 Philippe Ariès, *Centuries of Childhood*. Ariès's book has been intensively discussed, praised, criticized, and used by historians of childhood; see Adrian Wilson, 'The Infancy of the History of Childhood'; Richard T. Vann, 'The Youth of *Centuries of Childhood*'; Linda A. Pollock, *Forgotten Children*;

Ludmilla J. Jordanova, 'Conceptualizing Childhood in the Eighteenth Century' and 'New Worlds for Children in the Eighteenth Century'; Marie-France Morel, 'Reflections on Some Recent French Literature on the History of Childhood'; Brigitte H.E. Niestroj, 'Some Recent German Literature on Socialization and Childhood in Past Times'; and Hugh Cunningham, 'Histories of Childhood.' That Ariès's work continues to inspire and intrigue historians of childhood and the family is evident in the long passages devoted to it by Colin Heywood in *A History of Childhood* and Steven Ozment in *Ancestors*.

8 Besides the works already cited, see, for example, C.P. Hwang, M.E. Lamb, and I.E. Sigel, eds., *Images of Childhood*; Barbara Hanawalt, *Growing Up in Medieval London*; Anna Davin, *Growing Up Poor*; Christina Hardyment, *Dream Babies*; Tamara Hareven, 'The History of the Family and the Complexity of Social Change'; and Lloyd deMause, 'The History of Child Abuse.'

9 See Michel Foucault, *Discipline and Punish* and *The History of Sexuality, Vol. 1*. For a useful synthesis of work in the history of the human sciences, including an excellent bibliographic essay, see Roger Smith, *The Fontana History of the Human Sciences*.

10 Knowledge here must be understood not in the traditional philosophical sense of true belief but as a kind of discourse with a strong internal and external claim to scientific truth and authority. In *The Archaeology of Knowledge*, Foucault defined *knowledge* as the group of elements (objects, enunciations, concepts, or theoretical choices) formed in a regular manner by a discursive practice. He distinguished between *knowledge* and *science*: whereas only propositions that obey certain laws of construction belong to a domain of scientificity, knowledge may be found also in fiction, reflection, narrative accounts, institutional regulations, and political decisions. Although all sciences are constituted on the basis of a pre-existent knowledge, not all bodies of knowledge give rise to a science.

11 See Lorraine Daston, 'Introduction: The Coming Into Being of Scientific Objects,' and Ian Hacking, 'Historical Epistemology.' Hacking would not necessarily agree with my very unphilosophical use of 'historical epistemology.' For his recent reflections on history, ontology, and epistemology, see his *Historical Ontology*, especially 1–26.

12 The fascinating question as to whether DNA and quarks existed before their coming into being as scientific objects, hotly debated among students of science as a social and cultural practice, is not directly pertinent to the distinction I want to stress between objects like DNA and quarks on the one hand and dreams or children on the other.

13 Jean-Jacques Rousseau, 'Discourse on the Origin of Inequality.' See also Florence Lotterie, 'Les Lumières contre le progrès?' and Julia V. Douthwaite, *The Wild Girl, Natural Man, and the Monster*.

14 The 1987 edition of the American Psychiatric Association's *Diagnostic and Statistical Manual of Mental Disorders*, known as *DSM-III-R*, included as mental disorders of childhood a special class of 'Academic Skills Disorders' comprising 'Developmental Arithmetic Disorder,' 'Developmental Expressive Writing Disorder,' and 'Developmental Reading Disorder.' Academic Skills Disorders, diagnosed by means of 'standardized, individually administered tests,' are a subset of 'Specific Developmental Disorders,' all of which are 'associated with impairment in academic functioning in children who are in school' (*DSM-III-R*, 39–40).

15 On disciplinary history, see Stefan Collini, '"Disciplinary History" and "Intellectual History."' See also Georg Eckardt, Wolfgang G. Bringmann, and Lothar Sprung, eds., *Contributions to a History of Developmental Psychology*.

16 For an expanded version of this discussion of the Observers of Man and Buffon, see Adriana S. Benzaquén, 'Childhood, Identity, and Human Science in the Enlightenment.'

17 See Marcelle Bouteiller, 'La Société des Observateurs de l'homme, ancêtre de la Société d'Anthropologie de Paris'; George W. Stocking, 'French Anthropology in 1800'; Sergio Moravia, *La scienza dell'uomo nel Settecento*; Jean Copans and Jean Jamin, eds., *Aux Origines de l'anthropologie française*; and Jean-Luc Chappey, *La Société des Observateurs de l'homme (1799–1804)*.

18 Louis-François Jauffret, 'Introduction aux Mémoires de la Société des Observateurs de l'homme,' reprinted by Georges Hervé under the title 'Le premier programme de l'anthropologie.' Unless otherwise indicated, all translations are mine.

19 Jauffret, 'Introduction,' 482.

20 The prize was announced in *Magasin encyclopédique*, year 6, vol. 2, no. 8 (Fructidor year VIII [1800]): 531–535.

21 In its short life, the Society of Observers of Man was unable to carry out its ambitious research program. Still, the Observers were enthusiastic sponsors of Dr Jean-Marc-Gaspard Itard's experimental training of Victor, the wild boy of Aveyron, a landmark in the history of the sciences of childhood; see Benzaquén, 'Encounters with Wild Children.'

22 'Savages,' wild children, deaf-mutes, blind people, and the great apes were the privileged objects investigated by Enlightenment philosophers intent on finding out answers to questions of origins.

23 John Locke, *An Essay Concerning Human Understanding*; Étienne Bonnot, Abbé de Condillac, *Traité des sensations*, and Charles Bonnet, *Essai analy-*

tique sur les facultés de l'âme. See also Larry Wolff, 'When I Imagine a Child.' Sensationist epistemology denies innate ideas and proclaims that all knowledge originates in sensation. To 'study' the origin of knowledge and ideas, Condillac and Bonnet imagined a 'statue' inwardly organized like a human being and described the ideas it would acquire on being given use of each one of the senses. In 'Encounters with Wild Children' I suggested that a solution to Locke's problem was found at the turn of the nineteenth century by Itard in his work with the wild boy of Aveyron, in which the experimental study of the child came to be equated with medico-pedagogical (normalizing) intervention.

24 Georges Leclerc, comte de Buffon, *De l'homme*. Subsequent references to this work will be given in the text. On Buffon's life and work, see Jacques Roger, *Buffon*, and the many excellent articles collected in Jean Gayon et al., eds., *Buffon 88*. On Buffon's natural history of man, see Michèle Duchet, *Anthropologie et histoire au siècle des lumières*; Claude Blanckaert, 'Buffon and the Natural History of Man'; and Phillip Sloan, 'The Gaze of Natural History.'

25 J. Pivetau, ed., *Œuvres philosophiques de Buffon*, 338.

26 Rousseau had proffered his well-known portrait of 'natural man' as a solitary being in the 'Discourse on the Origin of Inequality.' A few years later he would rely on Buffon's account of childhood in his own famous discussion of child rearing in the first book of *Émile*.

27 *Œuvres philosophiques de Buffon*, 374. Subsequent references to this work will be given in the text.

28 Roger, *Buffon*, 5–6.

References

American Psychiatric Association. (1987). *Diagnostic and statistical manual of mental disorders* (3rd ed., rev.). Washington: American Psychiatric Association.

Ariès, P. (1962). *Centuries of childhood: A social history of family life*. (R. Baldick, Trans.). New York: Vintage.

Benzaquén, A.S. (1999). Encounters with wild children: Childhood, knowledge, and otherness. PhD dissertation, York University.

Benzaquén, A.S. (2001). On childhood, wildness, and freedom. *Public 21, special issue: 'Childhood,'* 33–41.

Benzaquén, A.S. (2004). Childhood, identity, and human science in the Enlightenment. *History Workshop Journal, 57,* 34–57.

Blake, W. (1971). *Songs of innocence*. New York: Dover. (Original work published 1789)

Blanckaert, C. (1993). Buffon and the natural history of man: Writing history and the 'foundational myth' of anthropology. *History of the human sciences, 6 (1)*, 13–50.

Bonnet, C. (1973). *Essai analytique sur les facultés de l'âme.* Hildesheim NY: Olms. (Original work published 1760)

Bouteiller, M. (1956). La Société des Observateurs de l'homme, ancêtre de la société d'anthropologie de Paris. *Bulletins et Mémoires de la Société d'Anthropologie de Paris 7, 10th series,* 448–465.

Boyden, J. (1990). Childhood and the policy makers: A comparative perspective on the globalization of childhood. In A. James & A. Prout (Eds.), *Constructing and reconstructing childhood* (pp. 184–215). London: Falmer.

Buffon, Georges Leclerc, comte de. (1971). *De l'homme.* (M. Duchet, Ed.). Paris: François Maspero. (Original work published 1749)

Burman, E. (1994). *Deconstructing developmental psychology.* London: Routledge.

Canguilhem, G. (1989). *The normal and the pathological* (C.R. Fawcet, Trans.). New York: Zone. (Original work published 1966)

Chappey, J.-L. (2002). *La Société des Observateurs de l'homme (1799–1804): Des anthropologues au temps de Bonaparte.* Paris: Société des études robespierristes.

Collini, S. (1988). 'Disciplinary history' and 'intellectual history': Reflections on the historiography of the social sciences in Britain and France. *Revue de Synthèse 3–4* (4th series), 387–399.

Condillac, É. B. de (1984). *Traité des sensations.* Paris: Fayard. (Original work published 1754)

Copans, J., & Jamin, J. (Eds.). (1978). *Aux origines de l'anthropologie française: Les mémoires de la Société des Observateurs de l'homme en l'an VIII.* Paris: Le Sycomore.

Cunningham, H. (1998). Histories of childhood. *American Historical Review, 103 (4),* 1195–1208.

Daston, L. (2000). Introduction: The coming into being of scientific objects. In L. Daston (Ed.), *Biographies of scientific objects* (pp. 1–14). Chicago: University of Chicago Press.

Davin, A. (1996). *Growing up poor: Home, school, and street in London, 1870–1914.* London: Rivers Oram.

DeMause, L. (1998). The history of child abuse. *Journal of Psychohistory, 25 (3),* 216–236.

Donzelot, J. (1979). *The policing of families* (R. Hurley, Trans.). New York: Pantheon.

Douthwaite, J.V. (2002). *The wild girl, natural man, and the monster: Dangerous experiments in the age of enlightenment.* Chicago: University of Chicago Press.

Duchet, M. (1971). *Anthropologie et histoire au siècle des lumières: Buffon, Voltaire, Rousseau, Helvétius, Diderot*. Paris: François Maspero.

Eckardt, G., Bringmann, W., & Sprung, L. (Eds.). (1985). *Contributions to a history of developmental psychology: International William T. Preyer symposium*. Berlin: Mouton.

Foucault, M. (1972) *The archaeology of knowledge and the discourse on language* (A.M. Sheridan Smith, Trans.). New York: Pantheon. (Original works published 1969 and 1971, respectively)

Foucault, M. (1979). *Discipline and punish: The birth of the prison* (A. Sheridan, Trans.). New York: Vintage. (Original work published 1975)

Foucault, M. (1990). *The history of sexuality: Vol. 1. An introduction* (R. Hurley, Trans.). New York: Vintage. (Original work published 1976)

Gayon, J., et al. (Eds.). (1992). *Buffon 88*. Paris: Vrin.

Gleason, M. (1999). *Normalizing the ideal: Psychology, schooling, and the family in postwar Canada*. Toronto: University of Toronto Press.

Hacking, I. (1990). *The taming of chance*. Cambridge: Cambridge University Press.

Hacking, I. (1993). Historical epistemology. Informal workshop discussion paper presented at the graduate workshop Historical Epistemology, University of Toronto.

Hacking, I. (1995). *Rewriting the soul: Multiple personality and the sciences of memory*. Princeton: Princeton University Press.

Hacking, I. (2002). *Historical ontology*. Cambridge, MA: Harvard University Press.

Hanawalt, B. (1993). *Growing up in medieval London: The experience of childhood in history*. New York: Oxford University Press.

Hardyment, C. (1983). *Dream babies: Child care from Locke to Spock*. London: Jonathan Cape.

Hareven, T. (1991). The history of the family and the complexity of social change. *American Historical Review, 96 (1)*, 95–124.

Hendrick, H. (1990). Constructions and reconstructions of British childhood: An interpretive survey, 1800 to the present. In A. James & A. Prout (Eds.), *Constructing and Reconstructing Childhood* (pp. 35–59). London: Falmer.

Heywood, C. (2001). *A history of childhood: Children and childhood in the west from medieval to modern times*. Cambridge: Polity Press.

Hwang, C.P., Lamb, M.E., & Sigel, I.E. (Eds.). (1996). *Images of childhood*. Mahwah, NJ: Erlbaum.

Ivy, M. (1993). Have you seen me? Recovering the inner child in late twentieth-century America. *Social Text, 37*, 227–252.

James, A. & Prout, A. (Eds.). (1990). *Constructing and reconstructing childhood: Contemporary issues in the study of childhood*. London: Falmer.

Jauffret, L.-F. (1909). Introduction aux mémoires de la Société des Observateurs de l'homme. In G. Hervé (Ed.), Le premier programme de l'anthropologie. *Bulletins et mémoires de la Société d'anthropologie de Paris, 10* (5th series), 476–487.

Jordanova, L.J. (1987). Conceptualizing childhood in the eighteenth century: The problem of child labour. *British Journal for Eighteenth-Century Studies, 10,* 189–199.

Jordanova, L.J. (1990). New worlds for children in the eighteenth century: Problems of historical interpretation. *History of the Human Sciences, 3(1),* 69–83.

Locke, J. (1979). *An essay concerning human understanding.* (P. Nidditch, Ed.). Oxford: Clarendon Press. (Original work published in 1690)

Lotterie F. (1998). Les lumières contre le progrès? La naissance de l'idée de perfectibilité. *Dix-huitième siècle, 30,* 383–396.

Magasin encyclopédique (1800).

Moravia, S. (1970). *La scienza dell'uomo nel Settecento: con una appendice di testi.* Bari, Italy: Laterza.

Morel, M.-F. (1989). Reflections on some recent French literature on the history of childhood. *Continuity and Change, 4(2),* 323–337.

Morss, J.R. (1990). *The Biologising of childhood: Developmental psychology and the Darwinian myth.* London: Erlbaum.

Morss, J. R. (1996). *Growing critical: Alternatives to developmental psychology.* London: Routledge.

Niestroj, B.H.E. (1989). Some recent German literature on socialization and childhood in past times. *Continuity and Change, 4(2),* 339–357.

Ozment, S. (2001). *Ancestors: The loving family in Old Europe.* Cambridge: Harvard University Press.

Pivetau, J. (Ed.). (1954). *Œuvres philosophiques de Buffon.* Paris: PUF.

Pollock, L.A. (1983). *Forgotten children: Parent-child relations from 1500 to 1900.* Cambridge: Cambridge University Press.

Roger, J. (1997). *Buffon: A life in natural history.* (L. Pearce Williams, Ed.; S.L. Bonnefoi, Trans.). Ithaca, NY: Cornell University Press.

Rose, N. (1985). *The psychological complex: Psychology, politics and society in England, 1869–1939.* London: Routledge.

Rousseau, J.-J. (1987). Discourse on the origin of inequality. In D.A. Cress (Ed. and Trans.), *The basic political writings.* Indianapolis: Hackett. (Original work published in 1755)

Rousseau, J.-J. (1961). *Emile* (B. Foxley, Trans.). London: J.M. Dent. (Original work published 1762)

Scheper-Hughes, N., & Sargent, C. (Eds.). (1998). *Small wars: The cultural politics of childhood.* Berkeley: University of California Press.

Sloan, P. (1995). The gaze of natural history. In C. Fox, R. Porter, & R. Wokler (Eds.), *Inventing human science: Eighteenth-century domains* (pp. 112–151). Berkeley: University of California Press.

Smith, R. (1997). *The Fontana history of the human sciences*. London: Fontana.

Steedman, C. (1995). *Strange dislocations: Childhood and the idea of human interiority, 1780–1930*. Cambridge: Harvard University Press.

Stephens, S. (Ed.). (1995). *Children and the politics of culture*. Princeton, NJ: Princeton University Press.

Stocking, G.W. (1968). French anthropology in 1800. In *Race, culture, and evolution: Essays in the history of anthropology* (pp. 13–41). New York: Free Press.

Vann, R.T. (1982). The youth of *Centuries of Childhood*. *History and Theory, 21*, 279–297.

Walkerdine, V. (1984). Developmental psychology and the child-centred pedagogy: The insertion of Piaget into early education. In J. Henriques et al. (Eds.), *Changing the subject: Psychology, social regulation and subjectivity* (pp. 153–202). London: Methuen.

Wilson, A. (1980). The infancy of the history of childhood: An appraisal of Philippe Ariès. *History and Theory, 19*, 132–153.

Wolff, L. (1998). When I imagine a child: The idea of childhood and the philosophy of memory in the Enlightenment. *Eighteenth-Century Studies, 31 (4)*, 377–401.

Wong, J. (1994). On the very idea of the normal child. PhD thesis, University of Toronto.

Wordsworth, William. (1981). *The poems*. (J. Hayden, Ed.). New Haven: Yale University Press.

2

Childhood in the Shadow of Parens Patriae

ANNE MCGILLIVRAY

Roman doctrine casts a long shadow over contemporary childhood. The doctrine, principle, power, jurisdiction, concept, or ideology of *parens patriae* – the state as the father of the people – is said to originate in Roman law, deriving from the emperor's title *pater patriae*, or father of the state. If so, it has overarched law and policy affecting children for some twenty-five hundred years. During these millennia, three legal paradigms of childhood emerged – as property of the father in Roman and common law, as vehicle of state interests in the nineteenth century, and as rights-bearer in the later twentieth century. These paradigms are extant in social and legal discourse in Canada as elsewhere.

Parens patriae was claimed as a power of the English Crown after the Norman Conquest. The responsibility of the king to care for the people, and in particular for those legally disabled, is now exercised under the equitable jurisdiction of the superior courts in individual cases, and in the form of social legislation. The phrase is rarely used in the modern legislation of the conditions of childhood, yet it impels and justifies such legislation. It underlies, for example, mitigation of criminal responsibility, the statutory powers of apprehension of endangered children, child allowances and tax benefits, and universal medical care and education. As an equitable jurisdiction of the superior courts of Canada (but not Quebec) and the legislative jurisdiction of the state, it is alive and well. It is a paternal jurisdiction, as the name implies, caught up in other Roman doctrines of criminal responsibility, legal capacity, wardship and emancipation, *pater potestas* and *familias*.

The limits of intervention into childhood are framed in terms of state and law, family and childhood. Reification of the terms of debate – state, law, childhood, family – hobble meaningful debate. The state is an agglomerate of courts, legislative bodies, agencies, schools, licensed charities, and licensed experts. Law, far from being 'at the top' of the social, is eclipsed in daily life by cultural affiliation, religious belief, or the daily horoscope. Childhood is socially produced, contingent on time and place, ideology and cultural practice.[1] Law defines childhood in different ways for different purposes at different times.[2] It made children criminally responsible and hanged or jailed them with adults from the age of seven, making the divide between child protection and criminal accountability a cognitive artefact with legal consequence. It sets bright lines for children's consent to sex but opens tests for consent to medical treatment.

Elusive in form, variously defined in law, the family is pivotal in child-state relations. The Roman familias has been resurrected to bolster state goals. The family came to occupy a new social space in the nineteenth century. Foucault posited a shift in the creation of the governed soul, from the public punishment of the body to the private discipline of the soul, a transformation aided by the new technologies of the 'psy' sciences. In this shift, the family became the 'privileged locus' of citizenship and subjectivity.[3] Jacques Donzelot saw the manipulation of the images of parenting that accompanied child welfare, schooling, and juvenile justice initiatives in nineteenth-century France as a 'tutelary regime' that would familialize society.[4] Although the aim of reform was the regulation of the poor, middle-class parents were the primary consumers of these projects of improvement, much as upper-class families had embraced the 'new childhood' influenced by Rousseau in the late eighteenth century.[5] Drawing on the work of Foucault and Donzelot, Nikolas Rose argued that the socialization of children is not an 'anthropological universal' but 'the historically specific outcome of technologies for the government of the subjectivity of citizens.'[6] The intense inspection of childhood by the 'psy' sciences in the twentieth century led Rose to conclude that childhood is now 'the most intensively governed sector of human existence.'[7]

Shaped by our discourses, the boundaries between child and law, family and state, are powerful markers of children's relations with the collectivity. 'Childhood is a submerged geography of pastoral or volcanic landscapes neither outgrown nor fully known.'[8] It is a touchstone of the public good and a lightning rod for social fears. Fear and sentimentality equally drive moral panics about children – poverty, delinquency, abuse, neglect, and mental, physical, or cultural difference. Generalizations are perilous. 'Here be dragons,' as the old maps declared of uncharted spaces. This essay is a rough cartography of parens patriae as it affects childhood. In the next two sections, I consider the origins and jurisdiction of parens patriae in English and Canadian law. I turn then to the rise of the statute and the opposition of judges, crime and child crime. I next consider the rise of social legislation and the introduction of child welfare legislation. By way of conclusion, I discuss the new paradigm of children's rights in the context of an enduring Roman doctrine, 'the discipline of minors.'

Parens Patriae, Pater Potestas, and the Common Law

The influence of Roman law on English common law is indirect. The early Roman occupation of Britain; the Norman Conquest of 1066, which imposed a common law on petty kingdoms and legal systems largely based on customary law; lawyers trained in Roman-influenced continental law; and the ecclesiastical courts (the arena of family dispute settlement for centuries) – these all informed the common law.[9] In frequent turns back to Roman doctrine and the Justinian Code, the courts and influential English writers such as Bracton in the thirteenth century and Blackstone in the eighteenth century shaped common-law constructs of childhood and capacity.

Parens patriae is an equitable jurisdiction of the courts and a residual jurisdiction of the Crown. Equity was meant to relieve the injustice of a strict interpretation of law. First administered by the king in court, it devolved to the Lord Chancellor, then to the Courts of Chancery, and finally to the superior courts of law, under the 1878 Judicature Act (UK). Equity, as law students learn, relieves the supplicant from the unfair application of law in the particular circumstances of the case. Parens patriae concerns the welfare of the population as well as those adversely affected by law and so remains in the residual jurisdiction of the state. Children, like others disabled by law or circumstance from acting for themselves, are said to be perpetually under parens patriae. As legal disability is manipulable, the jurisdiction has frightening potential for almost limitless legal intervention into people's lives.[10] Its early province in English history was not the good of the people but the care of children's estates and the profits to be had from them. Children without estates were rarely of interest. English courts early in the seventeenth century began to define parens patriae and confine its reach. The following cases illustrate the history attributed to the doctrine by the courts and suggest a shift of parens patriae to childhood in general.

Lord Somers LC explained the connection between wardship and parens patriae in 1696. 'In this court there were several things that belonged to the king as pater patriae, and fell under the care and direction of this court, as charities, infants, idiots, lunatics, etc. Afterwards such of them as were of profit and advantage to the king were removed to the court of Wards by the statute [32 Hen VIII, c 46 (1540)]; but upon the dissolution of that court [by the Tenures Abolition Act, 12 Car, c 24 (1660)], came back again to the Chancery.'[11]

With the demise of the lucrative trade in wardships, the focus of parens patriae shifted back to its Roman origins, in the duty of the state to take care of those 'not able to take care of themselves,' as Lord Eldon LC wrote in the case of *Wellesley v. Beaufort* (1827).[12] The duty is founded on 'obvious necessity,' but the focus should be only on 'cases in which it is clear that some care should be thrown around them.' In 1893, Esher MR called it a 'paternal jurisdiction' in which the court acts for the Crown as 'guardian of all infants as if it were the parent of the child, thus superceding the natural guardianship of the parent.'[13] *Patria potestas*, the power of the state, now trumps *pater potestas*, the father's power over his children. The court's jurisdiction over children supersedes even that of state officials, Wootten J wrote in 1983.[14] Donaldson MR wrote in 1991 that the jurisdiction 'is wider than that of parents [and is] not derivative from the parents' rights and responsibilities.'[15] It is 'the delegated performance' of the Crown's duty to 'protect its subjects and particularly children' to the courts.

The origin of parens patriae is 'lost in the mists of antiquity' according to Sir Henry Theobald,[16] its 'historic credentials ... of dubious relevance' according to Fortas J.[17] John Seymour argues that it was 'plucked out of the air' at the end of the eighteenth century 'to provide assurances about its respectable antiquity.'[18] Did the courts 'invent' the jurisdiction of parens patriae? Or did Constantine the Great declare it in the fourth century, as is sometimes claimed?[19] The Emperor Constantine indeed asserted in 316 that 'It is part of Our duty, and it is lawful for Us alone to interpret questions involving equity and law.' While Constantine outdid his predecessors in the core parens patriae area of childhood, jurisdiction over the legally disabled or incompetent neither began nor ended there. The earliest provision appeared eight hundred years before Constantine, in the Twelve Tables of 451 BCE: 'If a person is a fool, let this person and his goods be under the protection of his family or his paternal relatives, if he is not under the care of anyone.' The 'doctrine of fools' was extended by the Senate and by *praetors*, high-echelon elected judges, into the doctrines definitive of Roman law – *alieni juris* and *sui juris* – and the structure of wardship and capacity that defined childhood then, as it does today. Sui juris means legally competent. Alienis juris refers to those outside the law – children, the mentally disordered, the mentally disabled – who must be placed under someone's care, or wardship.

A child unable to speak is *infantia* and therefore under wardship and tutelage.[20] A child capable of intelligible speech is *intellectiae*, able to instruct her legal guardian, or *tutor*, depending on her *intellectus*, or capacity. This required examining the child, much as child witnesses are examined today in Canada for testimonial capacity. Infantia included young children, mutes, and those *non compos mentis* – idiots, spendthrifts, and lunatics. Children, spendthrifts, and the mentally disordered were *cura furiosa et minoris*, cured by the return of reason to the mentally disordered and by the child's emancipation into adulthood. By 407, children over seven were deemed to be intellectus without further examination. Children under seven were deemed infantia and thus legally incapable of *dolus*, or the intent to do wrong. These rules were codified by Justinian in the sixth century.[21] Puberty meant the onset of full criminal capacity and was established by physical examination of the child's body. In 529, Justinian decreed that 'Abolishing the indecent examination established for the purpose of ascertaining the puberty of males, we order that just as females are considered to have arrived at puberty after having completed their twelfth year, so, likewise, males shall be held to have arrived at that age after having passed their fourteenth year, and the disgraceful examination of the bodies of such persons is hereby terminated.' In these institutes of Roman law, we see the outlines of modern childhood.

The jurisdiction of the Roman *praetor* arose in the context of the *familia*. The familia was a social, legal, and religious structure peculiar to Roman society. It was the locus of law in the private sphere and the site of the worship of ancestors embodied in the household gods, *lares* and *penates*. Praetors conducted rites enabling the heir on death of the *paterfamilias* to take charge of *penates*, god of the storeroom.[22] The familia was headed by the paterfamilias, the father of the family, who represented the familia in public spaces. His *potestas* was a magisterial power over every member of the household – wife, servants, relatives, children (both young and adult) – including power of death, minor violence, exposure of newborns, control of marriage and divorce, selling or buying children, appointing children's legal tutors, and emancipating sons. *Patria potestas*, the power of the father, was 'essentially Roman: both in content, so great that it could be called *patria maiestas*, and in its lifelong duration, it had an intensity unknown to the paternal power in any of the systems with which Roman law came into contact.'[23] In later Roman law, family members could approach the praetor for protection or redress from the power of the father. By 287, for example, the Roman Senate had penalized paternal failure to acknowledge a child and ordered paternal support for children over three.[24] Patria potestas was diminished by edict in the late Roman Empire. The power to inflict death on members of the household – the discipline of minors – was restricted to 'moderate correction' (discussed below). The legal constructs of the familias and pater potestas shaped the modern family and its relationship to the state.

The pater familias was resurrected during the Protestant Reformation in the late sixteenth to mid-seventeenth centuries to bolster the middle-class father. In this time of political chaos and religious ferment, the closed nucleated father-headed family served a political purpose.[25] Unlike the open-kinship medieval family, which could draw upon multiple loyalties in opposition to the state and state religion, the nucleated family headed by the senior male could be constrained and manipulated. Manuals and broadsheets equated obedience to the father with obedience to God and king. A popular manual stated, 'The householder is called Pater Familias, that is father of a family, because he should have a fatherly care over his servants as it they were children.'[26] In 1609, James I told his subjects, 'Kings are compared to fathers in families: for a King is truly parens patriae, the politic father of his people,' and in 1618 he ordered that Mocket's *God and the King* be studied in schools and universities and purchased by all householders. Severe beating was a daily occurrence in grammar schools and colleges and was intended to reinforce filial, state, and religious obedience. Punishment of children mirrored Roman discipline – 'more children were being beaten in the sixteenth and early seventeenth centuries, over a longer age span, than ever before.'[27] Although pater potestas would never fully return under English law, the new father was similarly named temporal and spiritual head of the household, commanding the obedience of wife, children, and servants, inflicting corporal punishment, requiring religious observance, and controlling children's education, marriage, and inheritance in a sociolegal reflection of the Roman familias. The 'new childhood' of the late eighteenth century, influenced by Rousseau's *Émile* and seen in the upper middle classes, disrupted the paradigm.[28]

The nineteenth century saw a return to middle-class paternalism and a Victorian emphasis on family, paternal obedience, corporal punishment and control of marriage, education, and inheritance.

It is tempting to see in the familial origins of Roman law – the father's magisterial power, the familial concerns of the praetor, the paternal title and jurisdiction of the emperor, the law's concern with disability, legal incapacity and wardship, and emancipation of minors – a direct correspondence to the parens patriae jurisdiction of the modern courts. This is problematic.[29] Decisions of the praetors performed a quasi-legislative function in setting out circumstances in which future related legal actions would be considered. Although Cicero (106–43 BCE) described the praetorial edict in his day as 'basic to legal knowledge and development,'[30] reforms were minor and the legislative process was overtly political.[31] Even so, the ideology of Roman law left its mark on childhood, in doctrines of paternal power including the discipline of family members, the separation of family and state, and wardship and capacity.

Wardship and Potestas in the Courts

> The disabilities of an infant and his legal incapacity to manage his own affairs render it necessary that for the protection of his interests and the management of his property he should have a guardian, to whom he stands in the relation of ward.
>
> *Halsbury's Laws of England*

Wardship was central to the Roman structure of legal capacity and responsibility. That children were owned by their fathers was certain under Roman law and early common law.[32] The Crown asserted its power of guardianship and assignment of wardship to protect the property and persons of minor children where the father was dead or absent. Trade or holding in wardship underpinned the English economy. The thirteenth-century statute Praerogativa Regis (Prerogative of the King)[33] confirmed the power of the king as 'father of the people' to place orphaned children under his guardianship, assign wards, and put their estates into his trust and use. Although the benevolent doctrine of parens patriae was claimed, the real issue was the money to be made from the estates of minors. A West Virginia court observed that:

> much of the sovereign's revenue came from feudal incidents resulting from the King's control of persons under disabilities, the most well known of which were the wardships and marriages of the minor heirs ... there

was a thriving open market in much the same sense that there is a futures market today ... [T]he early development of *parens patriae* was in no way evidence of the sovereign's solicitude for the welfare of unfortunate subjects, but rather was the result of the King's need for revenue combined with medieval restraints upon the alienation of land which left valuable life estates in the hands of born incompetents ... [I]n those days it can be said with ironic force that the law was no respecter of persons.[34]

The Court of Wards and Liveries Act (1660) abolished socage (tenure of estates) and transferred parens patriae jurisdiction as a matter of equity to the Chancery Courts.[35] Wardship 'lost its connection with property and became purely prospective in nature.'[36] These are the statutory reforms noted by Lord Somers in 1696 (see above). Only children were subject in Roman law to both custodial jurisdiction and wardship. This jurisdiction was expanded by statute in the nineteenth century to include others legally disabled.[37] Again, the categories of disability are those founded in the Roman doctrine of fools.

The Judicature Act (1873) granted equitable jurisdiction to the superior courts of law. These courts now judge applications for custody and wardship. In *Re Eve* (1986), the Supreme Court of Canada denied a mother's application for non-therapeutic sterilization of her daughter, age twenty-four, who could not manage birth control due to mental disability but was sexually active. In his reasons for judgment, LaForest SCJ wrote, 'Wardship is merely a device by means of which Chancery exercises its parens patriae jurisdiction over children. Today the care of children constitutes the bulk of the courts' work involving the exercise of the parens patriae jurisdiction [and such cases] constitute a solid guide to the exercise of parens patriae power even in the case of adults. There is no need, then, to resort to statutes ... to exercise the jurisdiction in respect of adults.'[38]

Parens patriae jurisdiction is broad and 'situations under which it can be exercised are legion; the jurisdiction cannot be defined in that sense.' It 'can be invoked in such matters as custody, protection of property, health problems, religious upbringing and protection against harmful associations.' Courts can use it to prevent injury as well as correct it. While the scope of parens patriae is unlimited, in an individual case the court can do only 'what is necessary for the benefit or welfare of the protected person.' Judicial caution must be 'redoubled as the seriousness of the matter increases.' In denying the mother's application, the Supreme Court deferred to the legislative process.

Re Eve was put to the test in *D.F.G. G*, a woman of twenty-three who was addicted to solvents, had given birth to three infants, two of whom were congenitally disabled and in permanent care. A Winnipeg child protection agency sought custody of G, pregnant with her fourth child, to prevent further damage to her fetus. Schulman J of the Court of Queen's Bench granted the order under the Manitoba Mental Health Act despite expert opinion that G suffered no psychiatric disorder. Under a separate heading, the court asserted its parens patriae jurisdiction over G. That the concern was her fetus was clear: the order giving G into the custody of Child and Family Services terminated on delivery of the child. The decision was overturned by the Court of Appeal and by the Supreme Court of Canada. Extending the common law into fetal protection is beyond judicial reach. Lamer SCJ wrote that judges are confined to incremental change

> based largely on the mechanism of extending an existing principle to new circumstances ... major changes in the law should be predicated on a wider view of how the rule will operate in the broad generality of cases ... in a constitutional democracy it is the legislature, as the elected branch of government, which should assume the major responsibility for law reform ... where the revision is major and its ramifications complex, the courts must proceed with great caution.[39]

While Lamer in *D.F.G.* would defer to the legislature in resolving complex social questions, LaForest in *Re Eve* noted only that the Court is bound by existing legislation and that parens patriae requires no statutory authority. The Supreme Court made clear in both cases its reluctance to use its parens patriae jurisdiction in cases invoking complex legal and social problems.[40]

These cases raise troubling social issues – involuntary sterilization, the incarceration of pregnant women, the status of the fetus, the place of the mother. *Re Eve* begs the question of consent for those legally disabled from consenting for themselves. Who speaks for infantia? The law? The mother? Eve is in her mother's care but not custody, as would be a child born to Eve. *D.F.G.* begs the question of mental disorder and consent. A subtext of both cases is the history of the relationship between judge and legislator, common law and statute law, in setting the boundaries of legal capacity. The Supreme Court deferred to Parliament in its least bounded jurisdiction, that of parens patriae. *Re Eve* and *D.F.G.* reflect the historic rivalry of courts and legislature. This is evident in the history of criminal law.

Parens Patriae, Judge-Made Law, Statute Law, and Crime

The common law of England has fared like other venerable edifices of antiquity, which rash and inexperienced workmen have ventured to new-dress and refine, with all the rage of modern improvement ... [I]ts symmetry has been destroyed, its proportions distorted, and its majestic simplicity exchanged for specious embellishments and fantastic novelties.

Blackstone, *Commentaries* (1769)

Canadian courts routinely declare their law-making role to be interstitial, moving in minute increments from case to case. That they must defer to the legislator is now a tenet of the common law. Only in cases invoking the Charter of Rights and Freedoms can the courts overturn statute law, but parens patriae permits the courts to fashion remedies against the harshness of law in individual cases. As we see in *Eve* and *D.F.G.*, the courts are reluctant to push settled legal boundaries. 'Judge-made' law is the foundation of the common-law tradition. Legislation can cut through centuries of judicial development to impose new legal norms. Judicial development of both common and statute law is now seen as a necessary complement to legislation. Historically, the power of the judges and the power of the king (after 1688, the king-in-parliament) were opposed.

Blackstone's *Commentaries on the Law of England* (1769) was the recognized legal authority in England's colonies, having immense influence on the development of the law in the United States and early Canada. Employing an architectural metaphor, Blackstone equated legislation with 'specious embellishments' on the venerable edifice of judge-made common law. His aim was a 'science of legislation' that would improve the fit of statutes with common law.[41] Sir Francis Buller (1787) employed a horticultural metaphor. The statute 'like a powerful tyrant that knows no bounds ... mows down all before it' but the common law 'with a lenient hand ... roots out that which is bad and leaves that which is good.' Utilitarian philosopher Jeremy Bentham (1789) proposed a *Pannomium*, or codification of all law, on the premise that all law, judge-made or enacted, emanates from the legislator's will.[42] The sole limit on that will was to be 'the calculation of felicity' that ensured the greatest good to the greatest number.[43] His 'province of legislation' encompassed law, social practices, and the social system itself.

These eighteenth-century debates arose from the steep numerical rise in statutes after the 1688 English revolution that established the supremacy of the king-in-parliament over the king's courts.[44] On average, the parliament of William III (1689–1702) enacted 58 public acts per year; that of Anne (1702–14), 78; George I (1714–27), 58; George II (1727–60), 81; and George III (1760–1820), 254. The number of statutes produced by Parliament in the reign of George III was over four times the number under William III. Public statutes in this period total 12,485, of which 9,980 appeared under George III. Blackstone's disdain for statute law and Bentham's proposed Pannomium arose from this unruly output of legislation.

'Nowhere was the growth of legislation more striking than in the area of penal policy.'[45] The 'hanging acts' were a remarkable feature of English law in the eighteenth century. In his 1819 House of Commons speech, Thomas Fowell Buxton numbered capital statutes at 223, of which 150 were made capital in the eighteenth century. The output was such that William Eden wondered in 1771 whether 'the chief object of legislation in England' might be 'the extirpation of mankind' but Lord Hardwicke put the cause to 'the degeneracy of the present times, fruitful in the inventions of wickedness.' The hanging acts were icons of state power,[46] as much a tool of the mercantile state as was the spate of civil legislation in that same period.[47]

Parliament made capital offences of the theft of Brussels lace by street urchins at the London docks and pilfering of coal by children working in the mines.[48] Statutes governing new trades routinely prescribed the death penalty for theft, as an infringement on mercantile monopoly. The pomp and majesty of the 'bloody assizes' with their gorgeously gowned judges and the dangling hope of pardon or commutation of sentence served as much as execution, spiked heads, and instructive chronicles of the lives of felons to control society in the absence of public policing.

'Law was now a power with its own claims, higher than those of prosecutor, lawyers, and even the great scarlet-robed assize judge himself. To them, of course, the law was The Law. The fact that they reified it, that they shut their eyes to its daily enactment in Parliament by men of their own class, heightened the illusion. In short, its very inefficiency, its absurd formalism, was part of its strength as ideology.'[49]

The law's 'absurd formalism' lay in part in the strict interpretation of penal statutes. Judges might fail a prosecution on defects in the charge, for example, describing the accused as a 'farmer' rather than the requisite 'yeoman,' and thereby save many from hanging. Insistence on procedure strengthened law's popular ideology, as lying beyond the power of the people and the courts themselves. That judicial death could be commuted to penal servitude, or transportation to the colonies, or the crime pardoned under the royal prerogative of mercy, did not diminish law's majesty and its judicial sighs of care for the fate of convicts.

Judges claimed the power to declare new crimes in Sedley's Case (1663).[50] Debates came to a head in nineteenth-century movements to codify criminal law.[51] England appointed a Royal Commission to consider the question. The commission proposed abolition of judge-made crimes. Commissioner James FitzJames Stephen, author of a Draft Code that was influential in the drafting of Canada's first Criminal Code in 1892, explained in 1879:

> After the experience of centuries, and with a Parliament sitting every year, and keenly alive to all matters likely to endanger the public interests, we are surely in a position to say the power of declaring new offences shall henceforth be vested in Parliament only ... we run the risk of tempting the judges to express their disapproval of conduct which, upon political, moral, or social grounds, they consider deserving of punishment, by declaring upon slender authority that it constitutes an offence at common law ...[52]

English judges defeated both codification and the abolition of judge-made crime, arguing that legislation could not encompass all criminal circumstances.[53] The 1892 Canadian Criminal Code left the question open. In 1950, the Supreme Court of Canada ruled against judicial creation of criminal offences.[54] In 1955, Parliament amended the Code to provide that 'no person shall be convicted or discharged ... of an offence at common law.' In the area of juvenile justice, however, the courts could and did convict children of 'crimes' unknown to the law, under the wardship-based Juvenile Delinquents Act (1908). This ended with the enactment of the Young Offenders Act in 1984.

Parens Patriae, Crime, and Childhood

> The obscurity which hangs over the subject ... cannot be altogether dispelled until our existing ignorance as to the nature of the will and the mind ... is greatly diminished ... Much latitude must in any case be left to the tribunal which has to apply the law to the facts, in each particular case.
>
> Royal Commission on Indictable Offences (1879)

Roman doctrines of legal capacity were reflected in English law after the fourteenth century in a paradigm shift from deed to doer. Prior to that time, guilt was conduct based. Children of any age (and animals) were subject to prosecution.[55] Punishment included forfeiture of property, a virtual death penalty for the family of the one condemned. By the fifteenth century, pardons were granted in cases of accident and self-defence. As pardon requires proof of guilt, forfeiture was preserved but, as few children had anything to forfeit, young children were routinely acquitted as *doli incapax* – incapable of guile or deceit.[56] From the fourteenth to the seventeenth centuries, the indicia of criminal responsibility was puberty, proved by examining the child's body.[57] Criminal capacity in prepubertal children was established on the facts of the case. Judicial consensus emerged in the seventeenth century that children under seven should not be prosecuted, a direct echo of the 407 Roman doctrine of infantia. Baptismal records introduced late in the century meant that age could be established without physical examination, but judges disagreed on what age signified puberty. Sir Edward Coke set it at fourteen, claiming consensus of the medieval courts. There is no support for this. His precedent lies with Justinian (see above). After Coke, English common law recognized children under seven as doli incapax. From seven to fourteen, capacity must be established. After fourteen, capacity was presumed.

This scheme was incorporated into the 1892 Canadian Criminal Code. Crankshaw's *Annotated Canadian Criminal Code*, 1894 to date, was intended as a lawyer's guide and student text.[58] Early editions extensively quoted the Report of the English Draft Code Commissioners and judges' responses.[59] Crankshaw's notes on legal disability incorporated concepts of late-nineteenth-century science. Section 19 relieved from criminal liability

> persons who are insane or *non compos mentis* [including] idiots, lunatics, persons laboring under delirium tremens, imbeciles, persons suffering from delusions and hallucinations, monomaniacs, homicidal maniacs and children.
>
> A child within the age of seven is considered to be without any capacity to discern good from evil or right from wrong. Such a child is *so conclusively*, so *absolutely* presumed to be incapable of committing crime that the presumption of its incapacity cannot be rebutted.[60]

The test of criminal capacity in children was taken from M'Naughton's Case (1843). That case set the legal test for lack of capacity due to insanity (mental disorder). Thus, the child, like the mentally disordered, must be found competent to 'know the nature and consequences of his conduct, and to appreciate that it was wrong.'

Children of seven were jailed with adults in early Canada.[61] Jury nullification (refusal to convict) after 1800 led to two 1857 statutes in Canada West (Ontario): the Act for Establishing Prisons for Young Offenders, empowering the courts to sentence, and penitentiary governors to remove, those under twenty-one to a reformatory; and the Act for the More Speedy Trial and Punishment of Offenders, aimed at reducing pre-trial detention of children. Children were jailed with adults through the 1880s. Industrial schools and the new option of fostering replaced reformatories, as the welfare approach to child offending took hold (discussed below). The Juvenile Delinquents Act (1908) made 'delinquency' the sole head of criminal intervention, satisfied by immorality or breach of any law. The child's conduct was relevant only to the determination of her welfare. The new youth courts were empowered to place delinquent children in foster care, in industrial schools, or in the five remaining privately run reformatories until the age of majority.

The Charter of Rights and Freedoms (1982) mandated legal rights not recognized in the 1908 act. The Young Offenders Act (1984) introduced rights and limited criminal accountability, stressing diversion and alternative measures. The age of criminal responsibility was raised from seven to twelve, with the cut-off at eighteen. Limits were contested.[62] Judicial interpretation and parliamentary amendments lowered the threshold of transfer of children to adult court. Underuse of diversion and alternative measures vitiated the welfare aims of the 1984 act. Canada incarcerates more children per capita than any other industrialized state including the United States.[63] The Canadian Youth Criminal Justice Act (2002), in force April 2003, diverts more children from the justice system but returns adult criminal responsibility to others.[64] Abandoned in the statutes of 1984 and 2002 was the parens patriae 'welfare' approach of the 1908 statute.

Parens Patriae's Statutory Child – Social Legislation

Promiscuous alms giving is fatal ... it is the patent process for the manufacture of paupers out of the worthless and improvident. A poor law is a legislative machine for the manufacture of pauperism. It is true mercy to say that it would be better that a few individuals should die of starvation than a pauper class should be raised up.

The *Globe* (1874)

The focus of parens patria in the early courts of equity was the care of children's persons and estates upon death of the father. From Tudor times onward, the social problem posed by childhood was the incipient criminality of fatherless and impoverished children. These were dealt with under the Poor Relief Act (1536–1601), a series of statutes known as the Tudor Poor Law, for centuries the sole piece of social legislation in England and in the eastern colonies of Canada.

Social legislation is aimed at ameliorating social conditions by uniting disparate areas of law in new processes and social institutions.[65] Spurred by fear of disorder in times of social unrest, moral panics and calls for reform centred in the Hanoverian period (1790–1840) on unsocialized children (see below). While seen generally as a failure, the efforts of social reformers led to a 'radically different system of policy formation mobilizing government rather than public opinion.'[66] This 'made individual reformers and voluntary pressure groups such powerful influences on social legislation.' The Poor Law, education, factories and mines, prisons, policing, and public health fit the new reform model. Reform during the nineteenth century was enabled by the new medium of the Royal Commission. Sir Robert Peel warned his Home Secretary of the dangers: '[I]f you issue a Commission, you will excite to the utmost the hopes and fears of rival factions; the truth will be exposed in a light probably somewhat exaggerated, and the Government, which exposes to view so great a national deformity, ought to be prepared with an adequate remedy. A Commission is most useful to pave the way for a measure, which is preconcerted; take for example the Poor Law Inquiry.'[67]

The 1834 Commission on the Poor Law split discourses of self-improvement and philanthropy into Benthamite calculations of felicity and Malthusian calculations of shortage, leaving popular sentiment behind.[68] The unhappy residue of these reforms was exposed in *Oliver Twist*. In his 1850 speech to the London Freemason's Tavern, Charles Dickens praised those who 'found infancy was made stunted, ugly, and full of pain; maturity made old, and old age imbecile; and pauperism made hopeless every day [and] claimed for the metropolis of a Christian country that this should be remedied, and that the capital should set an example of humanity and justice to the whole empire.'[69]

The Dickensian project of nineteenth-century social reform – freedom from want, children cared for, disability provided for – became the scientific project of the Progressive Era, the era of Canada's formation. The British North America Act (1867) assigned social welfare to the provinces. Confederating provinces followed three models of welfare delivery – the church in Quebec, the Poor Law in Nova Scotia and New Brunswick, and a hodge-podge of services in Ontario, where the Poor Law was excluded on grounds that anyone wanting work could find it. Legislative innovation began with the 1874 Ontario Charity Aid Act for the deaf, blind, and mentally handicapped, 'a legislative machine for the manufacture of pauperism,' the *Globe* opined. The 'reluctant welfarism' of the years 1891 to 1940 spurred the formation of private associations in Canada for political, social, moral, and economic reform inspired by the social gospel movement and radical labour.[70] Worker's compensation, public health, and Depression relief projects set the stage for the boom years of the Canadian welfare state, 1941 to 1974. Second World War regulations, militant labour, and unemployment pushed further reform in the 1950s. Medicare, forged in Saskatchewan in 1961 under New Democratic premier Tommy Douglas, was the last major accomplishment of the welfare state. Childhood was a primary target of social legislation.

Parens Patriae's Statutory Child – Child Welfare Legislation

There is little or no difference in character or needs between the neglected and the delinquent child. It is often a mere accident whether he is brought before the court because he is wandering or beyond control or because he has committed some offence. Neglect [of moral training] leads to delinquency and delinquency is often the direct outcome of [moral] neglect.

Anonymous English reformer (1927)

Child welfare legislation is both a subset of social legislation and a reaction to it. The Tudor Poor Law, a series of statutes enacted between 1536 and 1601, required the parish on magistrate's order to receive or remove children of vagrant, destitute, or deceased parents and apprentice them to a trade, with the aim of boarding them out to a good middle-class family.[71] This was driven by a need for skilled child labour in an industrializing society and by the threat of uncontrolled children to the public order. Under Poor Law and vagrancy acts dating back to the bubonic plague, agents pressed children 'found wandering' into the ships and mines of the industrial revolution under specious apprenticeships. Reform was driven by sentimentality and fear.[72] Early charities stressed morality, family authority and social threat, not concern for children.[73] The Poor Law boarding-out model was replaced in the early to mid-nineteenth century by the new model of the asylum, desirable as it concentrated children under one regime for better inculcation of social behaviour, factory skills and Christianity.

Childhood management in the British Empire was guided by two government reports, the 1834 Report from His Majesty's Commission for Inquiring into the Administration and Practical Operation of the Poor Laws, and the 1837 House of Commons Report of the Select Committee on Aborigines concerning 'Native Inhabitants of Countries where British Settlements are made ... to promote the spread of civilization among them.' Both recommended overseers, training programs, and assimilation through education, civilization, and bringing into Christianity the young pauper or Aborigine. The Select Committee on Aborigines wrote, 'True civilization and Christianity are inseparable: the former has never been found, but as a fruit of the latter.' This was the hallmark both of reformatories and Indian residential schools in Canada.

The 1854 UK Act to make better provision for the Care and Education of Vagrant Destitute and Disorderly Children and for the Extension of Industrial Schools enabled charitable societies to place in industrial schools children under fourteen if found wandering, begging, or consorting with thieves, and under twelve if charged with a criminal offence or declared uncontrollable or truant.[74] The 1908 UK Children Act brought industrial and reform schools under one administration. Whether the child had been wronged or had done wrong was immaterial – both signalled moral degeneration. 'The evil was as much the spiritual harm which befell the abusers as the physical or moral damage sustained by their victims.'[75] Prosecutions of parents and guardians who killed or mutilated children are recorded,[76] but lesser cases were unlikely to come before the courts. The 1889 UK Prevention of Cruelty to Children Act expedited the prosecution of parents and guardians by making it a misdemeanour to wilfully ill-treat, neglect, abandon, or expose children 'if likely to cause unnecessary suffering.' Upper Canada's post–1850 urbanization spawned similar fears.

The leitmotif of child protection was the 1874 U.S. Mary Ellen case. The New York Society for the Prevention of Cruelty to Animals, concerned about a child mistreated by her guardians, was told that evidence was insufficient for criminal charges and the Department of Charities could not interfere with legal custody.[77] Arguing that children are human beings and hence members of the animal kingdom, the society was given legal authority to apprehend Mary Ellen, and sent out 'before' and 'after' pictures of her rescue. Humane societies represented both animals and children in Canada until the end of the nineteenth century.

Canada's Progressive Era (1880–1920) was infused by evangelical social purity linking moral, physical, and social hygiene, religion, and science to a new childhood and a new nation.[78] Social purity drew upon Canadian metaphors of untouched wilderness and imported ideas from abroad without much reflection on local conditions – for example, counting Winnipeg bedrooms as parallel to the London slum 'lodger evil' construct of child sexual abuse.[79] The stress on eliminating vice and degeneracy resembled British and American reforms, but Canadian progressivism had another goal. In the transition from colony to nationhood, Canada was to be sister to England in a new empire.[80] 'If Canada is to rear an imperial race, it will not be by children raised in slums.'[81] In Canada as elsewhere, social legislation regulating factories, mines, schools, asylums, delinquency, and child protection was in place by 1911. The Poor Law and asylums began to disappear. Manitoba, the first Western province, was the last to adopt the Poor Law, in its 1877 Apprentices and Minors Act.[82] Ontario, having rejected the Poor Law, closely followed American and British reform in its Humane Societies Act, which enabled the apprehension of children, and its 1888 Children's Protection Act, which empowered the courts to commit children to asylums. Toronto reformer J.J. Kelso campaigned for foster care and for separate humane societies for children. 'The difficulty is cropping up of keeping the animals and children from clashing, the two having their separate and distinct friends,' he wrote in 1890.[83] Under his motto 'It is wiser and less expensive to save children than to punish criminals,' Ontario enacted legislation in 1893 that gave the new Children's Aid Societies, carved out of the Humane Societies, the powers of custody and wardship in addition to the power to apprehend abandoned, neglected, abused, and truant children. Manitoba adopted the Children's Aid Society model in 1891 and enacted its Child Protection Act in 1898. The model is extant in Manitoba and provinces in the east, but not those further west.

Post-1920 child welfare philosophy shifted from child apprehension to family therapy. Professional social workers and university experts replaced the charitable amateur, statutes were renamed 'child and family services,' and the focus on abuse, exploitation, and parental delict was lost. Adoption legislation was introduced by the 1920s. New aims resembled the old: 'to avoid present and future expenditures on public welfare and to guarantee social peace and stability by transforming

ing dependent children into industrious, law-abiding workers.'[84] The new expertise legitimated the bias toward the patriarchal nuclear family.[85] In Canada's familialization of society, omitting kinship structures had stark consequences for Aboriginal children, first in residential schooling and its project of cultural conversion, second in the 'sixties scoop' of Aboriginal children by the child welfare system.[86]

The 1962 discovery of the 'battered child syndrome' returned child abuse to the forefront of child welfare.[87] Massive legislative reforms expanded categories of abuse and agency reach, resulting in the apprehension of thousands of Aboriginal children for placement in non-Aboriginal homes and institutions without explanation, home studies, or other protections long a part of the agency agenda. Northern expansion and constitutional quarrels over funding and jurisdiction between Canada, responsible for Indians, and the provinces, responsible for child protection, were to blame for deeply inadequate services.[88] Also to blame were dismal reserve conditions and generations of residential schooling premised on the long-discarded model of reformatories and industrial schools. Indian residential schools denigrated aboriginality, damaged family and cultural ties, and introduced child sexual abuse and corporal punishment into First Nations cultures. Overlooked even in the panic over battered children was the role played by the enduring Roman defence of moderate correction of children.

Pater Potestas, the Discipline of Minors, and the Rights of the Child

It follows, according to the actual progression of human beings, that the next influx or irradiation which our enlighteners are pouring on us, will illuminate the world with the grave descants on the rights of youth, the rights of children, the rights of babies.

– Hannah More (1799)

The corporal punishment of apprentices by masters was abolished in Canada in 1955, of criminals in 1972, and of those aboard ships in 2002. Children are now the only class of persons legally subject to corporal punishment.[89] 'Most of the ancient philosophers and law-makers were in favour of flogging children, not only as a means of inducing them to conduct themselves well and tell the truth, but also as an aid to education itself.'[90] A series of Roman novels (decrees) first emancipated cruelly treated children from paternal control,[91] next prohibited corporal punishment that exceeded 'moderate flogging' and equated the killing of children with the crime of parricide,[92] and finally limited the use of corporal punishment to the moderate correction of minors.[93] In 365, Valentinian and Valens advised the Senate on 'correction of relatives that correction is restricted to minors': 'We ... are not willing that the right to inflict extremely severe castigation for the faults of minors should be conferred, but that the exercise of paternal authority may correct the errors of youth, and repress them by private chastisement.'[94]

Roman annotators saw this as a defence to child assault and Bracton repeated the annotation verbatim, as English law, in his thirteenth-century text: 'Motive, as in whippings, which are not punishable if imposed by a master or parent (unless they are immoderate) since they are taken to be inflicted to correct not injure, but are punished when one is struck in anger by a stranger.'[95]

Masters justified flogging apprentices under 'custom of London' and common law. In a 1481 case of assault, battery, and false imprisonment brought by an apprentice against his hosier master, the master argued that his apprentice was 'negligent in learning his craft and would not apply himself, and so the defendant took him by the hand and beat him with a rod.' Littleton J replied, 'This is no plea. It is not lawful for someone to beat his apprentice, even if he does not apply himself to his craft, for the master may have a writ of covenant (for breach of contract) against him.'[96] He questioned 'whether a schoolmaster may justify beating, for it is no prejudice to him if the scholar will not accept learning.'

Lambarde's 1581 handbook for magistrates stated, 'Some are allowed to have privately, a *natural*, and some a *civile* power (or authoritie) [as husbands, masters, teachers] over others, so that they may be excused themselves if but (in reasonable manner) they correct and chastise them for their offenses.'[97] Blackstone called it a 'power of the father or his delegate' under English law's reduced pater potestas to 'lawfully correct his child being under age, in a reasonable manner for this is for the benefit of his education,' a right flowing from paternal duty.[98] Draft Code Commissioner James Fitzjames Stephen set out its nineteenth-century common-law limits. 'It is not a crime to inflict bodily harm by way of lawful correction ... to the person of another; but if the harm inflicted on such an occasion is excessive the act which inflicts it is unlawful, and, even if there is no excess, it is the duty of every person applying the force to take reasonable precautions against the infliction of other or greater harm than the occasion requires.'[99]

The 'power' made its first legislative appearance in the 1892 Canadian Criminal Code under 'Discipline of minors': '55. It is lawful for every parent, or person in the place of a parent, schoolmaster or master, to use force by way of correction towards any child, pupil or apprentice under his care, provided that such force is reasonable under the circumstances.' Revised in 1955, the Code states under 'Correction of child by force' that '43. Every schoolteacher, parent or person standing in the place of a parent is justified in using force by way of correction toward a pupil or child, as the case may, who is under his care, if the force does not exceed what is reasonable under the circumstances.'

A Roman doctrine, pater potestas, was modified by imperial edict to protect children. A protection measure became a defence, a paternal right, and a justification. 'The most startling feature of s. 43 is that, while conferring the right to correct with reasonable force, it nowhere defines the circumstances in which this correction can ensue.'[100] This is reflected in over a century of contradictory Canadian jurisprudence.

The United Nations Committee on the Rights of the Child chastised Canada for retaining the defence:

Further measures seem to be needed to effectively prevent and combat all forms of corporal punishment in schools or in institutions where children may be placed. The Committee is also preoccupied by the existence of child abuse and violence within the family and the insufficient protection afforded by the existing legislation in that regard [and] recommends that the physical punishment of children ... be prohibited. In connection with the child's right to physical integrity as recognized by the Convention ... and in the light of the best interests of the child, the Committee further suggests that the State party consider the possibility of introducing new legislation and follow-up mechanisms to prevent violence within the family, and that educational campaigns be launched with a view to changing the acceptance of legal prohibition.[101]

This reflects the combination of protective and equality rights in the UN Convention on the Rights of the Child. In 1999, a constitutional challenge to Section 43 was launched in the Supreme Court of Ontario under Section 15(1) of the Canadian Charter of Rights and Freedoms. This states that 'Every individual is equal before and under the law and has the right to the equal protection and equal benefit of the law without discrimination and, in particular, without discrimination based on ... age.'[102] The challenger, the Canadian Foundation for Children,

Youth and the Law, argued that as the family can be 'a very dangerous place for children, the *parens patriae* jurisdiction assumes greater importance.'[103] In 2004, the Supreme Court of Canada ruled that Section 43 does not offend the Charter nor does it offend the Convetion on the Rights of the Child as only 'mild corrective force of a truly transitory and trifling nature' is excused. The court set limits on the use of force not found in the law:[104]

> On the basis of current expert consensus, it does not apply to corporal punishment of children under two or teenagers. Degrading, inhuman or harmful conduct is not protected. Discipline by the use of objects or blows or slaps to the head is unreasonable. Teachers may reasonably apply force to remove a child from a classroom or secure compliance with instructions but not merely as corporal punishment. Coupled with the requirement that the conduct be corrective, which rules out conduct stemming from the caregiver's frustration, loss of temper or abusive personality, a consistent picture emerges of the area covered by s. 43 ... The gravity of the precipitating event is not relevant.

Outside this zone, corporal punishment risks criminal sanction. While children 'often feel a sense of disempowerment and vulnerability,' this must be set against 'the reality of a child's mother or father being pulled into the criminal justice system.' The court concluded that corporal punishment 'is not arbitrarily demeaning. It does not discriminate. Rather, it is firmly grounded in the actual needs and circumstances of the child.'[105] Three of the nine judges disagreed.[106]

Judges put the brakes on their role as 'legislators' in parens patriae cases, as *Re Eve* and *D.F.G.* show. While parens patriae is theirs to develop or restrain, the courts are necessary legislators in Charter cases, vested with an overarching jurisdiction where laws infringe on protected rights. The decision calls up old debates pitting familial and paternal power against the state and corporal punishment as ensign of that power. Children are non-actors, silenced, objects, not subjects, of reform.

Only in an era of children's rights would a legal defence to child assault be problematic. Children's rights were first raised in the international human rights context in 1923 by Eglantyne Jebb, drafter of the 1924 League of Nations Declaration of the Rights of the Child, who remarked, 'I believe we should claim rights for children and labour for their universal recognition.'[107] Second World War atrocities inspired a new era in international law. A binding convention on children's rights called for in 1978 resulted in the UN Convention on the Rights of the Child, adopted by the General Assembly 20 November 1989, in force 2 September 1990. State signing, the first stage of acceptance, was unprecedented in speed and number. Only the United States has failed to ratify the Convention. The Convention puts children both in and outside the parens patriae box, by naming child-specific protective rights together with, among others, rights to expression, association, and fair hearing. The Convention established a new childhood – the child as rights-bearer – and a new set of claims on the collectivity. If children's rights differ from the rights that accrue to all human beings, the difference must be justified.[108]

Anti-rights arguments take three forms. The first echos the tutelary scheme of *cura minoris* – childhood as a legal disability to be outgrown. We now know that childhood leaves its mark on society and that society is not relieved by specious argument from its responsibility to respect and protect all its members. That protection must now be read in terms of human rights and, in Canada, the Charter of Rights and Freedoms.

The second argument posits rights as the antithesis of relationship and relationship as central to childhood. 'Abandoning children to their rights' is portrayed as a stark consequence of children's rights. But 'individual' can have meaning only in reference to the collectivity.[109] Rights are less claims *against* the collectivity than markers of relationships of equality *in relation to* the collectivity. 'What makes autonomy possible is not separation, but relationship. This shifts the focus from protection against others to structuring relationships so that they foster autonomy.' Dependence is a precondition of relationship – parent-child, child-teacher, state-citizen – giving 'the security, education, nurturing, and support that make the development of autonomy possible.'

The third argument is that rights accrue only with equal measure of responsibility. This misstates the aim of human rights. Rights indeed invoke a mutuality of responsibility, but central to human rights is respect for the person. Rights accrue from birth. Responsibility accrues with maturity and capacity.

As Roman law recognized, some persons will not attain full legal capacity, yet we do not deny such persons the status of rights-bearer. To recognize children as rights-bearers is to respect and value them in the present, as ends in themselves as persons and not just means to other ends – parental power, agency increase, adulthood, nationhood. Legal constructs of capacity and the fashioning of parens patriae protections have the confusing result of either replacing rights with protection, thus denying capacity, or fostering capacity by protecting the person of the rights-bearer until capacity to exercise rights is attained. The logic either way recognizes the existence of rights and the status of rights-bearer.

Human rights set out in the UN Convention on the Rights of the Child and in the Canadian Charter of Rights and Freedoms portray the child as part of the collectivity, as citizen of a state, as belonging to an ethnic group, as a member of a family, and as a legal person. Although the family remains central, its internal hierarchies have shifted. If children remain the future of their nations, the concept of rights has recast the meaning of nationhood. The Convention on the Rights of the Child incorporates rights to a family and rights to protection with expressive and participatory rights, making the shift from protection and the *potestas* of others less disjunctive than portrayals of children as 'abandoned to their rights' make it appear. The test case for children's rights in Canada is the immunity derived from Roman law to child assault granted to tutors and parents. This question has now worked its way through the Canadian judicial system. Still, unless Parliament takes action in accord with Canada's international commitments, pater potestas trumps parens patriae and the basic human rights of children to be protected from assault.

The shift in children's status – from paternal ownership to perpetual state wardship to rights-bearer – is partial, painful, and resisted. Even so, the recognition of children's rights is the first new legal construct of childhood in some twenty-five hundred years. Short of violent revolution, this is how paradigms emerge.

Notes

My thanks to Trevor Anderson and Mark Golden for comments on an early draft. Initial research was supported by the Law Commission of Canada initiative on *Legislation*, for which law student Cary Clark provided able and enthusiastic research assistance.

1 George Lakoff, *Women, Fire, and Dangerous Things: What Categories Reveal About the Mind* (1987), discussed in Ainsworth, 'Achieving the Promise of Justice for Juveniles.' Ainsworth argues that essentialism justifies a separate youth court system and unequal treatment of older youth compared with adults (fewer legal protections, longer sentences); older youth are seen as more like the prototypical child (vulnerable, lacking judgment)

and less like the prototypical adult (autonomous, capable). We are fettered by unconscious classification.

2 McGillivray, 'Reconstructing Child Abuse' and 'Abused Children in the Courts.'

3 Foucault, *Discipline and Punish.*

4 Donzelot, *Policing of Families.*

5 McGillivray, 'Reconstructing Child Abuse' and 'Abused Children in the Courts.'

6 Rose, *Governing the Soul,* 130.

7 Rose, *Governing the Soul,* 103.

8 McGillivray, introduction to *Governing Childhood,* 1.

9 Holdsworth, *History of English Law.*

10 See, e.g., Manitoba Law Reform Commission, *Report.*

11 *Falkland v. Bertie* (1696), 23 E.R. 814 at 818; 2 Vern. 333 at 342. Citations in brackets are added.

12 *Wellesley v. Duke of Beaufort* (1827), 38 E.R. 236. 'It belongs to the King, as parens patriae, having the care of those who are not able to take care of themselves, and is founded on the obvious necessity that the law should place somewhere the care of individuals who cannot take care of themselves, particularly in cases where it is clear that some care should be thrown around them.'

13 *R. v. Gyngall,* [1893] 2 Q.B. 232 at 239. '[Parens patriae is] a paternal jurisdiction, a judicially administrative jurisdiction, in virtue of which the Chancery Court was put to act on behalf of the Crown, as being the guardian of all infants, in the place of a parent, and as if it were the parent of the child, thus superceding the natural guardianship of the parent.'

14 *Rolands v. Rolands* (1983), 9 *Fam. L.R.* 320 at 321. 'It has existed for many centuries, going back into the Court of Chancery in England, to act to secure the welfare of children. It has the power to override, when necessary, the views of those in charge of children, whether a parent, a minister of the Crown, government official or otherwise.'

15 *Re R* (a minor), [1991] 4 All. E.R. 177 at 186. '[T]he practical jurisdiction is wider than that of parents ... [It is] not derivative from the parents' rights and responsibilities, but derives from, or is, the delegated performance of the duties of the Crown to protect its subjects and particularly children.'

16 Theobald, *Law Relating to Lunacy.*

17 Qtd. in Graham, 'Parens Patriae,' 190.

18 Seymour, 'Parens Patriae and Wardship Powers,' 187–188.

19 *C.f.* 'In the fourth century A.D., Constantine the Great introduced the concept of parens patriae (the state as parent), the precedent for the legal

principle behind the state's intervention in family life when care falls below an established minimum.' Robert W. tenBensel, 'The Development of the Concept of the Needs of Children' (1987) 8 *Latham Letter* 1–4, cited in Schene and Ward, 'The Vexing Problem of Elder Abuse.'

20 Buckland, *Text-Book of Roman Law*, Cambridge, 157.

21 'The Code of Justinian,' in Scott, *Civil Law.*

22 Watson, *Spirit of Roman Law*, 148.

23 Buckland, *Text-Book of Roman Law*, 102.

24 'Justinian Code,' in Scott, *Civil Law*, s. 8, 47, 9, Emperors Diocletian and Maximian, ca. 287 (Appendix).

25 Stone, *Family, Sex and Marriage*, Ch. 5 and 408–411.

26 Stone, *Family, Sex and Marriage*, 27.

27 Stone, *Family, Sex and Marriage*, 117.

28 Steward, *New Child.*

29 '[T]he common notion that the praetors exercised an equity jurisdiction must be treated with great caution [as] there was basically only one system of courts ... and the innovations [of the Edict] were no more specifically equitable than is most legislation.' Watson, *Spirit of Roman Law*, 79–80.

30 Watson, *Spirit of Roman Law*, 77.

31 Watson, *Spirit of Roman Law*, quoting David Daube, p. 75: 'Legislation ... involved a cumbersome machinery, as a rule set in motion only for politicial purposes. In private law, it was something of a last resort.' Nor did legislation enjoy its modern supremacy. Gaius states, 'An imperial constitution is what the emperor ordains by edict or letter. It has never been doubted that this has the sovereign force of statute since the emperor himself receives his sovereign power by statute' (148). Emperors achieved status by military prowess, not precedent legislation.

32 Wardship arose in socage (feudal tenure), and by nature (for an heir apparent), custom, nurture, parental right, parental choice, and judicial appointment.

33 *Incert. temp.* cc. 11, 12; 17 Edw. 2, stat. 2., cc. 9, 10, Ruff.

34 *State ex. R. Hawks v. Lazaro*, 202 S.E. Rep. 109 at 117–118.

35 12 Car. 2, c. 24.

36 *Re Eve* (1986), 31 *D.L.R.* (4th) 1–37 at 14 (SCC).

37 The 1852 *Act for the Relief of the Suitors of the High Court of Chancery UK*, c. 87, s. 15 gave the courts 'custody of the Persons and Estates of Persons found idiot, lunatic or of unsound Mind.' The Idiots Act (1886), 49 & 50 Vict., c. 25 and the Lunacy Act (1890), 53 Vict., c. 5 granted custodial jurisdiction over such persons. Under 'The Crown as Parens Patriae,' Halsbury cites Blackstone: 'At common law idiots are persons born with-

out any glimmering of reason, including persons born deaf, dumb, and blind; whilst lunatics are persons who have become temporarily or permanently deprived of their reason, or *non compos mentis*, by disease, grief, or accident after birth.' This is the last reference in Halsbury to parens patriae; see *Halsbury's Laws of England*, 475 et seq.

38 *E. (Mrs.) v. Eve*, [1986] 2 S.C.R. 388. The judgment was criticized for its narrow view of the parens patriae 'best interests test,' in presuming that sterilization is non-therapeutic except on extremely limited medical grounds. There are therapeutic outcomes for a woman in Eve's position. See Shone, Case Comment.

39 *Winnipeg Child and Family Services (Northwest Area) v. D.F.G.*, [1997] 3 S.C.R. 925. G was put in hospital 'cold turkey' and went into convulsions, with potentially lethal consequences for her fetus and herself. She was delivered of a healthy baby, remained free of her addiction, and kept her baby. G had earlier sought admission to a drug treatment facility but no beds were available.

40 These judicial limits were set out by the Supreme Court of Canada in *R. v. Morgentaler*, a case involving fetal rights to life. The law recognizes rights in the human *in* being, which means born alive. In that case, the Supreme Court also deferred to the legislature.

41 Lieberman, *Province of Legislation Determined*, 63.

42 Bentham's Pannomium is reflected in Digests of the law that are so 'compendious' as to defy the simplicity inherent in the concept. Lieberman, *Province of Legislation Determined*, 282.

43 Bentham, *Introduction*, 33. A purpose of the Pannomium was to name all offences, one legacy of which is the Canadian Criminal Code. Another is the paradigm shift from natural law to legal positivism, from law as divine in origin to law as originating from the legislator.

44 Lieberman, *Province of Legislation Determined*, 13. Regular sittings of parliament facilitated legislation.

45 Lieberman, *Province of Legislation Determined*, 14.

46 Hay, 'Property, Authority and the Criminal Law,' 17–63. Dickens describes the reaction of the crowds to a dual public hanging in two letters to the *Times*, 14 and 18 November 1849. Disgusted by the crowd's 'wickedness and levity,' 'cries and howls,' 'screeching and laughing,' and 'brutal mirth or callousness,' he recommended that hanging be done secretly behind the prison walls. Ackroyd, *Charles Dickens*, 604–605.

47 Hanging acts are only a part of the legislative spate in this period. The eighteenth edition of Richard Burn's handbook for justices, published 1797, was three times the length of the first edition of 1775. For Alexander

Hamilton in 1788, in the United States, 'a voluminous code of laws is one of the inconveniences necessarily connected with the advantages of free government.' Lieberman, *Province of Legislation Determined*, 15.

48 Knell, 'Capital Punishment.' Knell documents 103 London cases between 1801 and 1836 in which children were sentenced to death; all sentences but one were commuted. The last, a boy of thirteen, was hanged for murder in 1831. Perhaps this is a parallel case to the boy of eleven sentenced to life in 2001 in the United States, for the brutal death by beating of a girl of four, attributed by the defence to the influence of televised, pre-staged wrestling.

49 Hay, 'Property, Authority and the Criminal Law,' 17–63 at 33.

50 The Court of King's Bench held in *Sedley's Case* (1663), 17 St. Tri. 155 that the court, as *custos morum* of the king's subjects and inheritor of the powers of the Star Chamber, can make criminal any conduct threatening the king's peace.

51 *Report of the Royal Commission appointed to consider the law Relating to Indictable Offences*, 1879, C 2345. See Friedland, 'R.S. Wright's Model Criminal Code' and Stephen, *Digest*. 'By far the greater part of the Code and of the Report was my own composition' (Stephen, *History*). The *Draft Code* was prepared for the English Colonial Office and based criminal codes in Canada (1892), New Zealand (1893), Queensland (1899), and the remaining Australian states later (Friedland, supra, at 340). The Canadian Code was substantially modified by colonial legal developments. England rejected codification.

52 The Canadian Criminal Code preserves common-law defences. 'The only result which can follow from preserving the common law as to justification and excuse is, that a man morally innocent, not otherwise protected, may avoid punishment. In the one case you remove rusty spring-guns and man-traps from unfrequented plantations, in the other you decline to issue an order for the destruction of every old-fashioned drag or life-buoy which may be found on the banks of a dangerous river.' Stephen, *History*.

53 Sir John Thompson assured Canadian Parliament that 'The common law will still stand and be referred to, and in that respect the code ... will have that elasticity which has been so much desired by those who are opposed to codification on general principles.' Qtd. in Crankshaw, *Criminal Code of Canada*, Introduction, xci–xcii.

54 *Frey v. Fedoruk*, [1950] S.C.R. 517. 'I think it is sager to hold that no one shall be convicted of a crime unless the offence with which he is charged is recognized as such in the provisions of the Criminal Code, *or* can be

established by the authority of some reported case as an offence known to the law. I think that if any course of conduct is now to be declared criminal ... such declaration should be made by Parliament and not by the Courts.'
55 This was the law of deodand, not abolished until 1846.
56 Buckland, *Text-book of Roman Law*. Ulpian defined dolus as 'Any craft or deceit employed for the circumvention or entrapping of the person' but later Roman law defined it simply as a wilful action with no requirement of deceit (594). Dolus attracted penal consequences unless restitution was made.
57 Anand, 'Catalyst for Change,' 517 et seq.
58 Crankshaw, *Criminal Code of Canada*. *Who's Who and Why in Canada* (1912) states that James Crankshaw 'In 1894 published work on criminal code, used as text-book throughout Canada, now in 3rd edition.' On the origins of the Code (Crankshaw is not mentioned), see Brown, *Birth of the Criminal Code* and *Genesis of the Canadian Criminal Code*.
59 Report of the Royal Commission appointed to consider the law Relating to Indictable Offences, 1879, C 2345. See text at note 1, above.
60 Crankshaw, *Criminal Code of Canada*, section 19. Emphasis in the original.
61 Carrigan, *Crime and Punishment in Canada*. A few were hanged in the eighteenth century.
62 Anand, 'Catalyst for Change.'
63 Schissel, *Blaming Children*, 8.
64 Children of fourteen to seventeen with two previous convictions for violent offences are now subject to adult penalties. See generally Smandych, *Youth Justice*.
65 Bureau et al., 'Development and Trends in Canadian Social Law,' 76. 'Common to [such] statutes is their presentation as measures of protection involving the establishment of institutions, structures and mechanisms to prevent injustice, correct situations and guarantee their beneficiaries a state of economic, social and cultural well-being.'
66 Eastwood, 'Men, Morals and the Machinery of Social Legislation,' 191.
67 Eastwood, 'Men, Morals and the Machinery of Social Legislation,' 200.
68 Eastwood, 'Men, Morals and the Machinery of Social Legislation,' 205.
69 Ackroyd, *Charles Dickens*, 616. That day, Dickens spoke at the inauguration of the Metropolitan Sanitary Association, instituted in response to the cholera epidemic of the previous winter and the horrors of London sanitation (supporating sewers, graveyards coughing up the dead).
70 Moscovitch and Drover, 'Social Expenditures,' 20. Associations included the Woman's Christian Temperance Union, the National Council of

Women, the Social Service Council of Canada, farmers' groups, consumer and agricultural co-operatives, and radical societies of working people.

71 Dingwall et al., 'Childhood as a Social Problem,' 210–211.

72 On moral panic, see Cohen, *Folk Devils*.

73 Dingwall et al., 'Childhood as a Social Problem, 214 et seq. The names of two London-based societies – the 1788 Philanthropic Society for the Prevention of Crimes, and the Reform of the Criminal Poor, by the encouragement of Industry and the Culture of Good Morals, among those Children who are now being trained up to Vicious Courses, Public Plunder, Infamy and Ruin; and the 1815 Society for Investigating the Causes of the Alarming Increase of Juvenile Delinquency in the Metropolis – make the point.

74 Enlarged 1861, consolidated 1866.

75 Dingwall et al., 'Childhood as a Social Problem,' 218. The Liverpool Society for Prevention of Cruelty to Children 'was not formed with a view to permanently housing, clothing, feeding or otherwise providing for children, but rather for the purpose of increasing and, if need be, enforcing such duties upon parents, guardians, or others entrusted with the care of children.'

76 Newspaper accounts from 1785 to 1860 shows some three hundred child assault prosecutions; see Pollock, *Forgotten Children* and *Lasting Relationship*.

77 Schene and Ward, 'Relevance of the Child Protection Experience.' The case was a media 'set-up' for statutory reform.

78 Valverde, *Age of Light*.

79 Social workers were to count bedrooms and household residents in the day, then return in the evening for a recount, to ensure that children were not sharing their beds with lodgers and thus in danger of sexual activity.

80 Valverde, *Age of Light*, 45. A speaker at the 1896 meeting of the National Council of Women orated, 'This vast Dominion, stretching as it does from ocean to ocean, endowed by nature so lavishly [gives] every sign and token, whether of natural resource or [white] racial heritage, [that] the future of Canada will be, must be, the golden future of a great and mighty nation.'

81 Valverde, *Age of Light*, 128.

82 Ursel, *Private Lives, Public Policy*. Chunn, *From Punishment to Doing Good*.

83 Diary, 10 January 1890. Kelso was a key figure in the development of the Canadian foster care system, Children's Aid Societies, statutory powers of apprehension, and the juvenile court. See Bullen, 'J.J. Kelso and the "New" Child-savers,' and Rutman, 'J.J. Kelso and the Development of Child Welfare.'

84 Bullen, 'J.J. Kelso and the "New" Child-savers,' 157–158. Children were placed on farms, given little education, subjected to 'many obvious injustices' and 'condemned to a working-class world that offered few opportunities for personal development and social mobility.'

85 Chunn, *From Punishment to Doing Good*, 36.

86 See Korbin, *Child Abuse and Neglect*, and Eichler, *Families in Canada Today*, and McGillivray, 'Therapies of Freedom.'

87 McGillivray, 'Reconstructing Child Abuse.'

88 McGillivray, 'Therapies of Freedom.'

89 McGillivray, '"He'll learn it on his body"' and 'Child Physical Assault.'

90 Scott, *Civil Law.* Ch. 8. Plutarch wanted whipping confined to slaves, as free-born children benefitted from encouragement and reproach and whipping young offenders provoked hatred and idleness. Quintilian denounced the whipping of schoolboys as a base and slavish practice that inured the child to blows, resulted in severe injury, and provoked the negligence of their teachers.

91 *The Digest of Justinian* 48.19.16. Alan Watson et al., eds., Philadelphia, PA. University of Pennsylvania Press, 1985. Respectively, Digest 37.12.5 (Trajan, 98–117); Digest 48.9.5 (Hadrian, 117–138); Code 9.17 (Constantine, 318–319). See also Sherman, C. P. (1937). *Roman Law in the Modern World*, 3d ed. New York, Baker, Voorhis.

92 *The Digest of Justinian* 8.46 (227).

93 The offender 'shall neither be put to death by sword, nor by fire, nor by any other ordinary method, but shall be sewed up in a sack with a dog, a cock, a viper, and a monkey, and, enclosed with these wild animals and associated with serpents, he shall be thrown into the sea.' This punishment for child killing is also the punishment for parricide.

94 Given on the day before the Kalends of December, during the Consulate of Valentinian and Valens. 365. The Code of Justinian, Book IX. Scott, *Civil Law.*

95 *Bracton on the Laws and Customs of England*, 299.

96 Anon. 1481. Free translation from YB 21 Edward IV, tr. John Baker, with thanks to Professor Baker.

97 Reference to the 'civile power' of a husband to correct his wife disappeared in later editions. See Doggett, *Marriage, Wife-Beating and the Law*, 5.

98 *Blackstone's Commentaries on the Laws of England* (1809), Book I, 15th ed., paras. 452–453.

99 Stephen, *Digest of the Criminal Law*, 147. The Draft Code was prepared for the English Colonial Office, rejected in England, and later adopted by a

number of English colonies. The Canadian version of this Code was substantially modified by post-settlement legal developments in the Canadian colonies.

100 Stuart, *Canadian Criminal Law*, 426 and subsequent editions. 'The loose drafting of the section may reflect the political impotence of the children whose interests are at stake rather than a considered response to the issues of parental and educational authority.' Colvin, *Principles of Criminal Law*, 227.

101 Holmstrom, *Concluding Observations*, 71–74.

102 *The Canadian Foundation for Children, Youth and the Law*, factum.http:// www.jfcy.org/corporalp/corporalp.html cf 29113.

103 *The Canadian Foundation for Children, Youth and the Law v. Canada* [2004] S.C.J. paragraph 40 http://www.lexun.umontreal.ca/csc-scc/en/rec/ html/2004scc 004.wpd.html

104 ibid., paragraph 68.

105 On the Supreme Court decision, see McGillivray and Durrant. On the challenge, the charter and decisions of the lower courts, see McGillivray (2003).

106 See Ontario Court of Appeal (January 15, 2002), http://www. ontariocourts.on.ca/decisions index/2002index.htm.

107 Save the Children, *Children's Rights: Reality or Rhetoric? The UN Convention on the Rights of the Child: The First Ten Years* [2000].

108 McGillivray, Why children do have equal rights.

109 Nedelsky, 'Reconceiving rights as relationship.'

References

Ackroyd, P. (1991). *Charles Dickens*. London: Minerva.

Ainsworth, J. (1997). Achieving the promise of justice for juveniles: A call for the abolition of juvenile court. In A. McGillivray (Ed.), *Governing Childhood*. Aldershot, UK: Dartmouth.

Anand, S.S. (1999). Catalyst for change: The history of Canadian Juvenile justice reform. *24 Queen's L.J.*, 515–559.

Bentham, J. (1789). In J.H. Burns & H.L.A. Hart, *An Introduction to the Principles of Morals and Legislation*. London.

Bracton on the laws and customs of England, vol. 2. (1256; 1968). S.E. Thorne (Ed.). Cambridge, MA: Belknap Press.

Brown, D.H. (1989). *The genesis of the Canadian criminal code of 1892.* Toronto: Osgoode Society.

Brown, D.H. (Ed.). (1995). *The birth of the criminal code: The evolution of Canada's justice system*. Toronto: University of Toronto Press.

Buckland, W.W. (1963). *A text-book of Roman law from Augustus to Justinian* (3rd rev.). Cambridge: Cambridge University Press.

Bullen, J. (1990). J.J. Kelso and the 'new' child-savers: The genesis of the children's aid movement in Ontario. *82 Ontario History 107*, 157–158.

Bureau, R.D., Lippel, K., & Lamarche, L. (1989). Development and trends in Canadian social law, 1940 to 1984. In I. Bernier & A. Lajoie (Eds.), *Family Law and Social Welfare Legislation in Canada* (pp. 71–131). Toronto: University of Toronto Press.

Carrigan, D.O. (1991). *Crime and punishment in Canada, a history*. Toronto: McClelland & Stewart.

Chunn, D.E. (1992). *From punishment to doing good: Family courts and socialized justice in Ontario 1890–1940*. Toronto: University of Toronto Press.

Cohen, S. (1972). *Folk devils and moral panics: The creation of the mods and rockers*. London: MacGibbon and Kee.

Colvin, E. (1991). *Principles of criminal law* (2d ed.). Toronto, Carswell.

Crankshaw, J. (1910). *The criminal code of Canada ... with commentaries, annotations, forms, etc., etc.* (3rd ed.). Toronto: Carswell.

Dingwall, R., Eekelaar, J.M., & Murray, T. (1984). Childhood as a social problem: A survey of the history of legal regulation. *11 J. Law & Society*, 207–232.

Doggett, M.E. (1993). *Marriage, wife-beating and the law in Victorian England*. Columbia: University of South Carolina Press.

Donzelot, J. (1979). *The Policing of Families*. New York: Pantheon Books.

Eastwood, D. (1994). Men, morals and the machinery of social legislation, 1790–1840. *13 (2) Parliamentary History*, 190–205.

Eichler, M. (1983). *Families in Canada today: Recent changes and their policy consequences*. Toronto: Gage.

Foucault, M. (1979). *Discipline and punish*. New York: Vintage.

Friedland, M.L. (1981). R.S. Wright's model criminal code: A forgotten chapter in the history of the criminal law. *Oxford J. Leg. Studies*, 307–346.

Graham, A. (1994). Parens patriae: Past, present, and future. *32 Fam. and Conciliation Cts. Rev.*, 184–207.

Halsbury's laws of England. (1907–17). London: Butterworth.

Hay, D. (1975). Property, authority and the criminal law. In Hay et al. (Eds.), *Albion's fatal tree: Crime and society in eighteenth-century England* (pp. 17–63). New York: Pantheon.

Holdsworth, Sir W. (1903). *A history of English law (Vol. 1)*. London: Methuen.

Holmstrom, L. (Ed.). (2000). *Concluding observations of the UN Committee on the Rights of the Child, third to seventeenth session (1993–1998).* London: Martinus Nijhoff.

Knell, B. E. F. (1965). Capital punishment: Its administration in relation to juvenile offenders in the nineteenth century and its possible administration in the eighteenth. *5 British Journal of Delinquency,* 198–207.

Korbin, J. (1981). *Child abuse and neglect: Cross-cultural perspectives.* Berkeley: University of California Press.

Lieberman, D. (1989). *The province of legislation determined: Legal theory in eighteenth century Britain.* Cambridge: Cambridge University Press.

Manitoba Law Reform Commission (2000). *Report on vulnerable adults and elder abuse.* Winnipeg: The Commission.

McGillivray, A. (1990). Abused children in the courts: Adjusting the scales after Bill C-15. *Manitoba L.J.,* 17, 549–579.

McGillivray, A. (1992). Reconstructing child abuse: Western definition and non-western experience. In M.D.A. Freeman & P. Veerman (Eds.), *The Ideologies of Children's Rights.* London: Martinus Nijhoff.

McGillivray, A. (1994). Why children do have equal rights: In reply to Laura Purdy. *2 International Journal of Children's Rights,* 43–258.

McGillivray, A. (1997). Therapies of freedom: The colonization of aboriginal childhood. In McGillivray (Ed.), *Governing Childhood.* Aldershot, UK: Dartmouth.

McGillivray, A. (1997). 'He'll learn it on his body': Disciplining childhood in Canadian law. *5 Int. J. Children's Rights,* 193–242.

McGillivray, A. (2004). Child physical assault: Law, equality and intervention. *30 Manitoba L.J.* 133–166.

McGillivray, A., & Durrant, J. (in press). Child corporal punishment; Violence, law and rights. In R. Alaggia & C. Vine (Eds.), *Cruel but not unusual: Violence in Canadian families, a sourcebook of history, theory & practice.* Waterloo, ON: Wilfrid Laurier University Press.

Moscovitch, A., & Drover, G. (1987). Expenditures and the welfare state. In Moscovitch & J. Albert, (Eds.), *The benevolent state: The growth of welfare in Canada* 13–43. Toronto: Garamond.

Nedelsky, J. (1993). Reconceiving rights as relationship. *Review of Constitutional Studies,* 1–21.

Olmesdahl, M.C.J. (1978). Paternal power and child abuse. In J.M. Eekelaar & S.N. Katz (Eds.), *Family Violence,* an international and interdisciplinary study (p. 253–269.) Toronto, ON: Butterworths.

Pollock, L. (1983). *Forgotten children: Parent-child relations from 1500–1800.* Cambridge: Cambridge University Press.

Pollock, L. (1987). *A lasting relationship: Parents and children over three centuries.* London: Fourth Estate.

Rose, N. (1989). *Governing the soul: The shaping of the private self.* London: Routledge.

Rutman, L. (1987). J.J. Kelso and the development of child welfare. In A. Moscovitch and J. Albert, (Eds.), *The benevolent state: The growth of welfare in Canada* (pp. 68–76). Toronto: Garamond.

Schene, P., & Ward, S.F. (1988). The vexing problem of elder abuse – The relevance of the child protection experience. *Public Welfare, 46*(2) 14–21.

Schissel, B. (1997). *Blaming children: Youth crime, moral panics and the politics of hate.* Halifax: Fernwood.

Scott, S.P. (Ed.). (1932). *The civil law.* Cincinnati: Central Trust Company.

Seymour, J. (1994). Parens patriae and wardship powers. *14 Oxford J. Leg. Stud.*, 159–188.

Shone, M.A. (1987). Case comment, *re Eve. 66 Can. Bar Rev.*, 635–646.

Smandych, R.C. (2001). *Youth justice.* Toronto: Harcourt.

Stephen, J.F. (1883). *A history of the criminal law of England, Vol. III.* London.

Stephen, J.F. (1887). *A digest of the criminal law (crimes and punishments),* 4th ed. London: Macmillan.

Steward, J.C. (1995). *The new child: British art and the origins of modern childhood.* Berkeley: University of California Press.

Stone, L. (1979). *The Family, sex and marriage in England 1500–1800.* Harmondsworth, UK: Penguin.

Stuart, D. (1987). *Canadian criminal law* (2d ed.). Toronto: Carswell; and subsequent editions.

Theobald, H.S. (1924). *The law relating to lunacy.* London: Stevens.

Ursel, J. (1992). *Private lives, public policy: 100 years of state intervention in the family.* Toronto: Women's Press.

Valverde, M. (1991). *The age of light, soap and water: Moral reform in English Canada, 1885–1925.* Toronto: McClelland & Stewart.

Watson, A. (1995). *The Spirit of Roman Law.* Athens: University of Georgia Press.

3

The Voices of Children in Literature

NAOMI SOKOLOFF

What is distinctive about literature as a way of knowing the world? Are there special ways that literature and literary studies may contribute to childhood studies?

These are large questions, prompted by the multidisciplinary focus of *Multiple Lenses, Multiple Images*. This volume takes as one of its points of departure the assumption that different disciplines construct under-standings of childhood through unique lenses. Different fields ask dif-ferent kinds of questions and define differently which information is meaningful and how it is to be collected, analysed, represented, and discussed.[1] In the field of literature, these issues are complicated by the very wide array of approaches scholarship has taken. In this essay I offer a few thoughts on narrative voice as one way to begin thinking about literary discourse and the representation of children.

One of the special strengths of literature and, in particular, narrative fiction, is in representing inner life. Writers often use their craft to explore the uncharted territory of another mind. In this connection, in *The Distinction of Fiction*, Dorrit Cohn writes of the 'fiction-specific privilege of mind-reading' (2000, p. 175).[2] A long critical tradition has emphasized the ways in which imaginative writing may depict the intimate, never-communicated thoughts of someone else and so reveal hidden aspects of experience or give voice to those not readily heard by society.

The point has special resonance for the literary treatment of children, for their voices are keenly in need of representation, being too often dismissed or heeded insufficiently by society. Moreover, these are voices that cannot freely assert themselves in writing. In this regard, they are unlike a variety of voices that have been marginalized by mainstream writing. Minorities and others can write their own stories and fight for recognition through them, but by the time children are ready to represent themselves in mature narrative, they are no longer children. In general, writerly sophistication seems to be something children arrive at relatively late. While precocious accomplishment is well known in the fields of music, math, painting, and computers, and while language learning is the special province of the young, prodigies and early achievement are rarely found in the area of belles lettres. Child authors are few and far between. Adult writing, as it sounds the consciousness and perceptions of children, is an attempt to represent voices that cannot represent themselves. With free rein for the imagination, fiction writers may capture children's perspectives or express aspects of children's consciousness in ways that enrich what other adults understand about young people.

Adult efforts to convey a child's voice are inevitably compromised, of course. They are necessarily an 'as if' proposition, a kind of ventriloquism, and disparities always exist between grown-up expression and youthful experience. Juvenile literature is doubly affected by the gap between adult and child voice, because it both represents children characters and also imagines the consciousness of a presumed reader who is a child. Adult estimations of what children think, know, and need affect several dimensions of the work. Moreover, child-authored texts that have been published have been controlled by adult editors, publishers, and audience expectations.[3] Altogether, children characters in literature – whether in adult texts or texts written for children – often tell us more about adult concerns that are projected onto children than about children themselves. Consequently, any literary construction of a child's thoughts works itself out in a highly equivocal realm, somewhere between appropriation and advocacy, artifice and insight. Still, novelistic prose may be one of the most effective tools to remind us that there is more to young viewpoints than meets the eye. The representation of consciousness, that peculiarly literary phenomenon, may help garner respect for young outlooks and for the inner, perceptual worlds of children that are ordinarily elusive and that we adults can all, at best, only imagine.

How have adults mediated children's thoughts and words in fiction? To explore this question, it is important to examine the construction of children at the level of narrative voice and to consider strategies of narration that allow an adult writer to coordinate his or her voice with that of a child character.[4] I choose this focus because in recent years an enthusiasm for ideological reading and cultural studies has sometimes led scholars to undervalue close reading. Increasingly, literary studies have brought literary texts together with other kinds of discourse – legal documents, journalism, political manifestoes, film, advertisements, and more – to investigate social constructions of childhood.[5] As valuable as these approaches are, charting broad cultural attitudes has at times eclipsed a look at the details of literary craft. I urge a return to textual analysis here in order to illuminate some of what is to be gained from literary texts in their distinctive sensitivity to perspective. As Robert Alter has noted so aptly, an 'essential defining feature of the novel is the variety, the subtlety, the unpredictability and the quicksilver mobility of its uses of perspective' (1989, 175–176). These qualities can be especially telling in depictions of children and childhood.

Armed with these convictions, let me move quickly to a specific example. I will revisit a book that has long been one of my favourites for its richly rewarding representation of a child's inner life: David Grossman's *See Under: Love*.[6] This Israeli novel was published in Hebrew in 1986 and appeared in English translation in 1989. The first section, which is the focus of my comments, features a nine-year-old boy named Momik who lives in Jerusalem. The year is 1959. Momik's parents are Holocaust survivors who are loath to speak to him about their traumatic past. He becomes increasingly curious about their secrets and about the wartime experiences that, though unspoken, dominate family life. He lives in a society that is deeply and extensively shaped by the events of the Holocaust and by an influx of immigrants who are survivors, but this society defines itself in opposition to them. Israel in its early years set itself the task of constructing a new society and new, proud, militarily strong Jews who were to be the opposite of the victimized Jews of the diaspora. The young state's relation to survivors was to be one of rescue and redemption, not identification. Momik has grown up absorbing those ideals from the society around him, yet he comes from a home all too familiar with trauma. Consequently, he struggles with the conflicting forces pulling at him and colliding within him. The following passage encapsulates some of those tensions as it conveys his inner world. Because of his youthful openness to his surroundings and his curiosity about that which has been silenced, to see the world through his eyes is to gain entrée to this realm where conflicting values intersect:

Dinner.

It goes like this: first Mother and Momik quickly arrange the table, and mother warms up the big pots from the fridge and then brings the dishes. This is when the danger begins. Mother and Father eat with all their strength. They begin to sweat and then their eyes begin to bulge. Momik pretends to eat but all the while watches them carefully and wonders how such a fat woman as his mother could have come out of Grandma Henny and how a scarecrow of a kid like himself could have come out of the two of them. He tastes just a little on the end of his fork, but the food sticks in his throat from all the tension, and that's how it is. His parents have to eat lots of food every night in order to be strong. Once already they managed to escape from death, but the second time, for sure, it wouldn't let them go.

Momik crumbles the bread into small balls and arranges them in the form of a square. After that he makes himself a bigger ball from dough, and cuts it precisely in two, and after that again in two. And again. You need the hands of a heart surgeon for that kind of precision. And again in two. He knows that at dinner they won't get angry at him for things like that, because no one's paying attention to him. Grandpa in his big wool coat is telling himself and Herrneigel a story and sucking on a piece of bread. Mother is already completely red from so much effort. It's impossible to see her neck, her mouth is working so hard. Sweat drips on Father's forehead. They clean the big pots with the help of big slices of bread and tear into them. Momik swallows saliva and his glasses steam up. Father and Mother disappear and peek out again from behind the piles of pots and pans. Their shadow dances on the wall behind them. Suddenly it seems to him that they are floating a little in the air on the hot vapors of the soup and he almost shouts from fear, God help them he says in his heart in Hebrew, and right away translates into Yiddish so God will understand, *mir zal zein far deine beindelach*, do something to me instead and have mercy on their little bones, like Mother always says about him.[7]

Though the parents never divulge details of their past, the son is highly aware of their terrible memories of hunger and of the fear that torments them even now. The first two sentences present events as Momik perceives them, but which he doesn't necessarily articulate. At the same time, the prose is tinged with verbal patterns and colloquialisms that might be ascribed to a child (*zeh holekh kakha* – 'it goes like this'; *maher maher* – 'quickly'). Such stylistic contagion helps create a closeness between author and fictional figure as it melds their voices together. Sentences 3, 4, and 5 introduce more distinct dissonance. The word 'danger' means different things for the adult and child. The boy would understand it as part of the vocabulary he often employs for spy games and for fantasies of being a war hero or a detective. For the adult reader, the danger is in the realm of psychic harm; the stressful atmosphere of family life clearly threatens the young child's well-being. The internal contradictions of the word 'danger' thus set off ironic resonance. For the boy, dinner holds the promise of a heroic mission; meanwhile, the adult perspective of the narrator casts the parents' eating habits as abnormal or damaged behaviour resulting from their suffering during the war. Because of such words as 'bulge' and 'sweat,' the actions of the mother and father seem pathetic or comically grotesque. Momik, who sees the scene in an idealized way, elevates the same actions into the terms of an ongoing struggle indicated by the phrase 'all their strength' (sentence 4). Within this framework, bulging and sweating take on the connotation of titanic effort.

That Momik inscribes his parents in a heroic code is made more explicit in sentences 8 and 9. It is not the mature narrator who suggests that overeating builds strength and staves off death. Instead, it is the child who sees the meal as part of a fateful battle. The technique Grossman uses to convey this opinion is narrated monologue – that is, the text maintains third-person narration while rendering the character's thought in his or her own idiom. The words in this line could be entirely the boy's except for the personal pronoun. A subtle shift has taken place, orienting the passage now to the child's utterance. The preceding line (sentence 6) has prepared the reader for just such a shift by using indirect discourse (*hu ḥoshev*, '[he] wonders') to present a summary of Momik's thoughts. Consequently, it provides a minimal but perceptible transition, signalling that the boy is struggling to crystallize his awareness of the situation and to put it into words. By sentence 8, the reader can accept the final pronouncements as Momik's evaluation of affairs, and at the same time the prose evades forcing the issue of whether or not a child would actually pronounce such a sentence to himself. The effect of this last line therefore is to make Momik's voice more pronounced and independent while also assuring that the actual text will fall short of direct quotation.

What is the advantage of achieving such an effect? Fundamentally, because the boy's words are retained within the voice of the narrator, his immature thoughts cannot be readily dismissed as childish prattle. The presentation of a child's view within the cogent narrative of someone older imputes seriousness to the character's inner world. As a result, the conclusions Momik reaches may be inadequate or comically distorted, and his innocence may raise smiles, but the passage insists that the readers take his inner life seriously. He shows impressive sensitivity and complexity in his thinking. Momik, in short, has discovered a profound truth: that his parents are perpetually engaged in a conflict of monumental proportions as they struggle with their own fears. The parents' compulsions therefore resist being judged by the standard norms of their society, which sees them as pitiful or contemptible victims. Momik's interpretation is at once misguided and somehow appropriate. Eerily in accord with the intensity of the parents' suffering, his understanding shifts heroism onto them, and a double-edged irony emerges. Working for and against Momik's views, it is created through the superimposition of voices that allows the narrator to exercise both distance from and identification with the character.

In the second part of the passage tension builds, as is evident in Momik's behaviour with the bread. Again, there is disparity between adult and child views. Momik casts his actions in positive terms, as evidence of scientific precision. He is an extremely bright and precocious boy who often entertains fantasies of himself as a scientist, and here he imagines he has the hands of a heart surgeon. Adult readers are likely to see things otherwise. The repeated cutting of the bread comes across as evidence of painful anxiety. This impression is much stronger on second reading, for Momik has many nervous habits that manifest themselves over the course of the plot. In this scene the child's feelings of anxiety and disorientation become paramount in an almost phantasmagoric moment when the parents seem to him to float in the air and loom over him.

The passage ends with humour as the homey Yiddish phrase brings everything back down to earth. Yiddish is the parents' everyday language and so it is familiar, a counterweight to phantasmagoria. Momik's childish notion that Yiddish is God's language, and that he must translate for God, makes for a gently humorous release of tension. The way that Momik wields a phrase appropriate for a mature woman but not for a child ('do something to me instead, have mercy on their little bones') also introduces an element of cuteness into the text. In a move that recalls Bakhtin's theories, Momik selectively appropriates words spoken by others and incorporates them into his psychic life; however, being very young, he absorbs this discourse uncritically and the youthful voice parroting the Yiddish phrase renders it comic.[8] To be sure, there is more than a little sadness in this comic moment. The child here takes on the parenting role, feeling he must protect his parents rather than the other way around. This is true throughout the story, and ultimately that painful burden becomes overwhelming to the young son.

Part of the success of Grossman's prose is that the shifts and glides between adult and child voices modulate the readers' impressions of Momik, requiring the reader to take an active role in appreciating the ways that the boy's perspective, that of the parents and that of the narrator clash or coincide. The movements may appear seamless or unobtrusive to readers. In some places it even takes a somewhat strenuous analysis to break them apart, and there are certainly lines that cannot be designated exactly as the words of the narrator or the child character. Yet, if this passage raises a smile, that is evidence that the incongruities are at work – that readers, so to speak, get it. This is an example of the kind of 'delicate, beautifully flexible dance of perspective' that Robert Alter suggests can be a most effective vehicle for our intimate knowledge of fictional characters. He refers to such 'narrative fluidity' as a defining feature of the novel as a genre (1989, 183). This feature, moreover, is one that helps to accomplish a pre-eminently novelistic task: that is, 'to attempt to express what cannot be expressed, because it exceeds all familiar norms, [and] flows from the ambivalent intensity of a unique relationship and a unique moment of experience' (1989, 183–184). To articulate that which is novel, to find expression for emergent experience and for things that have not previously been articulated: this description of the artistic function of fiction is especially apt for representations of a child's life. If the point is valid for fictional characters in general, how much more so in the case of characters for whom so much is new. And, in the example of Momik, the inner confusions that resist adequate expression – the discoveries he has yet to name – are especially keen, because he is a child for whom so much has been left unspoken.

A corollary observation: precisely because it touches on emergent experience, incipient feelings and those things previously left unsaid, literary art often has a visionary potential. That is to say, fiction may seem ahead of its time as it brings to light perceptions that only later find widespread recognition in society. Grossman, sensitive to issues that were soon to erupt as a major force in Israeli society, filled just such a role as a cultural bellwether. *See Under: Love* articulated tensions that in the early 1980s were not yet openly and publicly acknowledged, but that soon gained widespread and dramatic attention in the late 1980s and 1990s. Grossman's novel was followed by a series of literary works concerned with the Holocaust that showed a growing identification with survivors and a keen interest in the intergenerational effects of trauma. These attitudes emerged, too, in popular song, documentaries, historiography, and school curricula as well as other areas of Israeli life, leading to a greater identification with victims, with past Jewish history, and with Jews outside of Israel. The publication of David Grossman's novel was a highly visible event in the course of these developments, and it signalled a significant change in social discourse and cultural expression.[9]

Interestingly, according to at least one critic, the trend began with children's literature rather than adult writing (Zehavi 1992). Children's literature – because it usually operates outside the literary mainstream – may offer a setting conducive to experiment and to sounding out new ideas. As non-canonical writing, juvenile fiction may enjoy relative freedom from entrenched social values and reified images or discourse. Sometimes, too, because child characters have a marginal vantage point on society, they serve to open up new perspectives on social issues. This is what seems to have happened in Israel in the 1980s, contributing to changing cultural awareness about the Holocaust.

A case of particular interest is Gila Almagor's *The Summer of Aviya* (1986/1999), which took several forms; it appeared as juvenile fiction, as theatre, and, finally, in a film version.[10] While the prose of the original fiction is directed at young readers (ages ten to fourteen), the film is better suited to adults than children. It is a beautifully rendered but very intense and deeply troubling film. The stage version falls somewhere in between. It has been performed by children's theatres and also attended in large numbers by adults. Crossing generic boundaries, *The Summer of Aviya* achieved prominence in several cultural arenas as attention to the second generation came to spread throughout popular culture as well as more highbrow art.[11]

The Summer of Aviya makes for a telling contrast with Momik's story. Because they have much in common, their differences in artistic approach demonstrate what is gained by choosing different media, genres, and modes of presentation. The contrasts put into relief the distinctiveness of each art form.

Like *See Under: Love*, *The Summer of Aviya* presents a second-generation child. She is nine turning ten – the same age as Momik – and the story takes place in Israel in much the same era (1951). Like him, she takes on excessive responsibility in parent-child interactions. Her mother, a survivor, has been in a psychiatric hospital. Upon her release she brings Aviya home from boarding school for a summer, and throughout the summer the daughter struggles to look after her emotionally fragile mother. Much as was the case with Momik, the girl is an outsider, teased mercilessly by her peers. All the neighbours look on her mother with contempt as 'that crazy partisan.' Consequently, Aviya yearns to believe in a heroic version of her family history. The plot unfolds as some newcomers to town reinforce Aviya's hopes. Themselves survivors, they tell stories of her mother's role in the resistance in Poland, where was renowned for both courage and beauty.

A dinner scene from *The Summer of Aviya* invites special comparison with the earlier excerpt from *See Under: Love*. Here again, the dinner table is a site of potential tension, fraught with the importance of food and the challenging imperative of being together as a family. Moreover, in this scene Aviya struggles to understand her background, her family's past, and her current circumstance in unfriendly surroundings. The setting is the small shack where she lives with her mother, who works as a washerwoman and seamstress:

Mother fell on me: 'Where were you? I was worried!' Her shrill voice hurt my ears. She could have asked quietly where I had been. I was afraid of that voice and hurried to calm her down. I told her that Mrs Abramson invited me in and didn't let me go and then I helped her. [Anything] so that she'd calm down.

I ate dinner with Mother in silence. Suddenly in the middle of the meal I asked: 'Mother? What kind of name is Aviya?' And Mother said: 'A beautiful name! The most beautiful one! When you're big you'll understand.' And again silence stood between us. We ate yogurt. Mother insisted I finish my yogurt. She finished hers and a creamy moustache remained on her upper lip. I cleaned it with a napkin and both of us laughed. I was very close to Mother at that moment. It seemed to me that good times had come, and it seemed as though she had calmed down. I looked at her from up close and I didn't see the tension line that usually joined her two eyebrows. When the line disappeared, Mother's expression softened and then she was truly pretty. At that moment of the evening she was pretty and soft and suddenly I heard myself say: 'I'm already big, Mother, and I understand, I want you to tell me about him.'

Mother looked at me and didn't say a word, only looked and looked and afterward said: 'He had a beautiful voice, he was handsome. A handsome man.' And she sat that way for another moment and then got up and went to her room. And I remained alone with her words. I wanted to hear more, I wanted to know more, and she left me only crumbs.[12]

The emphasis here is on the child's hunger for parental love. Aviya yearns for tenderness from her mother, who is fearful and given to rages. The little girl also yearns for her father, who died during the war before Aviya's birth. Her name, about which she inquires, in fact means 'her father.' The mother has named her that as a kind of memorial, the significance of which Aviya only vaguely grasps. When she presses for an explanation, her mother leaves her only crumbs of information that do not satisfy her appetite for knowledge. As Aviya's peaceful moment gives way to renewed tension, the imagery of food intertwines with the theme of parental loss.

These issues work themselves out in a play of words and silences. Attention is drawn first to the mother's voice, and later to the father's absent voice. In between, and between mother and daughter, stands silence until the child's emerging voice inquires about the meaning of the name 'Aviya.' The child is asserting herself as someone ready to take command of her own life story, to identify her origins and construct her own version of her childhood. An insightful feminist reading of the text has pointed out that Aviya's attempt to understand her name will entail a special struggle; her very name works against her autobiographical impulse as it represses female identity. To reclaim the name and invest it with her own experience, Aviya will have to claim recognition for all sorts of things marginalized and disregarded by her community – the feelings of a child mistreated by her peers; the perspective of her mother, a survivor and an outcast; and most fundamentally, the life of a girl whose name 'signifies perpetual absence' (Halpern, 1995).

The dinner scene marks the beginning of Aviya's autobiographical journey, as she first articulates her sense of self. This process will culminate eventually in her retrospective narrating of this story. It is notable that the narrative presentation of this scene includes plenty of direct discourse dialogue. There is no counterpart in *See Under: Love*, where speech is presented indirectly or as part of Momik's inner life. (The absence of direct discourse is striking, in fact, throughout the narrative, not just in the one scene.)

There are advantages and disadvantages to Almagor's artistic approach. The disadvantage is that we lose the interanimations of voice, the ironies and multiple dimensions that lent *See Under: Love* so much richness. In *The Summer of Aviya* the discourse of the narrator and that of the character are closely aligned. The mature Aviya who narrates retrospectively chooses simple language, not just for the child's words, but for the entire passage. This narrows disparities between the older and younger voices. Although the adult is clearly in control of the narration – which is to say, no ten-year-old would write a story this way, producing the carefully ordered structure of the paragraphs – the mature voice is constrained. The overall result is simplicity and clarity.

This passage lacks the poignant complexity and comic grotesquerie that challenges Grossman's readers, but at the same time there are clearly advantages to simplicity. This style confers a certain measure of dignity and solemnity to the exchange between mother and daughter. In addition, Almagor's prose is much less demanding than Grossman's, producing a text highly accessible to young readers. McCallum (1999) notes that in many children's novels, the character's point of view and the narratorial point of view tend to be implicitly aligned, 'so that the attitudes of character, narrator and implied reader coincide' (p. 35). The result is that the reader takes a more passive role than in cases such as Momik's story, where the reader must assess the overlap, the disparities and shifts between young character and older narrator, and where ironies and multi-voicing encourage active analytic and inferential reading.

Another element of alignment strengthens the central thematic concerns of this scene. Even as the adult voice is constrained to simplicity, the child's voice emerges as more adult-like: Aviya announces, 'I'm already big.' Through this statement, which diminishes the disparity between narrator and character, Aviya takes a step toward one day telling her own story and becoming a mature narrator. The text, however, does not detail what that process of maturation feels like internally. The narrator does not enter the child's mental world attempting to capture subtleties of inner speech. Instead, she narrates the child's view as simple memory handily summarized from an adult vantage point (for example, in the words 'I was close to Mother'). Significantly, when the child's voice sounds, it is described (on two occasions) as emerging 'suddenly.' That is, the movement here, as with Momik, is from inner perception toward articulation, but Aviya speaks out loud while Momik speaks to himself. In Aviya's case attention is thus deflected away from inner complexity to simple external dialogue.

An advantage to this narrative approach is that *The Summer of Aviya* is highly adaptable to stage and screen. Direct discourse easily converts to spoken dialogue. In the film version, the voice of a live child is undeniably appealing as it grants the story dramatic immediacy. Yet, translated into a new medium, the story is not quite the same. The film brings out the key issues with slightly different emphases. To begin with, there is more actual dialogue in the dinner scene and it draws attention to the value of food. While the prose version states, 'Mother insisted I finish my yogurt,' providing a very brief summary of parental admonishments, the film spells out the conversation. The child says that she doesn't like yogurt, and the mother then retorts that food is not for liking, it is for eating. She also remarks explicitly on how expensive the yogurt is. These comments recall the scarcity of food during the war and also remind the viewers of the family's current poverty and their low social status as outsiders.

Other modifications in the film take place more in the visual realm, for instance, through attention to the yogurt 'moustache.' In the film, Aviya has one first and the mother wipes it away. This is a protective, tender gesture, followed by a reciprocal gesture from the daughter. In the text, however, it is Aviya who takes care of the mother. There is less of a sense of mutual tenderness. In both the screen and the prose versions we find an inversion of parent/child roles, much as we found in *See Under: Love*, and time bears out this impression. As the mother's mental illness becomes increasingly severe and ultimately unmanageable, Aviya must look after her, and not the other way around. But in this particular scene the mother's affection for her daughter is evident. Because a lot is conveyed through facial expression and gesture, the mother appears as a more sympathetic character on screen than in the book. This portrayal makes the eventual deterioration of the relationship that much more painful to observe.

Beyond these emendations to the scene that distinguish the film from the novel, there are other differences that emerge specifically because of the change of medium. Importantly, for example, images that are implicit in the text, but visually explicit in the film, suggest an undermining of gender boundaries. The moustache, a playful, amusing reference to gender reversal, conjures up the absent father who is the focus of conversation at the table. Furthermore, the film explicitly associates Aviya with masculine images. Aviya has a shaved head and wears boyish clothing – worn shorts and a T-shirt. The clothing, as good as the family can afford, contrasts painfully with the frilly dresses Aviya so desires. And the baldness is Aviya's great shame; her mother has cut off all her hair to get rid of lice. This act is an overreaction on the mother's part and is linked to her Holocaust experience, but Aviya experiences it above all as an assault on her femininity. Each of these matters does surface earlier in the text, and they are a notable component of the plot. However, they take on new energy in the visual medium of film because they are clearly in sight, present in an ongoing way for the viewer to notice and keep in mind. Their significance is that, together, they suggest Aviya serves as a substitute for the absent male or as a reminder that he is not there. She is 'her father,' as her name implies. This impression is cemented as the film progresses: later the mother comments that the daughter's eyes are just like her father's, and subsequently there is also a dance scene in which Aviya and her mother waltz while her mother recounts what a wonderful dancer the father had been. All these moments add up to a troubling picture. For the mother, Aviya is a constant reminder of loss, and she is also someone to rely on rather than someone to nurture.

The eroticized element to their interaction merits comment in connection with James Kincaid's highly publicized and (in my view) very problematic work, *Erotic Innocence*.[13] Kincaid claims that many films which feature children actually put youngsters on display for the erotic gaze of adult viewers. In addition, he documents at length plots in which youngsters purportedly look for parental love and protection but instead find adults whose feelings toward them could more aptly be described as romantic or even explicitly sexual. Kincaid overstates his case, but he does make a noteworthy point. It is true that, by converting *The Summer of Aviya* to a visual medium, the film version creates an eroticizing lens. With her expressive acting, the young girl who plays Aviya is a very appealing figure and the camera focuses the gaze of the audience on her, shifting emphasis away from her view of the world and onto the viewing of her. The film thereby also accentuates one aspect of the troubling mother-daughter relationship, the child as substitute for the father, which is lightly hinted at in this scene and developed more later on. I would argue, however, that the film does not collude uncritically with the kind of phenomenon that Kincaid describes. Instead, it makes explicit the emotional danger of a situation in which an adult misdirects inappropriate yearnings and feelings toward a child. What matters for this current discussion, then, is that the issue of displaced on misplaced emotion is more evident in the film, and less central to Aviya's story as told in the book. It arises here, to a significant degree, as a function of the film medium, in contrast with narrative fiction.

All of this is also quite different from Momik's story, which does not lend itself to cinematic presentation. It would be very difficult to make a film depicting Momik's life. One attempt to dramatize parts of the Momik narrative aired on Israeli television in the 1990s,[14] but it largely focused on external plot events and downplayed matters of inner life. As such it did not deal with the most riveting part of the fiction, which is what takes place in the child's head, in his mental processes and evolving thoughts. It is hard to imagine capturing those qualities on camera. In contrast, inner life is conveyed most effectively through the densely layered prose, the shifting perspectives, and the representation of consciousness that make *See Under: Love* such a distinctively literary accomplishment.

Both *See Under: Love* and the various versions of *The Summer of Aviya* show a child sizing up parent-survivors, wanting to believe in their strengths and at the same time all too aware of their fears and short-comings. Each piece, in its own way, presents those youthful perspectives in an exceptionally moving way, undermining or dismantling the rigid opposition of heroes/victims that was prevalent in the social setting depicted. The children respond to and resist that dichotomy, yielding more nuanced portraits of survivors and revisioning them as both wounded and heroic, impressive despite or even because of their suffering. It should not be forgotten, of course, that at play here are not children's voices but literary constructs, products of the adult imagination crafted out of memory and invention. And that fact raises an inevitable question: do these pieces convey how a child might truly have felt in Israel in the 1950s? To what extent are these images of childhood an expression of adult attitudes from the 1980s, projected backward onto the past in the guise of a child's views? Even the most sensitive, perspicacious, and densely layered novel, one that yields multiple meanings and implications as it mediates and modifies a child's voice, runs the danger of misappropriating that voice. As many recent studies have demonstrated, the treatment of children in literature is never free from adult concerns, and ultimately, some claim, it is necessarily an act of manipulation, contaminated by adult power.

At its most sinister, the artistic attempt to enter the mind of the child could be an act of invasion. This possibility brings to mind the child at the end of the 1999 movie *Being John Malkovich*. In that film, a quirky portal allows the main character to enter the consciousness of others and see the world from their eyes – at first as an observer, but eventually as a force that takes over control of their thoughts. The disturbing final scene shows a little girl inhabited by a lustful, jealous adult male; he uses her as a perch from which to spy on the woman he desires, her mother. This is an extreme and unsettling example of appropriating a child's perspective. But are depictions of children's voices in literature necessarily an evil distortion, or can they play a more benign and beneficial role? While admittedly an artifice, the fictional representation of a child's inner life – that peculiarly literary phenomenon – may provide a special vehicle to speak on behalf of children by reminding adult readers that very young people have multiple and multidimensional experiences, perceptions, understandings, and interpretations of the world that they themselves are not yet ready to express.

Notes

1 See the introduction to this volume.
2 See also her excellent and extensive discussion in *Transparent Minds* (Cohn, 1978).
3 Even accomplished writers considered extraordinary for their youth – Anne Frank and Rimbaud come to mind – produced their famous work from the age of fourteen. These are clearly adolescents, not children. It will be interesting to see how the advent of desktop and web-based publishing figures into the future of children's writing, and if young writers will find more or less power to control their own publications in the face of widespread technological change. The complicated issue of children's voices in literature is the point of departure for a variety of discussions in *Infant Tongues* (Goodenough, Heberle, & Sokoloff, 1994).
4 Along with Cohn, others who have provided very useful overviews of the field of narratology and insights into narrative voice include Gerard Genette (1980) and Shlomith Rimmon-Kenan (1983). On the representation of children's language, see especially McHale (1994).
5 Earlier studies on images of children in literature were primarily descriptive or broadly thematic (e.g., Coveney, 1957; Pattison, 1978). For a more recent survey of twentieth-century constructions of childhood, see Pifer (2000). In its contemporary move toward cultural studies, the field of literature has been drawing closer to the field of history, which has devoted growing attention to childhood since the 1960s. For an overview of the debate in the field of history, see Cunningham (1998). Berry (1999)

provides a telling example of cultural studies – exploring the image of the child victim in nineteenth-century English literature while investigating the discourse of child welfare and the welfare state through court documents and public rhetoric. Another emerging body of research deals with the sociology of reading – that is, who wrote what for whom, when, where, and under which circumstances – and integrates that material directly into analysis and interpretation of fictional texts. See, for example, Rose (1984) and Lerner (1997).

6 See my discussion of Grossman in my book *Imagining the Child in Modern Jewish Fiction* (1992), pp. 153–176.

7 All translations in this essay are mine. The passage quoted here is from p. 46 of Grossman's novel. An English version of the novel was published in 1989, translated by Betsy Rosenberg.

8 For further discussion of Bakhtin's applicability to narratives of childhood, see Sokoloff (1992) and McCallum (1999).

9 For discussion of these changes in Israeli culture, see, for example, Holtzman (1996), Morahg (1997), Yaoz (1998), and Brenner (2002). Most prominently in the arena of fiction, Nava Semel and Savyon Liebrecht have dealt with the second generation. A series of documentaries and pop songs turned to these issues as well, for instance, in the music and film of Yehuda Polliker. Historians have challenged the once cherished self-image of Israelis as rescuers and have documented Israeli rejection of survivors. Also of particular interest is the rising number of high-school students who participate in visits to Holocaust sites in Eastern Europe.

10 The film, screened first in 1988, was written and produced by Gila Almagor and Eitan Evan.

11 That neither Grossman nor Almagor is personally the child of survivors, and so not of the second generation in that literal sense, is in itself very telling. It indicates both a widespread identification with and empathy for the second generation, and also the success of imaginative writing that has filled a special function in these cultural developments along with documentary and memoir.

12 My translation, from pp. 30–31 of the original. A complete English translation of the novel, by Hillel Halkin, appeared in 1991.

13 Kincaid (1998) egregiously misreads or misinterprets some films to bolster his arguments. In general, I find the book troubling in its excessive eagerness to downplay the dangers of pedophilia and child pornography.

14 The TV presentation was aired as a segment of Gershon Shaked's series, 'Leshon hamar'ot: 'al sifrut vehevrah,' 1993–94. For a review of the series, see Berg (1996).

References

Almagor, G. (1986). *Hakayits shel Aviyah*. Tel Aviv: Am Oved.

Almagor, G. (1991). *The summer of Aviya*. (H. Halkin, Trans.). London: Collins.

Alter, R. (1989). *The pleasures of reading in an ideological age*. New York: Simon and Schuster.

Bakhtin, M. (1981). *The dialogic imagination*. C. Emerson & M. Holquist, Trans. Austin: University of Texas Press.

Berg, N. (1996). A cavalcade of Hebrew literature on TV. *Prooftexts 16(3)*, 301–312.

Berry, L.C. (1999). *The child, the state and the Victorian novel*. Charlottesville. University of Virginia Press.

Brenner, R. (2002). The Holocaust and its fifty-year-old commemoration. In L.Z. Eisenberg, N. Caplan, N. Sokoloff, & M. Abu-Nimr (Eds.), *Traditions and transitions in Israel studies: Books on Israel* (Vol. 6). Albany: SUNY Press.

Cohn, D. (1978). *Transparent minds: Narrative modes for presenting consciousness in fiction*. Princeton, NJ: Princeton University Press.

Cohn, D. (2000). *The distinction of fiction*. Baltimore: Johns Hopkins University Press.

Coveney, P. (1957). *The image of childhood: The individual and society: A study of the theme in English literature*. Harmondsworth, UK: Penguin.

Cunningham, H. (1998). Histories of childhood. *American Historical Review, 103(4)*, 1195–1208.

Genette, G. (1980). *Narrative discourse*. Ithaca, NY: Cornell University Press.

Goodenough, E., Heberle, M., & Sokoloff, N. (1994). *Infant tongues: The voice of the child in literature*. Detroit: Wayne State University Press.

Grossman, D. (1986). *'Ayen 'erekh: 'ahavah*. Jerusalem: Hakibbutz Hameuhad.

Grossman, D. (1989). *See under: love* (B. Rosenberg, Trans.). New York: Farrar, Straus & Giroux.

Halpern, R. (1995). The summer of Aviya: Writing the storms. Presentation at the Association for Jewish Studies Annual Meeting.

Holtzman, A. (1996). Nos'e hasho'ah basiporet hayisra'elit: gal hadash (The Holocaust in Israeli fiction: A new wave). In *Dapim lemehkar besifrut (10)*, 131–158.

Kincaid, J. (1998). *Erotic innocence: The culture of child molesting*. Durham, NC: Duke University Press.

Lerner, L. (1997). *Angels and absences: Child deaths in the nineteenth century*. Nashville, TN: Vanderbilt University Press.

McCallum, R. (1999). *Ideologies of identity in adolescent fiction*. New York: Garland Press.

Morahg, G. (1997). Breaking silence: Israel's fantastic fiction of the Holocaust. In A. Mintz (Ed.), *The boom in contemporary Israeli fiction* (pp. 143–183). Hanover, NH: Brandeis University Press.

McGavran, J.H. (Ed.) (1999). *Literature and the child: Romantic continuations, post-modern contestations.* Iowa City: University of Iowa Press.

Mchale, B. (1994). Child as ready-made: Baby-talk and the language of Dos Passos' children in *U.S.A.* In E. Goodenough, M. Heberle, & N. Sokoloff (Eds), *Infant tongues* (pp. 202–224). Detroit: Wayne State University Press.

Pattison, R. (1978). *The child figure in English literature.* Athens: University of Georgia Press.

Pifer, E. (2000). *Demon or doll: Images of the child in contemporary writing.* Charlottesville: University of Virginia Press.

Rimmon-Kenan, S. (1983). *Narrative fiction: Contemporary poetics.* London: Methuen.

Rose, J. (1984). *The case of Peter Pan, or the impossibility of children's fiction.* London: Macmillan.

Sokoloff, N. (1992). *Imagining the child in modern Jewish fiction.* Baltimore: Johns Hopkins University Press.

Yaoz, H. (1998). Inherited fear: Second generation poets and novelists in Israel. In E. Sicher (Ed.), *Breaking crystal: Writing and memory after Auschwitz* (pp. 160–169). Chicago: University of Illinois Press.

Zehavi, A. (1992). Reaching out: Israeli Holocaust literature for children and youth. *Modern Hebrew Literature,* 89, 40–42.

4

Muscle Memory:
Reflections on the North American Schoolyard

SUSAN HERRINGTON

The lens of landscape architecture focuses on built environments as well as pictures and writings that reference landscapes. Because built landscapes are physical, they are like artefacts that can be studied or interpreted. By examining landscapes as artefacts we can begin to learn something about the culture that created them. This notion of the built landscape as an artefact of culture is an underlying assumption of landscape architectural historians. It is also a type of lens that is shared with numerous other disciplines such as archaeology, art history, and cultural studies.

According to historian Robin Evans, 'ordinary things contain the deepest mysteries' (1997, p. 56). Schoolyards are ordinary spaces that one encounters throughout North America. By looking closely at their size, organization, placement within the city, and other characteristics we can gain clues to who created them and for what purpose. For researchers interested in the history of childhood in North America, the large number of schoolyards created in the nineteenth and twentieth centuries, and which continue to evolve in the twenty-first century, provide us with a very important type of landscape as artefact. This is because schoolyards were designed for children; thus, they not only reflect a shared cultural idea of what children needed, but how that space could shape them as future adults.

Landscapes as artefacts may suggest to us aspects of a culture not usually revealed through what a culture says about itself. Likewise, there are dimensions of a culture that can't be understood by studying only the landscapes it has produced. By examining both, we can further glean information about their inspirations and intentions, and ideally reflect more thoughtfully on the schoolyards we produce for children today.

This chapter traces the way concepts and beliefs about the North American schoolyard have changed over time, and how these changes are connected to shifts in notions about childhood, nature, and society. In this chapter I focus on the nineteenth and early twentieth centuries, when romantic beliefs about the nature of childhood and society were replaced with determinist explanations of the industrial era. This change in lens is captured in a letter composed by kindergarten advocate Elizabeth Palmer Peabody, when she writes to a teacher in Chicago, 'I think it is rather misleading to look at children in the kindergarten as they may when they grow up – I think they are to be estimated in the present' (Peabody, ca. 1880). This observation points to the heated debate that occupies North American educators in their unfolding discovery of childhood during the late nineteenth century. Peabody and other kindergarten proponents, as well as child play advocates, consider education a vital experience where experimentation and play foster self-expression and moral reasoning.

The romantic idea of childhood believes that reasoning is attained through analogy rather than cause and effect. Likewise, the spatial imperatives of education, the school and its yard, are the unworded texts that communicate a range of moral and intellectual precepts. In contrast to this romantic perspective, more scientifically oriented educators and scholars during the twentieth century contended that education is the primary vehicle for producing industrious, healthy, and morally fit citizens and saw the school and its yard as a space for exercising these skills. They argued over whether the character of children should be shaped by education to emulate and perpetuate certain values, or whether children are free agents whose inner selves are revealed and nourished through the educational experience. These are important questions for any society in that by 'saying what we wish a child to become, we are saying what we are' (Postman, 1982, p. 63).

Parallel to these conflicting views of childhood at the turn of the century is the development of the school itself as a public institution, and the schoolyard as an armature to this system. Not surprisingly, this time period coincides with provincial and state legislation to educate all children, and ambitious plans to build public schools throughout the burgeoning cities of North America. Many of the schools and schoolyards seen today are remnants of these grand plans. Schoolyards are mnemonic spaces that reflect previous as well as contemporary beliefs regarding education, childhood, and even nature. They are much like important muscles, layers of tissue connecting to the skeletal frame of the city, providing open spaces and supporting a range of physical and cultural needs. Given the pressures – ecological, social, and economic – that weigh upon contemporary cities, some reflection on these open spaces may be helpful in addressing the future of our urban landscapes.

German Beginnings

Romantic notions of childhood in North America were greatly inspired by the work of the nineteenth-century German educator Friedrich Fröbel (1782–1852). Fröbel, inventor of the kindergarten, was one of the earliest pedagogues to value childhood and play. His school motto 'Kommt, laßt uns unsern Kindern leben' [Come, let us live with our Children] and his books, such as *The Education of Man* (1826/1887) and *Mother Songs, Games, and Stories* (1843/1914), a compilation of illustrated chimes that combine narrative songs with the fine-motor movements of children's fingers, encouraged adults to cherish childhood. Key to Fröbel's educational system was a series of 'gifts,' the forbearer of play blocks, and 'occupations,' activities like weaving or gardening that are performed by the children. The 'gifts' and 'occupations' were introduced gradually to children and required their manipulation. For Fröbel, playing and learning intermingled and revealed children's independent and versatile learning abilities (Allen 1988, p. 437). During the 1840s, his first kindergartens in Germany contained actual gardens that he designed to reflect the philosophical underpinnings of his school. Fröbel was deeply moved by the transcendental qualities he found latent in plant life, and the potential for the garden to symbolize children's growth and an idealized garden culture (Herrington, 1998). Excursions into the surrounding farms, forests, and towns provide children with living templates that fuse the material and ethereal realms. Observation and exploration of natural processes, like the life cycles of plants, and cultural conditions, such as the spatial organization of a village, afforded the contemplation of their abstract analogues. While Fröbel emphasized the relatedness of animals, plants, seasons, and weather, reminding kindergarteners that 'again natural objects should be referenced to the time of their appearance' (Fröbel, 1887, p. 257), the reverent capacity of the unknowable in these experiences is a consistent backdrop to the moral lessons found outside the school.

While the practices of the kindergarten seem harmless from a contemporary viewpoint, they were highly controversial during Fröbel's time. He received considerable criticism from the Prussian government about the long hair and folk attire of his students and his employment of women. Yet it is his conflation of nature and God that infuriated both governmental authorities and the church. Added to this, the study of plants, an important aspect of Fröbel's pedagogy, was considered inappropriate for women because Linnaean categorizations (a system developed by Carl von Linné to describe vegetation) classified plants based on their sexual parts. In 1851 the kindergartens were banned and were not reopened in Germany until the 1860s. However, this banning provoked Fröbel's student teachers to spread the idea of the kindergarten throughout the world.

Canada was one of the earliest countries to incorporate Fröbel's pedagogy into its public education system. In 1877, Ada Marean, a student of Maria Kraus-Boelte's kindergarten training school in New York, opened the first Canadian kindergarten in Saint John, New Brunswick. In 1883, with Toronto School Inspector James Hughes, Ada Marean (later Ada Marean Hughes) opened the first public kindergarten in Toronto (Corbett, 1989). The action-oriented activities and outdoor focus of the kindergarten appealed to many Canadians. James Hughes noted in his *Annual Report* that in the kindergarten 'a child learns and remembers what a cube is in the same way that it learns and remembers what a spoon is, by using it'(*Annual Report*, 1883, p. 23). By 1891, there were twenty-seven schools that offered kindergartens in Toronto. This number grew to 120 by 1900 (Kreutzweiser, 1982, p. 23). The growing inclusion of this new educational system into the burgeoning school system of Ontario inspired programs such as nature study and gardening in elementary schools (Phillips, 1957, p. 423). The enthusiasm for utilizing natural processes for cognitive development was expressed in James Hughes's widely read *Froebel's Educational Laws for All Teachers*. Here, he emphasizes the multiple learning experiences to be found in kindergarten education:

> The germination of a seed, the growth of a plant, the unfolding of a bud, the blooming of a flower, the structure of a leaf, the song of a bird, the love and mystery of a bird's nest, the home-making of an insect, the evolution of a worm into a butterfly, the rippling of a brook, the vastness of the ocean, the majesty of a mountain, the movement of the trees in the wind – all these Froebel uses to quicken the intellectual and spiritual life of the child. (Hughes, 1897, p. 268)

Largely in response to this educational philosophy, the Niagara school in Toronto in the late nineteenth century featured the first outdoor play space specifically for kindergarten children. However, in many urban schools there was no room for gardens or extensive outdoor walks. Many teachers responded by using window boxes for cultivated plants and took the children on city strolls or walks in nearby parks.

Countering this verdant lens on childhood was the emerging notion of childhood as a Darwinian trajectory that must be shaped and controlled by public institutions including schools. Darwin's theory of natural selection and his scientific approach to understanding natural processes had a profound effect on the way society viewed children and other elements of the natural world. Equipped with Darwin's theory and the determinism of scientific reasoning, professional educators saw nature as something to be dissected, analysed, and controlled, and this influenced the way children were educated and why. While Darwin never distinguished between acquired characteristics and those that are passed down genetically, later interpretations of his work and the notion of the 'survival of the fittest' suggested that childhood was a key time to teach specific skills and values that would not only ensure the survival of society, but steer its future development. The verdant lens on childhood was counter to the notion of childhood as a Darwinian trajectory because it portrayed children as possessing a fundamental nature that would be revealed and developed during the educational process. This could be seen in Fröbel's kindergarten, where the wonder of a growing plant was the ideal analogy for the developing child. The plant analogy not only evoked metaphysical reflections regarding the organic dimensions of education, but the tending of plants by children made visible to educators the inherent character of each child. For educators informed by Darwin's theories, children were not born with a fundamental nature; this needed to be instilled in them. Plants were not used to reveal the essence of each child, but were specimens of nature that could be identified, memorized, and tested.

Coinciding with the notion of childhood as a Darwinian trajectory was the rise of industrial cities in North America. Cities such as Toronto, Boston, and New York emerged as critical armatures to the capitalistic system, employing, processing, and reproducing vast quantities of human and 'natural' resources. Thus, budding public institutions like schools were assigned the task of shaping and aligning the idea of childhood as part of this trajectory. Scientific and pragmatically minded urban reformers who understood education as a way to control the future linked labour-inspired training with the formation of adult character. For reformers, vocational training prepared children to become 'socially efficient citizens' as adults. It engendered them with 'directive intelligence, habituating them in the new industrial work rhythms and work norms' (Jones, Sheehan, & Stamps, 1979, p. 248). 'While some educators worried about the erosion of scholarly values by business and labour-market pressures, prominent school reformers joined the campaign to link education to industrial life' (Axelrod, 1997, p. 110). By the late nineteenth century this notion had taken hold in many cities across Canada and the United States where rapid industrialization, urbanization, and immigration brought an unprecedented number of children under the agency of public schools. The Darwinian trajectory, which found its launching point in schools, was distinguished by a preoccupation with physical fitness. Schools were key sites for 'corporeal regulations' (Axelrod, 1997), and schoolyards provided the physical spaces where children's bodies and souls were shaped in preparation for adulthood.

The Rise of Physical Education

The reputation of Canada as a home to vigorous youths who flourished in the bounty of its natural resources coupled with the dominance of Canada's Anglican and Catholic population, who raised physical exertion and discipline to the level of religious absolution (McNiven, 2001), whetted the appetite for exercise programs in Canadian public schools. In Johann Christoph Friedrich Guts Muths's renowned *Gymnastik fur die Jugend* (1803), Guts Muths admired the inhabitants of Canada, a country he considered 'the Germany of North America.' For Guts Muths, the people of Canada were 'strengthened by the climate, not denied sufficient nourishment, hardened by ingenious education, perfected by hunting, and warlike exercises, not exhausted by care, not borne down by oppressive labor' (as cited in Moolenijzer, 1973, p. 298). The physical fitness programs that emerged in the school systems were critical in the preparation of children for military and industrial life as adults, and the reparation of children caught in the clutches of the immense machine of the city. As the *Annual Report for Toronto Schools* contended, 'Drills and Calisthenics: These have a most important influence on industrial training by strengthening the body and training the muscular system to respond definitely to the commands of the mind' (1888, p. 35).

Exercise is not so much a reward for industrial life as it is a necessary counterpoint. This is the moral lesson, a case in point voiced in the popular *How to Get Strong and How to Stay So* (1879), read throughout the United States and Canada. Here, the author notes that sickly adult labourers might have avoided their ailing state 'had their body been early shaped, and hardened, and made rigorous' (Blaikie, 1879, p. 109). The strategy to shape children's 'supple bodies' was pervasive in the literature regarding children's education in the early twentieth century. Schools became 'key to bourgeois incitement to discourse on sexuality and a means of regulating and normalizing children's bodies' (Kirk, 1998, p. 15). Children were viewed as evidence of the biological workings of nature, while simultaneously these workings were controlled to produce what this nature could and should be (Foucault, 1978, p. 104). Exercises and organized sports that honed the masculinity of boys and the reproductive capacity of girls concurrently addressed looming health problems and helped to maintain the population growth of European descendants in North America.

The time and space of childhood was catapulted forward with the speed of a first-rate production line. The desire to mould the supple muscles of children's bodies was matched only by the will to shape the future of the province and the nation. This lens on childhood was also disseminated into school curricula through military exercise books disguised as instructional manuals for children's physical fitness. The *Syllabus of Physical Training for Schools*, which was inspired by the British Army and Navy and used in the Normal Schools of Vancouver, British Columbia, noted the schoolyard 'yields an abundant harvest of recreation, improved physique, and national health (Board of Education, 1933, p. 8). Outside the classroom doors, the schoolyard mirrored the school's obligation to regulate the safety, morals, and fitness of children. The spatial distribution of schoolyards throughout the early-twentieth-century city was a legacy to current reflections and inventions regarding childhood and the urban environment.

The Legacy of Schoolyards

These schoolyards are landscape artefacts that reveal a palimpsest of ideas concerning childhood. As a case in point, at the school across the street from where I live in Vancouver, I find a range of material factors that suggest how the space is used and valued in the past and present.

Similar to other schools in my neighbourhood, the space of this educational institution occupies the entire city block and is bounded by four streets. A majority of Vancouver is laid out in a grid pattern and the school adheres to the system of infrastructure – the sewer lines, the sidewalks, the electrical wires – from below grade to the ground plane surface to overhead. The school's name, Bay View, suggests that at one time I could see English Bay from its upper floors. This is probable, given that only a fraction of the houses that now densely surround the school are present on city maps from the early twentieth century.

The school is bound on the north by a tree-lined street where a linear tapestry of canopies casts a soft dappled light for three blocks to the west and twelve blocks to the east. The original school, built in 1913, faces this tree-lined street. Later additions, in 1930 and 1962, expanded the school to the northeast corner of the block, allowing for an ample yard to the west. A stream once meandered diagonally across the yard, and neighbours are reminded of this buried hydrological feature when heavy rains flood the area. Nonetheless, the surface of the playing field that covers this stream is the dominant feature of the schoolyard. Surrounded by a 2.5-metre-high cyclone fence, this perceptibly flat space is rectilinear in shape, reflecting not only the grid of the city, but the kind of surface that is needed for the calisthenics and drills for which it was designed.

One of the earliest specifications for schoolyards built in British Columbia cites that 'the rear of the school building should be utilized for a good large schoolyard and nothing should be done to diminish this all important breathing space' (Mott, 1986, p. 58). The emphasis on 'breathing spaces' is significant not only for overcrowded nineteenth-century schools, but also for the urban dwellings of poor families, which are viewed as moral and physical contagions. Within the packed chambers and passageways of these dwellings, which were distinguished by their inadequate ventilation, lurked the makings of diphtheria and tuberculosis. Drills at school that involved breathing exercises, marches, calisthenics, and movement games, 'preferably outdoors' in the bright of day, were valued antidotes to these life-threatening conditions (Axelrod, 1997, p. 116). The generally deleterious appearance of children was equally disturbing. The physical deterioration of youthful bodies was a visible sign of failure to the newly emerging industrial societies of North America. Casting an unsettling eye on the state of childhood in the late nineteenth century, one European visitor to

Boston observed 'that almost every man is born middle-aged' (Cavallo, 1981, p. 19).

To combat these circumstances and as a precondition to the foundation of a virile adult population, physical exercises performed in schoolyards were carried out with military zeal. In 1909, the Strathcona Act, a federal undertaking, furnished money for physical education in schools 'to assist in the development of citizens for a strong Canada' (Munro, 1965, p. 5). Money was distributed by the National Department of the Militia to public schools throughout the country. In many Canadian schoolyards, children were instructed to stand upright in a grid and perform, in unison, movements dictated by the teacher. This was a stark contrast to the disorder of children's homes while a mirror to the rational superstructure of the city. British Columbia's 'Physical Exercises for Infants,' for teachers of children from age five to seven, gives a glimpse of the detailed instructions that guided teachers in this important activity:

> *Breathing exercises* form an extremely necessary part of the lesson and may be given freely between the other exercises. Whenever possible the lesson should be commenced with 'handkerchief drill,' to ensure a free passage for the air through the nose. Breathing may be taken with the 'Hands on the chest,' or in the 'Hips firm,' position and in this exercise little children may be directed to breathe audibly, keeping the mouth shut during expiration as well as inspiration.
>
> *Crow Hop* – Heels raise and knees bend as far as they will go. Keep the back quite straight. Then hop forward with both feet together. At first only one hop at a time, later 2 or 3 hops in succession; finally several hops, but the children should stop before they become breathless. The children can also hop round each other in pairs, or round in a ring holding hands. (Consentino & Howell, 1970, p. 114–115)

An extension to the idea of exercising the body and respiratory system in the open air was the more radical notion of the Forest School. In Forest Schools, children with particular ailments were removed from the school itself. They were relocated to nearby parks and forests, where lessons were conducted with a particular emphasis on hygiene. Noting that 'we are not dealing with a diseased child but rather a diseased environment,' Forest Schools sought 'any piece of park land well drained and free from factory smoke and dust, and adjacent to transportation' as suitable (Burke, 1928, p. 12). Another German import, the first municipal Forest School was located in Charlottenburg, Germany, in 1904, followed by Bostall, England, in 1904, and Providence, Rhode Island, in 1908. High Park Forest School, the first school of its kind in Canada, was established in 1914. Its goal was to provide a setting free from urban pollution where 'school work is carried out in conjunction with a well regulated programme which blends hygiene and academics' (Burke, 1928, p. 10). The Forest Schools began in Toronto as a school program; yet, by 1917, these schools were under the jurisdiction of the Department of Public Health (Burke, 1928, p. 18). Forest Schools were eventually phased out in the 1930s and replaced with a more common approach to integrating the outdoor environment into the public school experience. This approach involved changing the schoolyard itself with the installation of school gardens.

School Gardening Programs

Children's gardening programs, one of the favoured initiatives of industry-linked education, played a significant role in legitimizing the creation of large schoolyards during the late nineteenth century (Herrington, 2001). These programs were key to reform in both the urban and rural context. Connecting to city beautification projects and rural outreach programs that galvanized civic pride with children's efforts, school gardening was intended to provide practical skills and moral training to immigrants in the city, and to help keep rural children on the farm. In Canada, two significant funding sources for school gardens materialized at the exact historical moment when provinces such as British Columbia embarked on an unprecedented school-building initiative. The Macdonald Rural School Fund which supported school gardening programs in elementary schools, and the Federal Agricultural Instruction Act of 1913 were established to imbue public schoolyards throughout Canada with the 'benefit of the greatest bounty Canada had to offer' (Axelrod, 1997, pp. 113–114).

Under these programs, school garden plots, which contained vegetables or flowers, measured approximately fifty square metres for each class, and they were often configured production style, in a uniform grid pattern. In North American school gardens, teachers noted that children learned a valuable trade when instructed to properly stake out, till, hoe, plant, water, prune, and harvest plants. In addition to these fruits of labour, school gardens also included children in the process of economic production, as their gardens were cultivated for profit. Typically, each plot was numbered for identification and records were maintained over several years to determine which crop was most profitable. With a focus on skill development, civic pride, and economic output, school gardens were a stark contrast to the early German kindergartens discussed earlier. Fröbel's symbolically composed gardens were respites for individual growth where exploration, manipulation, and contemplation helped to reveal a child's divine essence (Herrington, 2001). By the 1930s, most Canadian schools no longer maintained gardens as part of standard practices. Hand-gardening skills could not compete with the technology required of the large-scale agriculture that came to dominate the North American landscape. Likewise, teachers often resented the burden of maintaining a garden. Eventually, these garden spaces became 'mud plots' (Shipp, 1937, p. 32) and were forfeited to the growing spatial demands of organized sports.

Organized Sports

Organized sports offer a glimmer of the workings that lie between the illusion of the game and the physical perimeters of the schoolyard. According to proponents of organized sports, these games are the primary means to shape the 'mental and moral faculties of children' (Cavallo, 1981, p. 22). By introducing organized sports into the urban schoolyard, 'young girls and boys promised discipline, citizenship, and team work' (Hardy, 1982, p. 14). Perfect sports fields, with their sacred dimensions applied to the surfaces of the schoolyard, extolled virtue, health, and the lessons of sportsmanship. In fact, these fields become the localized embodiment of the perfectly behaved children.

The first organized sports in Canadian schools were diverse. End ball, scout, volleyball, newcombe, rounders, stoolball, football, shinty (informal hockey), and cricket are only a sample of the wide variety of team games that were played in the early schoolyards of North America. By the early twentieth century these games served as the main course to an appetizer of calisthenic activities, and an armature of physical education established in the nineteenth century. An instructional book for physical training used in British Columbia offered the following recommendations:

The games period of 20–30 minutes for younger children should be planned to include:
   (i) A vigorous opening activity in which all take part.

(ii) A short period devoted to 'ball sense' training for which purpose sufficient apparatus will be required for all to be actively employed.

(iii) One or more simple group games of short duration – scores and results being noted to encourage improvement in the standard play.

With large numbers a teacher will need to exercise a guiding hand most of the time, though the children should be left as free as possible to gain their own experience from the fortunes of the game. (Board of Education, 1933, p. 49)

Football, baseball, hockey, and cricket emerged as the most highly skilled games, 'where unless suitable conditions are available, the game should not be attempted' (Board of Education, 1933, p. 40). Emphasis was placed on the accuracy of the field, the equipment, and the player in preparation for inter-school matches at the high-school level. Delivered through the formalities of the game, the horizontal plane of the field, and the matching uniforms that blur class, race, and gender, the ideas of sportsmanship and game are powerful metaphors for a society at a moment of transformation from agrarian to industrial production.

The agrarian ethos where notions of self-sufficiency were tied to the land, ordered by the seasons, and bound by the family unit gave way to participation in a system ordered by the clock and controlled by the shop, the factory, or the business of the city. Organized sports provided a microcosmic mirror image of the industrial society, giving children further insight into the inner workings of these worlds. Implicit in these children's organized sports is the social mileage to be gained as a prerequisite to success in this society. The rules of the game and the rationality of the playing field had the power to transcend social economic class. Networking, sportsmanship, and team effort eclipse individual talent, and recall the opening lines of an old school chime, *The Short Cut*: 'That you need not score a larger amount, But the shortest cut to the heights of fame is to get to know the chaps who count.'

Stanley Eitzen (1986) argues that baseball and football each elaborate two fundamentally different myths in North America: agrarian and industrial. 'Baseball represents an island of stability in a confused and confusing world' and belongs to the rural, self-sufficient farmer, while football resonates with the highly bureaucratized urban society (Eitzen, 1986, p. 45). Like the farmer whose work is not finished until the chores are complete, the game of baseball reflects rural time, and it is often not finished until it is won. The baseball player stands alone to bat with the intent of getting home, ultimately seeking to deviate from the perimeter of the field with the ball to score a 'home run.' Baseball terms like 'pitcher's mound,' 'dugout,' 'infield,' and 'outfield' also evoke a rural legacy. Time on the traditional farm is in sync with the changes of the seasons, whose cyclical movements are mirrored in the revolution of the baseball players around the bases of a shared field. While the shape of the baseball field is called a diamond, its actual outline is not so well defined; it suggests a residual space between a town and a field, or a barn and tilled land.

Conversely, the gridiron shape, regularized spatial segmentation, and exact dimensions of the football field, which is comparable in size to a city block, resonate with the language of the twentieth-century city. Like the urban factory, the clock strictly regulates the game of football or soccer, and the players are highly specialized. Football and soccer players seek to 'penetrate deep into the opponent's territory' (Eitzen, 1986, p. 41) within a set amount of time. Factory employees work for exact periods of time on specific tasks, rarely seeing the end result of the process in its entirety. Likewise, members of a football team must pass the ball between players who are assigned positions in planned strategic formations.

While Bay View school is occasionally the setting for organized sports like soccer, the activities of Tai Chi, frisbee, and fetch are the chief uses of the yard today. The play equipment scattered throughout the schoolyard is also a setting where play is located, simultaneously signifying play outside and orchestrating the repetitive movements of the body. Bay View's main entrance is flanked on either side by two islands of ganged play equipment. These are circa 1970s wooden structures with slides and ladder extensions. Turning the corner of the building are more ancient renditions of these token gestures of play, a set of metal parallel bars and a ball pole. At the rear of the school, the playing field is bordered to the south by a set of swings and a new play apparatus. Recently the giant tire tractor and a favourite slide built into the hill were removed for safety reasons. The location of this equipment to the margins of the schoolyard conforms to the early twentieth-century guidelines noted by Lerbert H. Weir, field secretary of the Playground and Recreation Association of America for the Pacific Coast. He recommends that 'in placing apparatus, place it whenever possible near the edge of the ground so as to leave as large as space as possible in the center' (Weir, 1912, p. 742).

The Dominance of Play Equipment

The earliest play apparatuses to occupy schoolyards in North America are the open-air gymnasiums inspired by Friedrich Ludwig Jahn at his school Die Deutsche Turnfest in Germany. These play structures were large space frames, often reaching three metres in height, that offered multiple opportunities for climbing, swinging, and hanging. The objectives of these apparatuses are similar to other fitness equipment, which strive to develop the muscles and lungs through physical exercise. Salem, Massachusetts, touted one of the first open-air gymnasiums at a schoolyard in 1821 (Frost, 1989, p. 17). The open-air gymnasiums were typically fenced off from the rest of the schoolyard, and the first gymnasiums were reserved for older boys. Towards the end of the nineteenth century, these mega-structures were replaced or augmented with isolated pieces of equipment geared for younger children and girls. As early as 1897, Sears Roebuck was selling jumpers for younger children, the predecessor to swings (Calvert, 1992, p. 125), and by the early twentieth century self-propelled merry-go-rounds, giant slides, sand tables, and swings were found throughout North American schoolyards (Jones, 1925, p. 388). For both economic and pragmatic reasons, the schoolyard was the ideal setting for the play-equipment playground. According to Weir, 'the school grounds furnish a ready made basis, in as much as they are in effective radius of every child in every community of the city. The school building does away with immediately, as a general rule, with the necessity of erecting special buildings such as a lavatory, field house or recreation building which represents a great economic savings to the community' (1912, p. 740).

By 1910, catalogues distributed by play equipment manufacturers featured a range of mass-produced equipment for schools and communities to purchase. Manufacturers aligned themselves with advocacy groups, like the Playground Association of America, contending that manufactured equipment could conveniently satisfy gross-motor activity and in turn improve the physical health of urban youth. Some advocates also claimed that play-equipment playgrounds fostered 'loyal as well as more efficient citizens' (Cavallo, 1981, p. 14). The idea of solving social and health problems cheaply and efficiently with mass-produced equipment was greatly appealing to the burgeoning production-line industrial cities of North America. Thus, by the 1920s, the placement of play structures at schools, parks, and community centres became synonymous with the creation of playgrounds at these locations. The manufactured play-equipment playgrounds and the large playing fields reserved for organized sports still dominate schoolyards today. Joe L. Frost (1989) maintains that by generating schoolyards where play equipment and sports fields dominate, physical development becomes the chief focus of children's outside experiences. Indeed, the schoolyard's narrowed scope of contribution to the daily lives of children is a contrast to Elizabeth Palmer Peabody's lens cited earlier that eventually inaugurates the kindergarten and nature study into the public school system. Peabody, Fröbel, and Hughes valued children as children, and not just as future adults. They also found a multitude of social, cognitive, and emotional opportunities outside the school building. This perspective had long vanished by the first quarter of the twentieth century.

Conclusion

Children's bodies make visible the mechanics of life and the primacy of physical, cognitive, and social development. The strategy of late-nineteenth- and early-twentieth-century schools seeks to control, regulate, and determine this trajectory of development. Schoolyards, with their moral certitudes of physical fitness and fresh air, are strategic components of the schools' spatial imperative. The drills performed in unison, the sports played by rules, the crops harvested through effort, and the repetitive movements conditioned by play equipment hone the muscle memory of children. This memory adheres to the demands of the city's pervasive hierarchies, spatial arrangements, codes of conduct, and the ethos of industrial capitalism. Muscle memory is the 'electronically encoded blueprint(s)' for the activation of muscles in previously exercised patterns of coordinated movement (Devore & Devore 1981, p. 9). It engenders the internal mechanics of the body with the externalized workings of society. Muscle memory enables one to perform a range of precise movements, for example, riding a bicycle or singing the alphabet, without consciously dictating these movements. It is the physical imbued with the cognitive. Likewise, visualizing the workings of a city like the mechanics of the human body, the schoolyard becomes a muscle memory of the city.

The twentieth century has left a legacy of schoolyards that form a pattern of open spaces across the urban landscapes of North America. For example, Vancouver contains a patchwork of schoolyards evenly distributed throughout the city. While most of these schoolyards have their origins in the first decade of the twentieth century, they have continued to support numerous programs that address sweeping changes regarding public health and education. These range from absorbing many cultural missions, hosting a long list of recreational activities, mediating a prescribed culture and nature, and providing the daily environment for many children who spend unprecedented hours there. Most schoolyards in North America are typified by expanses of grass or gravel, chain-link fence, and dilapidated play equipment. However, these spaces of reform envisioned by previous generations may now offer ecological conditions to the city as reprieve from the dense physical development that has grown up around them.

John Claudius Loudon, a nineteenth-century author and garden designer, was one of the first to draw an analogy between the mechanics of the city and the workings of the body. In the *Gardener's Magazine* (1829), lungs are a leitmotif for the green spaces in the urban landscape. Using a drawing that demarcates concentric circles of green belts, he notes that these open spaces function as 'breathing zones' for London. Given the one hundred years of existence of many schoolyards and their systematic location throughout Canadian cities, their role as a vital organ or muscle should not be overlooked. Schoolyards are open spaces, facilitating a direct connection between air and water at the surface and the systems that lie below this surface. Schoolyards could supply a green infrastructure that provides habitats for observation and exploration by children, addressing not only a diverse range of human activity, but serving as collection points for the conveyance of storm water. The Darwinian lens of childhood perceives the schoolyard as a space that shapes future adults; unfortunately, this lens focuses on the physical deficiencies of children found there. Perhaps by shifting this lens to the yard itself, a new set of considerations may come into view. These considerations address the diverse interests held by children, the green infrastructure of the whole city, and the range of potentials that the schoolyard has to offer.

References

Allen, T.A. (1988). 'Let us live with our children': Kindergarten movements in Germany and the United States. *History of Education Quarterly, 28(1)*, 23–48.

Annual report of the inspector of the public schools of the city of Toronto, year ending December 31st 1882. (1883). Toronto: G.C. Patterson & Co.

Annual report of the inspector of the public schools of the city of Toronto, year ending December 31st 1887. (1888). Toronto: G.C. Patterson & Co.

Axelrod, P. (1997). *The promise of schooling education in Canada, 1800–1914.* Toronto: University of Toronto Press.

Blaikie, W. (1879). *How to get strong and how to stay so.* New York: Harper & Brothers.

Board of Education (1933). *Syllabus of physical training for schools.* London: H.M. Stationery Office.

Burke, F.S. (1928). Forest school as an adjunct to school health. *The Public Health Journal, 19(1),* 9–19.

Calvert, K. (1992). *Children in the house: The material culture of early childhood.* Boston: Northeastern University Press.

Cavallo, D. (1981). *Muscles and morals: Organized playgrounds and urban reform, 1800–1920.* Philadelphia: University of Pennsylvania Press.

Consentino, F., & Howell, M. (1970). *A history of physical education in Canada.* Toronto: General.

Corbett, B.E. (1989). *A century of kindergarten education in Ontario 1887–1987.* Mississauga, ON: Froebel Foundation.

Devore, S., & DeVore, G. (1981). *Muscle memory: Programming for everyday sports.* Chicago: Chicago Review Press.

Eitzen, D.S. (1986). *Sociology of North American sports.* Dubuque, IA: W.C. Brown.

Evans, R. (1997). *Translations from drawing to building.* Cambridge, MA: MIT Press.

Foucalt, M. (1978). *The history of sexuality: An introduction* (Vol. I). New York: Random House.

Fröbel, F. (1887). *The education of man* (W.N. Hailman, Trans.). New York: D. Appleton and Co.

Frost, J.L. (1989). Play environments for young children in the USA: 1800–1990. *Children's Environment Quarterly, 6(4),* 17–24.

Hardy, S. (1982). *How Boston played.* Boston: Northeastern University Press.

Herrington, S. (2001). Garden pedagogy from romanticism to reform. *Landscape Journal: Design Planning and Management of the Land, 21(1),* 30–47.

Herrington, S. (1998). The garden in Fröbel's kindergarten: Beyond the metaphor. *Studies in the Histories of Gardens & Designed Landscapes, 18(4),* 326–337.

Horrigan, O.K. (1931). *Creative activities in physical education.* New York: A.S. Barnes & Co.

Hughes, J. (1897). *Froebel's educational laws for all teachers.* New York: D. Appleton and Co.

Jones, D.S., Sheehan, N.M., & Stamp, R.M. (1979). *Shaping the schools of the Canadian West.* Calgary, AB: Detselig.

Jones, H.S. (1925). A playground in Brooklyn: A playground established by Emil Bommer. *The Playground, 14(7)*, 388–389.

Kirk, D. (1998). *Schooling bodies: School in practice and public discourse, 1880–1950*. London: Leicester University Press.

Kreutzweiser, E. (1982, July 23). Kindergartens: A century of change in the 'child's garden of learning.' *Globe and Mail*, Regional Section.

McNiven, L. (2001). *Schoolyards: Socialization tools*. Unpublished Report. Vancouver: University of British Columbia.

Moolenijzer, N. (1973). The concept of 'natural' in physical education. In E.F. Ziegler (Ed.), *A history of sport and physical education to 1900*. Champaign, IL: Stipes Publishing.

Mott, M. (1986). Confronting modern problems through play: The beginning of physical education in Manitoba's public schools. In N.M. Sheehan, J.D. Wilson, & D.C. Jones (Eds.), *Schools in the west: Essays in Canadian education history*. Calgary, AB: Detselig.

Munro, Iveagh (1965). The early years. In M.L. Van Vliet (Ed.), *Physical education in Canada* (pp. 1–11). Scarborough, ON: Prentice Hall of Canada.

Peabody, E.P. (undated letter to Mary Whiting) 48–21. Cambridge, Massachusetts: Schlesinger Library, Radcliffe College.

Phillips, C.E. (1957). *The development of education in Canada*. Toronto: W.J. Gage and Co. Ltd.

Postman, N. (1982). *The disappearance of childhood*. New York: Delacorte Press.

Shipp, H. (1937). *The problems of the school garden. Landscape and Garden, 4(1)*, 32–35.

Weir, L.H. (1912, May). Public Schools and the playground movement. *The American City*, 740–743.

5

Disability in Childhood:
Views within the Context of Society

MARCI J. HANSON

I first met Annie when she was eight weeks old. She had received a diagnosis of Down's syndrome at birth and her family was referred to the early intervention program that I directed. Annie was small and fragile. Not only was she diagnosed with Down's syndrome, but she also suffered from a heart condition – an opening between the chambers of her heart. Her parents were extremely worried about her diagnosis and the heart condition. Both a health-care professional and a family friend recommended the parents institutionalize their daughter.

Annie was born nineteen years ago. I received a greeting card from her mother this last holiday season with photographs and a note. I had not seen the family for years and was delighted to learn that Annie had just graduated from a local community college.

Why is there such a difference between the developmental expectations for Annie two decades ago and the more hopeful outlook we have for her life today? In that time period, much research has been devoted to the study of the human genome and the effects of the trisomy condition that manifests itself as Down's syndrome. Despite these exciting efforts, no cures or means of remediating the chromosomal anomaly that produces Down's syndrome have been discovered.

The difference today lies within our views about disability and our knowledge about the effects of education and intervention services. We know, of course, that human development is the result of a complex and dynamic interplay between genetic or hereditary factors and environmental factors. Though the child's genetic or constitutional status is determined prior to birth, the child's growth and developmental outcome is ultimately formed by the environment in which she or he is raised.

This article explores these concepts about the dynamic nature of development with respect to the meaning of developmental disability. The first part reviews developmental contexts for children and primary models of development. The second part examines concepts of developmental disability. The third, and final, part presents an overview of research findings from a study of inclusive services in early childhood education in order to highlight contemporary challenges in services for children with developmental disabilities.

Developmental Contexts

A useful model for analysing the contexts that influence child development is the *ecology of human development* framework as postulated by Bronfenbrenner (1979). This ecological-systems framework provides a model for understanding the relations between the developing person and the environment. It is a particularly robust model for the study of children who are disabled or at risk in that it enables one to describe the range of influences on children and their families and the interactions among systems over time (e.g., Bernier & Siegel, 1994; Berry, 1995; Hanson et al., 1998; Odom et al., 1996).

Bronfenbrenner (1979) describes the ecological environment as a set of structures or systems nested within one another like Russian dolls. This set of structures includes the microsystem, mesosystem, exosystem, and macrosystem. Briefly, the *microsystem* is 'a pattern of activities, roles, and interpersonal relations experienced by the developing person in a given setting with particular physical and material characteristics' (p. 22). The family is the primary microsystem, of course, for a young child. Other microsystems, such as childcare settings and early-education programs, may also be considered. The next layer of the model is the *mesosystem* – the interrelationships among these microsystems. Mesosystem factors for the young child with a disability, thus, may include the relationships that occur between home and childcare, home and early-intervention programs, and home and hospital, to name a few. The next level, the *exosystem* level, is defined as 'one or more settings that do not involve the developing person as an active participant, but in which events occur that affect, or are affected by, what happens in the setting containing the developing person' (p.25). Examples for young children include childcare and early-education-program policies and institutions, neighbourhoods, families' social networks, parents' employers, and employment policies. These networks outside the family can have an impact directly on the child and family. At the broader systems level, or *macrosystem*, are societal and cultural beliefs and values that serve to shape and influence the other systems. These macrosystem factors can include factors such as societal views of disability, childrearing, early education, health, and education, and intervention philosophies and policies.

More recently, Bronfenbrenner and colleagues (Bronfenbrenner & Ceci, 1994; Bronfenbrenner & Morris, 1998) have expanded this model to incorporate the developmental influences of the individual's own personal characteristics and the influence of time. This expanded model has been termed "bioecological" and is useful as we examine the impact of disability in early childhood.

For a moment, consider the ecological contexts for Annie's development. She was born to a family who wanted her and had the resources to care for her. Societal pressures (macrosystem influences) had an impact on those within her sphere of professional and personal caring (e.g., attitudes of health-care professionals, neighbours). The availability and policies of health-care, education, and social-support systems (exosystems) greatly influenced her developmental trajectory as well (e.g., the availability of cardiac surgery and the technology and belief that it could and should be conducted, the provision of early-intervention services in her community). The support her parents experienced from personal and professional sources (mesosystem) allowed Annie's family to keep her at home and provide the needed medical and educational supports to enable her to develop more fully within their family (microsystem).

Models of Development

Let us turn now to consider models of development. Three primary models have been applied to the study of child-developmental outcomes. They include the main-effect model, interactional model, and transactional model (Sameroff & Chandler, 1975).

Main-Effect Model

The main-effect model, often referred to as the medical model, is based on the premise of linear relationships between constitutional or environmental factors and the child's developmental outcome. For instance, under this model our genetic endowment for intelligence would predict our intellectual abilities. Another example is that of a child suffering a brain injury prior to or during birth that would produce a disorder such as cerebral palsy and the consequent assumption of limited developmental capabilities due to that condition.

The main-effect model has failed in predictive efficacy. While environmental factors, injury, or genetic factors have a profound impact, the child's development simply cannot be predicted solely on the basis of one of these factors.

Interactional Model

Little debate occurs today among clinicians, theoreticians, or scientists regarding the importance of both hereditary and environmental factors as contributors to children's development. Data from longitudinal studies (reviewed in Sameroff & Chandler, 1975) provide further evidence for the interactional nature of these factors in influencing developmental outcomes. We know, for instance, that children with poor constitutional conditions fare better when raised in supportive, nurturing environments. Likewise, children without constitutional risks can fare poorly if raised in suboptimal or non-supportive environments. Thus, the interaction of both hereditary and environmental influences is deemed crucial for studying, analysing, and predicting developmental outcomes.

Transactional Model

The most compelling model for explaining developmental trajectory is the transactional model. This model acknowledges the complex interplay between nature and nurture forces and the remarkable plasticity in the development of the human organism. Research on early brain development (reviewed in Shore, 1997) only serves to underscore this plasticity and the influence of environmental factors on neurological development in the early years. The transactional model expands on the notion of interactional relationships and examines the transactions that occur throughout the individual's life. The transactional model also more fully accounts for the contributions the individual makes to her or his own development. Personality, physical state, and temperamental characteristics, for instance, all influence the child's experiences in environmental interactions. Further, the transactions between the organism (child) and her or his environment produce transformations in both the organism and the environment such that the contributions of each at a later point in time are not the same.

We can look back at Annie's life to demonstrate this model. We know that Annie was born with a genetic defect, Trisomy 21, or Down's syndrome, that is typically associated with some degree of mental retardation, particular physical features, and, sometimes, medical complications such as Annie's heart condition. Annie was also born into a supportive environment. She had loving and caring parents who were able to mobilize professional medical and educational resources to support her development. Thus, she was given the medical care she needed to survive (cardiac surgery, pediatric health care) and the educational services she needed to thrive (early intervention educational and therapeutic services, support for family). As she became physically stable and developmentally competent, her parents felt competent and supported. Annie was able to participate in more advanced education services and activities, which continued to provide hope for her parents, and on and on. A kind of positive spiral of transactions occurred. Had we used a main-effect model to examine Annie's development, we would have predicted little hope for Annie's developmental outcomes given her heart condition and Down's syndrome diagnosis. Rather, her developmental trajectory continues to surprise many who predicted a less favourable outcome on the basis of her early life events and diagnosis.

Human Diversity: Concepts about Disability
Defining Disability

In 1980, the World Health Organization issued a document, *ICIDH: International Classification of Impairments, Disabilities, and Handicaps*. This classification system referred to an *impairment* as an 'abnormality or loss of any physiological or anatomical structure or function' (Scheer & Groce, 1988, pp. 23–24). A *disability* was defined as the consequence of that impairment and the term *handicap* signified the resulting social disadvantage of the disability or impairment (Scheer & Groce, 1988). These terms remain accepted and in general use today.

However, this 1980 classification system has been replaced by a more contemporary classification system as reflected in the recent document *International Classification of Functioning, Disability and Health (ICF)* (2001) (see web site http://www.who.int/icf). This new classification system replaces the 'disease' model with a 'health' model. It is organized into components of 'functioning and disability' and 'contextual factors.' Thus, bodily functions, structures, and impairments are viewed with respect to types of activity, participation, activity limitations, and participation restrictions. Contextual environmental and personal factors are also considered. This new system is in greater accord with models of functioning and development that examine the child's or individual's behaviour within various contexts or environments.

Common Assumptions about Disability

In 1988, Fine and Asch reviewed and critiqued assumptions about disabilities typically found in the research and literature. These assumptions are summarized as follows:

1. Disability is a biological issue.
2. Impairment is the primary source of problems faced by the individual.
3. The person with a disability is a 'victim.'
4. Disability is central to the person's 'self-concept, self-definition, social comparisons, and reference groups' (p. 11).
5. 'Disability is synonymous with needing help and social support.' (p. 12).

While this critique was issued over a decade ago, these views continue to pervade our thinking about persons with disabilities today. In the last year, I have had parents tell me their child was not selected for a preschool program because his type of disability was not 'includable.' Others did push through the gate because their children's personalities were so social that they were selected 'despite their child's disability.' Some of these same parents have lamented that if they were having a bad day, it was always assumed it was because their child was disabled. As children met new teachers and engaged in new activities, typically it was the disabilities that were seen and discussed rather than the children themselves. These clinical impressions go on and on. Despite more enlightened educational and health policies and practices and our greater knowledge about development and developmental disabilities, these assumptions form barriers for children and their families.

Culture and Context: Constructs of Disability

Concepts regarding disabilities can only be understood in respect to the norms for that culture and context. Whether we see an individual's behaviour as deviant or different is derived from the cultural context. Our competence and ability to survive and thrive, for example, undoubtedly would differ radically depending on whether we were dropped in the outback of Australia or in downtown San Francisco or Vancouver.

Today, in our richly diverse societies, we also experience tremendous cultural variation with respect to views of children and child rearing, education and intervention, medicine and healing, as well as views on causation and the meaning of disability (Hanson, Lynch, & Wayman, 1990; Lynch & Hanson, 2004). In the United States, the dominant cultural perspectives on disability typically ascribe disability to genetic or environmental causes or a combination of these factors, and great faith is placed in interventions that highlight technological advances, the potential for and focus on change, and the impact of the individual and her or his family in creating that change.

Many cultural groups, however, instead place a strong emphasis on the role of fate in determining each person's outcome. From that vantage point, the individual is viewed as having little power to escape her or his fate. Acceptance and living in harmony are the primary focus. For some, individuals are seen as responsible for these misfortunes; in other cultures, the disorder is viewed as bad luck or misfortune with little personal culpability. Beliefs about the family's role or responsibility for the disorder may also vary. In some cultures, the disability is viewed as punishment for the sins or transgressions of the parents or even the ancestors, and the disability is associated with great shame brought on the family (Chan, 1986). For others, disability can be attributed to ghosts, evil spirits, or demons, or to an imbalance of mind-body relationships, the yin and yang. Clearly, these cultural differences not only signify differences in beliefs about attribution or causation, but they also lead to different methods for treatment and different outcomes. Views differ on whether or not change is possible, necessary, or desirable. Further, the sources of support and change agents vary markedly for different cultural groups from Western-trained physicians to shamans, spiritual guides, and elders. The potential for cultural clashes is great as children with disabilities or risk conditions enter standard

Western health, education, and social services. A sensitive story about the complex issues surrounding these cultural variations can be found in Fadiman's (1997) book, *The Spirit Catches You and You Fall Down: A Hmong Child, Her American Doctors, and the Collision of Two Cultures.*

Anthropologists McDermott and Varenne (1995) maintain that 'perceptions of ability organize perceptions of disability' (p. 332). They state: 'We might just as well say: "No ability, no disability. No disability, no ability."' These cultural norms establish and define who is considered disabled and who is not.

Definitions of disabilities such as learning disabilities, thus, are highly related to the culture in which the child lives. Cultural values and academic performance standards virtually define this condition. Cultural norms and environmental contexts dictate the importance of various responses and skills. Cultural norms also establish who will be included or accepted and who will be excluded or separated.

Over the course of history, we have seen children with disabilities vilified and shunned, pitied, accepted but separated, and accepted into activities and services that are available to all others (Safford & Safford, 1996). As research, service models, and belief systems have come to focus on an individual's competence and strengths in various situations regardless of behaviour or developmental labels or diagnoses, we come closer to a fully inclusive society.

Inclusion: Belonging and Participation

In closing, I would like to examine systems and services for young children with disabilities in terms of participation as members within their peer group in an inclusive society. I will review some of the findings from a multi-university research project in which I have been engaged with a number of colleagues for the past several years, the Early Childhood Research Institute on Inclusion (see overview on web site http://www.fpg.unc.edu/~ecrii and in Odom, 2002; other references include Beckman et al., 1998; Hanson, Gutierrez, Morgan, Brennen & Zercher, 1997; Hanson et al., 1998; Lieber et al., 1998; Lieber et al., 2000; Odom et al., 1996; Odom et al., 1999). This project was a five-year, federally funded project designed to identify barriers to inclusion for young children with disabilities and their families and to develop strategies to facilitate inclusion. Over the course of the research project we engaged in a variety of research studies that examined family issues, children's participation in programs, classroom teacher and staff concerns, and policy issues. For dissemination purposes, we endeavoured to synthesize the findings from these many studies of inclusion into several key points. Those synthesis points are summarized in the discussion that follows.

Synthesis Point #1: Inclusion is about belonging and participating in a diverse society.

- Inclusion is not just a school issue – it extends to the communities in which children and their families live.
- Inclusion is not only a disability issue – all children and families have a right to participate and be supported in their schools and communities.

Synthesis Point #2: Individuals – teachers, families, administrators – define inclusion differently.

- Levels of the ecological system, priorities, and responsibilities influence definitions of inclusion.
- People within the same system (e.g., one school or school district) may have extremely different views of inclusion.

Synthesis Point #3: Beliefs about inclusion influence its implementation.

- The beliefs about schooling that families and professionals bring with them to the classroom influence how inclusive practices are planned and implemented. These beliefs are influenced by many complex factors.
- Beliefs about human diversity – culture, race, language, class, ability – influence how inclusion is implemented in schools and communities.

Synthesis Point #4: Programs, not children, have to be 'ready for inclusion.'

- The most successful inclusive programs view inclusion as the starting point for all children.
- Inclusion can be appropriate for all children. Making it work successfully depends on planning, training, and support.

Synthesis Point #5: Collaboration is the cornerstone to effective inclusive programs.

- Collaboration among adults, from different disciplines and often with different philosophies, is one of the greatest challenges to successful implementation of inclusive programs.

Synthesis Point #6: Specialized instruction is an important component of inclusion.

- Participation in a community-based or general education setting is not enough. The individual needs of children with disabilities must be addressed in inclusive programs.
- Specialized instruction can be delivered through a variety of effective strategies, many of which can be embedded in the ongoing classroom activities.

Synthesis Point #7: Adequate support is necessary to make inclusive environments work.

- Support includes training, personnel, materials, planning time, and ongoing consultation.
- Support can be delivered in different ways and each person involved in inclusion may have unique needs.

Synthesis Point #8: Inclusion can benefit children with and without disabilities.

- The parents of children without disabilities whose children participate in inclusive programs often report beneficial changes in their children's confidence, self-esteem, and understanding of diversity.
- High-quality early-childhood programs form the necessary structural base of high-quality inclusive programs; thus, all children benefit from them.

In the work of this institute to understand and facilitate the inclusion of young children with disabilities into programs and services available to their typically developing peers, we were struck by the impact of belief systems. In service systems and places where diversity was valued and disability was seen as one form of human diversity, children with developmental disorders were more likely to be welcomed as participating members.

The following story told by a school principal demonstrates the power of these belief systems and this commitment:

> This is just a little story that kind of illustrates the levels at which this impacts people. We had one of our parents come to me and say, 'I don't want my child eating with this other child.' ... And I said, 'then you don't want your child at this centre, because that's what we do. It's really important to us. And I'd feel terrible if your child left the centre, but I can't separate the two groups of children because one of the things that's very important to us is to educate the heart as well as the head and that's what we want for all our children.' And then she was kind of troubled and I just asked her if she would do me a favour and come to lunch one day so she could see what happens when the children are mixed. So she came to lunch and ... she came to me afterwards, and I'm pretty sure she had tears in her eyes, and she told me it was all right. I mean, you know, that's really powerful stuff.
>
> But it all seems to us that everything flows from what our ethical underpinnings are. So that what we want to do is really look at what are the values that we hold dear and that we want for our children. And that the curriculum should flow from those values ... That there's much more to teach children and in that context of that body of knowledge, all those other things, like circle and squares can come, but the real key is what do we really believe? What do we hold to be really sacred about life and about what we want for kids? ... And the idea is that all of us together want to come up with a curriculum that is really site-based, that flows from our sense of importance of diversity, importance of building community and seeing the child in the context of the community. – School Principal
>
> (cited in Hanson et al., 1998, pp. 206–207)

Summary

As we have come to recognize that the concept of disability is not merely an abnormality or impairment, but rather that disability is integrally linked to the demands and supports within the developmental context of the child, we have developed services to better support young children. As we come to accept that disability is yet another form of human diversity and that individuals with disabilities should enjoy the same opportunities for membership and belonging in the society as others, we will realize the concept of full inclusion. Indeed, when this goal is realized, we will not need to have a separate lecture on disabilities in a lecture series on child development.

References

Beckman, P.J., Barnwell, D., Horn, E., Hanson, M.J., Gutierrez, S., & Lieber, J. (1998). Communities, families and inclusion. *Early Childhood Research Quarterly, 13(1),* 125–150.

Bernier, J.C., & Siegel, D.H. (1994). Attention-deficit hyperactive disorder: A family and ecological systems perspective. *Families in Society, 75,* 142–150.

Berry, J.O. (1995). Families and deinstitutionalization: An application of Bronfenbrenner's social ecology model. *Journal of Counseling and Development, 73,* 379–383.

Bronfenbrenner, U. (1979). *The ecology of human development.* Cambridge, MA: Harvard University Press.

Bronfenbrenner, U., & Ceci, S.J. (1994). Nature-nurture reconceptualized: A bioecological model. *Psychological Review, 101,* 568–586.

Bronfenbrenner, U., & Morris, P.A. (1998). The ecology of developmental processes. In R. Lerner (Ed.), *Handbook of child psychology (5th ed.): Vol. I. Theoretical models of human development* (pp. 993–1028). New York: Wiley.

Chan, S. (1986). Parents of exceptional Asian children. In M.K. Kitano & P.C. Chinn (Eds.), *Exceptional Asian children and youth* (pp. 36–53). Reston, VA: Council for Exceptional Children.

Fadiman, A. (1997). *The spirit catches you and you fall down: A Hmong child, her American doctors, and the collision of two cultures.* New York: Farrar, Straus, and Giroux, Noonday Press.

Fine, M., & Asch, A. (1988). Disability beyond stigma: Social interaction, discrimination, and activism. *Journal of Social Issues, 44(1),* 3–21.

Hanson, M.J., Gutierrez, S., Morgan, M., Brennan, E.L., & Zercher, C. (1997). Language, culture and disability: Interacting influences on preschool inclusion. *Topics in Early Childhood Special Education, 17(3),* 307–336.

Hanson, M.J., Lynch, E.W., & Wayman, K.I. (1990). Honoring the cultural diversity of families when gathering data. *Topics in Early Childhood Special Education, 10(1),* 112–131.

Hanson, M.J., Wolfberg, P., Zercher, C., Morgan, M., Gutierrez, S., Barnwell, D., & Beckman, P.J. (1998). The culture of inclusion: Recognizing diversity at multiple levels. *Early Childhood Research Quarterly, 13(1),* 185–209.

International Classification of Functioning, Disability and Health (ICF) (2001). Web site: http://www.who.int/icf.

Lieber, J., Beckman, P.J., Hanson, M.J., Janko, S., Marquart, J.M., Horn, E., & Odom, S.L. (1997). The impact of changing roles on relationships between professionals in inclusive programs for young children. *Early Education and Development, 8(1),* 67–82.

Lieber, J., Hanson, M.J., Beckman, P.J., Odom, S.L., Sandall, S., Schwartz, I., Horn, E., & Wolery, R. (2000). Key influences on the initiation and implementation of inclusive preschool programs. *Exceptional Children, 67(1),* 83–98.

Lynch, E.W., & Hanson, M.J. (2004). *Developing cross-cultural competence: A Guide for working with children and their families* (3rd ed.). Baltimore: Paul H. Brookes.

McDermott, R., & Varenne, H. (1995). Culture as disability. *Anthropology & Education Quarterly, 26(3),* 324–348.

Odom, S.L. (2002). *Widening the circle: Including children with disabilities in preschool programs.* New York: Teachers College Press, Columbia University.

Odom, S.L., Horn, E.M., Marquart, J., Hanson, M.J., Wolfberg, P., Beckman, P., Lieber, J., Li, S., Schwartz, I., Janko, S., & Sandall, S. (1999). On the forms of inclusion: Context and individualized service delivery models. *Journal of Early Intervention, 22(3),* 185–199.

Odom, S.L., Peck, C.A., Hanson, M.J., Beckman, P.J., Kaiser, A.P., Lieber, J., Brown, W.H., Horn, E.M., & Schwartz, I.S. (1996). Inclusion at the preschool level: An ecological systems analysis. *Social Policy Report: Society for Research in Child Development, 10(2 & 3),* 18–30.

Safford, P. L., & Safford, E. J. (1996). *A history of childhood and disability.* New York: Teachers College Press, Columbia University.

Sameroff, A.J., & Chandler, M.J. (1975). Reproductive risk and the continuum of caretaking casualty. In F.D. Horowitz (Ed.), *Review of Child Development* (Vol. 4, pp. 187–244). Chicago: University of Chicago Press.

Scheer, J., & Groce, N. (1988). Impairment as a human constant: Cross-cultural and historical perspective on variation. *Journal of Social Issues, 44(1),* 23–37.

Shore, R. (1997). *Rethinking the brain.* New York: Families and Work Institute.

6

Developmental Theory and Public Policy: A Cross-National Perspective

MICHAEL E. LAMB

It is important to note at the outset that I am not a student of the policy-making process and that I have never formally engaged in either the construction or evaluation of public policy. Instead, I offer in this essay the perspective of a developmental psychologist raised far from North America who has (perhaps as a consequence) long argued that cross-cultural research should constrain the widespread tendency of Western social scientists to overstate and overgeneralize their findings. In addition, the international experts and organizations that increasingly direct and evaluate public policies affecting children should, but seldom do, pay attention to a number of interrelated issues that may sharply affect their relevance and impact. Some of these issues are pertinent to any communication between researchers and policy-makers, whereas others are of special concern only to those with cross-national interests or tendencies to seek lessons from the experiences of other countries. Clearly, my goal is not to discourage multinational communication, but to suggest ways in which it can be maximally fruitful to all concerned.

In this chapter, I first note that the apparent and the implicit goals of any policy may differ, and that similar ostensible goals may disguise discrepant implicit motives in different countries. As a result, generalization from one country's experiences is often problematic, and it is almost always necessary to analyse the cultural and historical assumptions behind any policy, as well as the cultural history of those who might be affected by the policy. I then briefly discuss issues that may impede effective cross-national policy-making and analysis, including cultural differences in the definition of desirable outcomes and in the interpretation and conceptualization of the tests used to measure the effects of public policy. Regardless of cultural context, furthermore, researchers and policy-makers have different responsibilities and must perforce ask different questions, guided in part by the policy-makers' need to distribute limited resources among competing programs and thus to focus on cost-effectiveness as well as optimization. These issues are the focus of my final section. All the issues discussed in this chapter have broad relevance across the lifespan, but to keep my analysis manageable, I focus my discussion narrowly on the care and socialization of children in the first few years of life.

'A rose by any other name would smell as sweet' – But What About Brambles Called Roses?

It is important to note at the outset that superficial similarities between the policy and service needs of different countries may obscure substantial differences between the actual needs, ideologies, and policy goals of different nations. Careful examination and articulation of these differences is necessary in order to benefit from the experiences of agencies and policy-makers in other countries. An analysis of national policies and experiences with respect to non-parental care policies is illustrative. Non-parental childcare has become increasingly common throughout the developed world, and superficial analysis suggests that we should be able to learn much by studying and borrowing from the experiences of other countries. In fact, cross-national exchanges have been neither common not particularly helpful, for reasons that I hope to make clear.

Although developmentalists often assume, and politicians, especially in developed countries, may claim, that 'family policies' have children's welfare as their primary concern, policy-makers are likely to focus on the interests of all family members and to consider their concerns as parents, workers, and dependants. When these interests are in conflict, trade-offs are sometimes necessary, but there may be compelling political reasons to disguise the conflicts of interest and to represent policies in a misleading way. Parents have long had to make arrangements for their children's care and supervision, for example, and a diverse array of non-parental care arrangements are evident in the developed and developing world (Lamb, Sternberg, Hwang, & Broberg, 1992; Olmsted & Weikart, 1989). Individual choices among the available options are influenced by local social demography, history, and cultural ideology, but economic forces – particularly the need for women to work outside the home in conditions that are incompatible with childcare to support their families – universally play a major role in determining whether and what types of non-parental care arrangements are made. Non-parental care arrangements have thus proliferated because parents need to seek employment and cannot simultaneously care for their children, not because parents (let alone policy-makers) simply sought to enhance the quality of their children's lives. Especially when there is a real choice between feeding their families and providing 'quality care,' this may help explain why concerns about the adverse effects of non-parental care have had such little impact.

Independent of the economic pressures driving families to seek non-parental care, childcare policies in many countries, including those in the former Communist bloc, were designed to facilitate and promote female employment and to equalize the potential employment opportunities of men and women (Cochran, 1993; Lamb et al., 1992). Despite costly and extensive investments in childcare facilities, however, equality of opportunity has never been achieved anywhere. Even in countries such as Sweden, with a long-established and popular commitment to gender equality, almost all childcare providers are women. Ironically, therefore, many employed women are engaged in female-typed activities – often the same activities they would otherwise perform at home without pay. And in most countries (the Nordic countries excepted), women do not enjoy equitable pay, whether or not their professions are integrated. Nonetheless, the availability of non-parental care facilities has indeed facilitated – sometimes coercively – the increased participation of women in the paid labour market.

Childcare facilities have frequently been used to facilitate acculturation or ideological indoctrination as well. Pre-school education was made widely available to Japanese four- and five-year-olds in 1941 because the government wanted to foster nationalism (Shwalb, Shwalb, Sukemune, & Tatsumoto, 1992). The number of Italian children in pre-schools nearly doubled in the 1960s because pre-schools were believed by philosophers such as Ciari to provide cultural foundations for children from different socio-economic backgrounds (Corsaro & Emiliani, 1992), while in the People's Republic of China, universal childcare in the early 1950s permitted parents to participate in political re-education programs (Lee, 1992). In Israel, meanwhile, the speed with which successive waves of Jewish immigrants have risen to positions of economic and political power is largely attributable to the participation of immigrant children in pre-school and school programs where they learn

Hebrew and the norms of Israeli culture (Rosenthal, 1992). The children in turn socialize and teach their parents.

Childcare facilities have also been provided to facilitate job training or paid employment and thus to reduce dependence on public assistance. In the United States, pursuit of this goal energized major revisions of the welfare system in the 1990s. Ironically, this goal was often promoted with greatest vigour by conservative politicians generally opposed to other governmental involvement in the support or regulation of childcare. Critics in turn argued that the childcare provided to children whose mothers were encouraged or required to work was often of marginal quality. Whether or not such arguments were valid, critics missed the point: childcare was designed to facilitate maternal employment and economic self-sufficiency while reducing government outlays, not to enhance children's well-being.

At least some childcare facilities and policies have been developed because policy-makers *did* want to enrich the lives of children, of course. The impetus to develop and invest in intervention programs thus grew in the early 1960s following the determination by experts that poor children in the United States experienced understimulation, over-stimulation, or inappropriate stimulation, which in turn led them to perform poorly in school and on achievement tests (Fein & Clarke-Stewart, 1973; Hess, 1970). The development of the Head Start program in 1965 exemplified a desire to enrich the lives of children from the poorest and most disadvantaged families in the United States (Zigler & Valentine, 1979), and comparable programs like Turkey's Fair Start (Bekman, 1998) have had similar goals. Likewise, despite its strong opposition to non-maternal care, the Catholic Church in Italy came to view pre-schools as an effective technique for socializing children whose impoverished parents were considered incapable of effective socialization (Corsaro & Emiliani, 1992; New, 1993). Only later was pre-school deemed acceptable for children in better socio-economic circumstances. In Great Britain, daycare is still considered a service for children at risk because their parents cannot cope (Melhuish and Moss 1992). Popular disapproval of daycare is reinforced there by a policy of channelling government funding to daycare centres serving disadvantaged, troubled, and disabled children. In Canada, meanwhile, it took the recommendations of a government task force in the mid-1980s to recast daycare as a service of potential value to all Canadian families, rather than as a service for disadvantaged and immigrant children (Goelman, 1992; Pence, 1993).

With these important exceptions, however, concern with enriching the lives of children did not motivate the initial development of institutions serving young children, and there is ample evidence that parents often accept care of lower quality because they simply have no choice but to make such arrangements (National Academy of Science, 1990). Where parents, groups, and societies have seriously considered the needs and best interests of children these have often been secondary considerations.

Regardless of their specific motivations, of course, most developed and developing countries have initiated childcare policies. This does not mean that such policies and programs have been embraced with enthusiasm. In particular, it is crucial to consider international variations in the extent to which the provision of childcare is viewed as a public responsibility rather than a private or individual concern. The United States and the United Kingdom probably hew most closely to the extreme position that decisions about childcare should be left to parents, that the cost and quality of care should be set by the competition between the unregulated forces of supply and demand, and that governmental intrusions of all kinds should be resisted because they simply reduce efficiency (Cohen, 1993; Lamb et al., 1992; Spedding, 1993). At the other extreme stand the democratic-socialist countries of Scandinavia and the formerly Communist countries of Eastern Europe in which society as a whole was believed to share responsibility for the care and welfare of all children (Ahnert, 1998; Stoltenberg, 1994; Kamerman & Kahn, 1978, 1981; Hwang & Broberg, 1992). Canada often seems to fall between these two extremes, with the Western provinces leaning toward the U.S. model and the Eastern provinces looking to Europe for their inspiration. Interestingly, a comparative analysis suggests that the best-quality non-parental care tends to be provided and/or regulated by governmental agencies in the context of comprehensive family policies (Lamb et al., 1992). By contrast, countries or regions that have failed to develop comprehensive family policies and eschew governmental intervention tend to provide care of much poorer average quality.

Further complicating the picture and confounding attempts to derive simplistic lessons from other countries are national variations in the extent to which childcare is viewed as a social welfare program rather than an educational program. Since all industrialized countries and most developing countries regularly assign responsibility for children older than five or six years of age to educational authorities, many countries have expanded the availability of care settings for young children by emphasizing the educational value of pre-school care. Because public education is a widely accepted concept, it has proven relatively easy to direct public finances to the support of pre-schools. By contrast, when non-parental care is viewed as a custodial babysitting service addressing the goals of social welfare, it has proven harder to obtain public financial support, and harder yet to make quality of care a relevant dimension. This discrepancy is not new; O'Connor (1995) and Cahan (1989) have chronicled emergent distinctions of this sort at the turn of the century. In St Louis, Missouri, for example, kindergartens came to be seen as part of the educational process and flourished, whereas day nurseries experienced the struggle for support that continues to this day. Thus, the perceived character and purpose of non-parental care has major and far-reaching implications for the quality, type, and public support for non-parental care services. In Italy, the United Kingdom, France, and the Netherlands, for example, the portrayal of daycare for pre-schoolers as an educational rather than a welfare service altered perceptions of its value by middle- and upper-class families and thus legitimized its widespread utilization (Clerkx & van IJzendoorn, 1992; Corsaro & Emiliani, 1992; Lamb et al., 1992; Melhuish & Moss, 1992). Particularly in the developed countries, higher percentages of pre-schoolers are enrolled in non-parental-care settings when they have educational rather than custodial goals (Olmsted, 1992).

We need to consider these ideological and philosophical issues when evaluating the policies and systems of diverse countries because international differences of these dimensions make it generally inappropriate and perhaps dangerous to generalize from one country to another or to use any country's social policies as models for adoption by others. Only when they attempt to understand the social structures and the ideologies that led to the development of a particular childcare system are social scientists likely to learn from the experiences of other societies. Even though Sweden's family policies are widely envied and often cited as exemplary models for the rest of the world, for example, that nation's history, economy, and ideology are about as unique as its family policies. Sweden is a culturally and linguistically homogeneous country of about 8 million people; it experienced relatively little immigration for several centuries. The dominant political ideology – democratic socialism – is so well established that the Social Democratic Party has remained in power for all but three of the seventy years since 1932, and the country has a long and sincere history of commitment to the attainment of gender equality. Historically, Sweden switched with re-markably rapidity from a basically agrarian economy to a highly indus-trialized country. After remaining neutral and relatively untouched by the two world wars that ravaged the rest of Europe, Sweden emerged from the Second World War as the only European country with a functioning, undamaged, and modern industrial base capable of pro-viding consumer goods to the rest of the world. As a result, Sweden has since experienced a degree of affluence shared by few other countries. The generous family policies that Swedes still enjoy were made pos-sible by all of these factors, which in turn ensure that Sweden does not constitute a good model for countries like the United States, the United Kingdom, or Canada that are characterized by cultural heterogeneity, ideological diversity, economic inequality, and insistent commitments – except perhaps in Eastern Canada – to individualism and capitalism.

More generally, this analysis of the diverse ideological, economic, and historical factors that shape each country's approach to non-parental childcare offers important lessons to those who aim to learn from the experiences of other countries. Clearly, it is essential that assumptions about similarities between the cultural, economic, politi-cal, and historical circumstances of any two countries be carefully ex-amined and evaluated before attempts are made to transplant policies from one to another. In addition, once a policy direction has been set, it is important that it build upon, incorporate, and be responsive to local cultural beliefs and practices.

Cultural Differences in Values, Goals, and Means

Differences in parental and national goals lead to differences in the implementation and effects of programs and policies that appear simi-lar, and the evaluation of those outcomes differs from society to society as well. For example, some Americans might see assertiveness as a desirable goal, whereas the British might recognize it as one manifes-tation of undesirable aggression. The Japanese view it as a marker of immaturity and ill-socialization (Fiske, Kitayama, Markus, & Nisbett, 1998; Trommsdorff & Friedlmeier, 1993). Everywhere debate persists over the relative value of individualism and cooperation. Is compliance an index of passive acquiescence or of being well socialized? As long as disagreements concerning the desirability of such characteristics exist, it is inappropriate to state that a program or pattern of care has 'posi-tive' or 'negative' effects except in a clearly specified cultural context. In psychological development, things are not always what they seem – the perspective of the beholder is often critical. Furthermore, we cannot assume that practices associated with assertiveness in one cultural context would have the same effect in another cultural space, or that an index behaviour means the same thing in different cultural contexts.

The relative importance of differences in the conceptualization and character of policies and outcomes depends in part on divergent conceptions of childhood and developmental processes. Most 'experts' in the Western industrialized countries are steeped in the post-Freudian belief that early experiences are crucially important; they seldom step back and acknowledge this belief as an ideological statement of faith, rather than as an empirically proven statement of fact. Where philosophers instead emphasize the formative effects of experiences occurring after the age of reason (six or seven years) rather than before, as do many in Asia and West Africa (Lee, 1992; Riseman, 1992; Shwalb & Chen, 1994–95), the ages of the children concerned may affect the types and quality of care that they need. It is neither morally nor scientifically appropriate for us to assert, given our current state of knowledge, that the Western conceptualization is superior.

Cultural Variations in Socialization Goals

Any intervention designed to enhance children's development must be sensitive to cultural variations in the definitions of acceptable, appropriate, and inappropriate parenting and care. Adolescent initiation rites provide obvious examples (Korbin, 1981). In many African tribes, for instance, adolescent boys are beaten, circumcised without anaesthesia, and forced to fast before being accepted as men. These rituals are considered so crucial that boys who fail to complete them are doomed to remain children forever, unable to marry or own land. Neighbouring tribes often consider these practices barbaric, and when their boys are coerced into participating in order to prepare for commerce with tribes who practice such rituals, their relatives attempt to smuggle food and soothing medication to them. Both groups, of course, would perceive the ritual circumcision of newborn males in North America as barbaric, but it is often endorsed and practised by those who criticize female genital mutilation in parts of West and East Africa.

Cultural relativity is even more problematic when one attempts to define potentially harmful practices. By the standards of Western childcare specialists, for example, the Japanese tradition of indulging young children during the pre-school years must be deemed harmful, particularly since indulged children would seem peculiarly ill-prepared to face the relentless rigidity of the Japanese school system. To the Japanese, changing demands are believed to catalyse changes in the child's personality. Judgments about poor parenting are particularly sensitive to the individual, professional, and cultural values of raters or judges, and this creates a potentially dangerous situation in which quality of interaction may be determined more by value orientation than by empirical evidence demonstrating the context and circumstances under which certain behaviours may be harmful to children. This is particularly problematic when those who are authorized to label behaviour often have different values and backgrounds than those whose behaviours are being labelled. Furthermore, the same practices may have very different effects on children's behaviour depending on the cultural context. Baumrind (1972), for example, has shown that 'authoritative parenting' promotes socially competent behaviour in white, middle-class children, while 'authoritarian parenting' promotes social competence in black, middle-class children. In all, the evaluation of parental behaviour and the relationship between parent-child interaction and child outcomes vary dramatically across cultural contexts. One cannot, therefore, make assertions about the universal harmfulness of certain parental practices or behaviours:

> The lack of clarity and certainty does not lie merely in the absence of a factual basis on which to answer the question of harm. It also lies in the nature of the question. What is 'harmful to children' can only be answered with respect to some questions on the basis of social values. Scientists, including social and behavioural scientists, can answer with facts about given sets of conditions and about the likelihood that they will lead to particular outcomes. The 'harmfulness' of these outcomes, or conversely their desirability, becomes a question of values, not of facts. (Giovannoni, Conklin, & Iiyama, 1978, p. 88)

Setting aside the complexities that attend the definition of high-quality parenting and desirable outcomes, let us now consider the different needs of researchers and practitioners, including policy-makers, where it comes to the differences between categorical and continuous definitions of childcare quality and, especially, child maltreatment. For researchers, it is perfectly reasonable to think of a continuum of parental quality, particularly as they may lose statistical power by viewing parental quality categorically, in terms of adequate parenting and 'maltreatment.' But even if one believes that psychological maltreatment lies at one end of a continuum of parental quality, and that there are linear relationships between quality of parenting and child outcomes, the implications for policy-makers and researchers are quite different. The researcher's role is facilitated by the knowledge that better-quality parent-child interaction is associated with more desirable outcomes, and that the poorer the quality of interaction, the poorer the developmental outcome for the child. For policy-makers and practitioners, however, recognition of a continuum poses a profound dilemma. These practitioners must use a concept of maltreatment to make decisions about a child's placement, which in turn requires both that they be sensitive to issues of fairness, equity, clarity, and due process and that they recognize and take steps to avoid the dangers associated with inappropriate intervention and failure to intervene.

If a continuum of more and less desirable parental practices and child outcomes exists, who is to decide where the line should be drawn? No Western political system permits public authorities to intervene directly in the day-to-day lives of parents and children in order to ensure the best possible futures for all children. Traditionally, such interventions have been tolerated only when the child's safety or overwhelming social benefits are at stake. Most industrialized countries have thus sought to define minimal acceptable standards of care for safeguarding the child's growth and development (Goldstein, Freud, & Solnit, 1973). Contrast this with the view that parental behaviour associated with a sub-optimal outcome could be deemed psychologically harmful (McGee & Wolfe, 1991); who would sanction intervention under these circumstances? As Wald (1975, pp. 1016–1017) wrote:

> While emotional damage to a child should be a basis for intervention in some cases, it is essential that laws be drafted in a manner consistent with our limited knowledge about the nature and causes of psychological harm. Intervention should not be premised on vague concepts like 'proper parental love' and 'adequate affectionate parental association.' Such language invites unwarranted intervention based on each social worker's or judge's brand of folk psychology.

'When I use a word, it means exactly what I want it to mean'

To complicate matters further, it is clear that the behaviours or tests that we use to quantify the effects of either parental quality or specific interventions may mean very different things in different temporal and cultural contexts. The complex ways in which cultural differences in everyday experiences may affect the fundamental validity of instruments used to assess the effects of various practices and policies are well illustrated by research on the Strange Situation (Lamb, Thompson, Gardner, & Charnov, 1985). The Strange Situation was developed by Ainsworth and her colleagues in 1962 to assess individual differences in the security of infant-mother attachment (Ainsworth, Blehar, Waters, & Wall, 1978). In the Strange Situation (see Figure 6.1), infants are subjected to several everyday sources of stress, including the appearance of an unfamiliar adult and brief separations from the parent. Researchers closely examine the infants' reactions, particularly their use of the parent for comfort and assistance in dealing with these stresses. Securely attached infants actively seek reassurance from their parents and are effectively soothed by them. By contrast, insecure infants either avoid their parents or direct anger toward them.

In part because these patterns of behaviour in the Strange Situation appear to have degrees of external validity (especially regarding antecedents and correlates) lacked by other measures of socio-emotional development, the Strange Situation became extremely popular among researchers, and it has been a central component of research in North America for the last quarter century. Secure behaviour in the Strange Situation is implicitly viewed as evidence that the child has enjoyed sensitive care from the adult in question and is destined to be socially adept in interactions with those he or she encounters in the future, whereas insecure behaviour implies insensitive care and a less desirable prognosis (Thompson, 1998).

As the Strange Situation achieved prominence as a procedure for assessing individual differences in parent-infant attachments, it came to be used in many countries other than the United States. Quite unexpectedly, the results of these studies have forced researchers to question the assumptions that (1) similar patterns of Strange Situation behaviour necessarily have the same origins and the same relationship to future behaviour in different cultures, and thus that (2) Strange Situation behaviour is isomorphic with security of attachment.

Research using the Strange Situation outside the United States began in the late 1970s and early 1980s in West Germany (Klaus and Karin Grossmann), Sweden (Michael Lamb, Philip Hwang, and Ann Frodi), Israel (Michael Lamb and Avi Sagi), the Netherlands (Marinus van IJzendoorn), Japan (Kazuo Miyake), and in other parts of Germany (the

Figure 6.1   The Strange Situation

	Parent and child enter
Episode 1*	Parent and child
	Stranger enters
Episode 2	Stranger, parent, and child
	Parent leaves
Episode 3	Stranger and child
	Parent returns; stranger leaves
Episode 4	Parent and child
	Parent leaves
Episode 5	Child alone
	Stranger returns
Episode 6	Stranger and child
	Parent returns; stranger leaves
Episode 7	Parent and child

*All episodes are three minutes long, although separation episodes may be abbreviated and reunion episodes extended if the child is very distressed.

Grossmanns, Helggaard Rauh, Lieselotte Ahnert). Interestingly, the distribution across Strange Situation groups and subgroups reported by these researchers often deviated from the distribution considered typical in the United States, although with one exception (the Grossmann, Grossmann, Huber, & Wartner, 1981, study of infants in Bielefeld) the secure (B) classification was modal in all cultural contexts, whereas the division of infants between the insecure-avoidant and insecure-resistant groups varied markedly between and within cultures. Although van IJzendoorn and Kroonenberg (1988) argued there are no culture-specific patterns or distributions that fall outside the range of distributions evident in the United States, it remains important to explain why the distribution observed in any study deviates from the 'normative' pattern.

In their first study, the Grossmanns reported that the various ratings of maternal and infant behaviour were interrelated in Bielefeld as they were in Baltimore. The mothers of infants who later behaved securely were rated as more sensitive when the infants were two and six months old than were the mothers of infants who were later resistant, although mothers of both insecure and secure infants were equivalently sensitive when observed with their ten-month-olds.

When observed in the Strange Situation, however, a surprisingly large number (49 per cent rather than the expected 20–25 per cent) of these German infants were assigned to the insecure-avoidant group and similar distributions were evident when the infants were observed with their fathers at eighteen months of age (Grossmann et al., 1981). The Grossmanns suggested that North German mothers begin socializing their infants to be independent at a much earlier age than American mothers do, and that behaviours designed to foster independence may have been rated as rejecting and insensitive by observers applying Ainsworth's rating scales. From this perspective, increased demands to behave in a culturally appropriate fashion (i.e., independently) produced avoidant behaviour in the Strange Situation, with 'our infant's ... avoidance in the Strange Situation [being] an indication of the difficulty coping with demands that the infants have not learned to cope with yet' (Grossmann & Grossmann, 1983, p. 6). 'Initial avoidance of attachment figures appears to be a first indicator of infants' application of cultural rules, as well as their acceptance of demands and requirements which are not neglectful' (p. 7). Importantly, then, factors other than parental insensitivity appear to be associated with Strange Situation behaviour, may be rated as indices of insensitivity on Ainsworth's rating scales, and may also be culturally normative in North Rhine-Wesphalia. The implication, as Grossmann, Grossmann, Spangler, Suess, and Unsner (1985) noted, was that 'insensitivity for the sake of complying with cultural norms is not equivalent to rejection' (p. 255). In addition, constitutionally based infant characteristics may have influenced the behaviour of the Bielefeld infants in the Strange Situation. Grossmann and Grossmann (1983) reported that twelve of the sixteen infants who behaved securely in the Strange Situation were 'good orienters' neonatally compared with only nine of the twenty-four avoidant infants.

By contrast, the distribution across attachment categories observed in Göteborg, Sweden, by Lamb, Frodi, Frodi, and Hwang (1982) was quite similar to that reported by Ainsworth et al. (1978). Like the Bielefeld infants, however, these Swedish infants appeared to show less distress in the Strange Situation than American infants typically did. For some reason, therefore, the Strange Situation appeared to perturb these North German and Swedish babies less than it typically stressed American infants, although earlier measures of parental attitudes, parental behaviour, infant behaviour, parent-child interaction, or infant temperament were not related to Strange Situation behaviour in Sweden. What, then, did the Strange Situation behaviour of these Swedish infants really mean? The possibility that it may not mean very much at all – and thus may not tap some fundamentally important aspect of the developing infants' personalities or of the infant-parent attachments – is strengthened by the fact that classifications of the infant-mother attachments were unrelated to measures of infant sociability with unfamiliar adults (contrary to findings obtained in the United States and Israel) and that Strange Situation behaviour with fathers was only weakly associated with stranger sociability.

Sagi et al. (1985) studied eighty-six infants on 'traditional' Israeli kibbutzim where children lived in group homes rather than with their parents. Each child was seen in the Strange Situation three times – once each with his or her mother and father and the *metapelet* (caretaker) primarily responsible for his or her care – and an unusually high number were rated as insecure-resistant. Does this mean that kibbutz childcare arrangements fostered insecurity? Such arrangements entail multiple caretakers and conditions in which infants' cries may go unanswered for long periods of time (especially at night), and thus the higher proportion of resistant attachments would be consistent with predictions from attachment theory.

Instead of variations in the quality of care, however, the distribution of infants across attachment categories could perhaps be explained by differences in the infants' interpretations of the Strange Situation procedure. More than a third of the sessions on the kibbutzim had to be abbreviated because the infants were inconsolably distressed. Most of these infants later behaved resistantly. When children whose sessions were abbreviated were excluded, however, the distribution across attachment categories did not deviate significantly from the distribution reported by Ainsworth et al. (1978). Thus the unusual distribution across attachment categories was accounted for by a group of infants who consistently manifested unusual degrees of distress and were extremely difficult to soothe.

These levels of distress may have reflected unusual levels of stranger anxiety. Prior to each Strange Situation session, the researchers assessed the infants' sociability using what is, to American infants, an innocuous and non-intrusive procedure. The mean sociability scores were substantially lower than those obtained with American infants (Sagi, Lamb, & Gardner, 1986; Stevenson & Lamb, 1979; Thompson & Lamb, 1982). Furthermore, the subsequent appearance of another stranger in the second episode of the Strange Situation provoked considerable distress on the part of many infants – most notably those whose sessions had to be abbreviated or modified. As a result, the Strange Situation procedure was substantially more stressful for many kibbutz infants than it was for most American infants.

Of course, the greater distress evinced by the kibbutz infants may have reflected their insecurity, but it is also possible that these infants were more distressed by strangers because they lived in fairly small, closed groups in which they were, as a consequence, less frequently exposed to total strangers, or that they were temperamentally prone to high distress. If the kibbutz infants were indeed more distressed, for whatever reason, one cannot simply compare their behaviour to that of American infants in essence responding to a psychologically different experience.

Similar issues were raised by Miyake, Chen, and Campos (1985), who studied twenty-nine middle-class Japanese mothers and their infants. More than a third of these infants were classified as insecure-resistant, and none were deemed insecure-avoidant. As in Israel, the Strange Situation procedure seemed to arouse more stress among these Japanese infants than it typically did in the United States – again suggesting that the Strange Situation may have a psychologically different meaning to infants in different cultures (see also Nakagawa, Lamb, & Miyake, 1987–88). Differences between the child-rearing practices and goals of Japanese and American parents may help account for the different Strange Situation behaviour of Japanese and American infants (Rothbaum, Pott, Azuma, Miyake, & Weisz, 2000). Because Japanese infants are rarely if ever separated from their mothers, even at night, they may have been unusually stressed by the brief separations involved in the Strange Situation procedure, and their mothers may have been unusually concerned about behaving appropriately. Their unease may have unsettled their children as well. In addition, Grossmann and Grossmann (1987–88) argued that the Strange Situation was implemented differently in Japan than in other countries, and that the more stilted behaviour of the mothers also affected the infants' interpretation of the procedure. Rothbaum, Weisz, Pott, Miyake, and Morelli (2000) went further, arguing that attachment theory is laden with Western perceptions and assumptions regarding both the characteristics of appropriate or sensitive parenting and the desirability of some of the outcomes (such as outgoing sociability) viewed as the desirable consequences of secure attachment.

Clearly, it is important to ensure that the Strange Situation procedure creates a psychologically comparable and similar experience for different infants (both intraculturally and interculturally), to recognize that factors other than variations in maternal sensitivity may affect the Strange Situation behaviour, and that the behaviour of both parents and infants, inside and outside the Strange Situation, may mean different things in different cultural contexts. Just because two infants behave similarly in the Strange Situation does not mean they do so for the same reason. In the absence of validation in a particular culture, therefore, we cannot assume that the same behaviour denotes similar qualities of 'attachment security.'

Whatever the relationship between maternal sensitivity and Strange Situation behaviour, in sum, the findings of studies done abroad are particularly helpful in demonstrating how factors other than adult sensitivity may have a powerful effect on infant behaviour in the Strange Situation. The Strange Situation was designed to provide a context for observing how infants organize their attachment behaviour around attachment figures when mildly or moderately distressed. All infants – regardless of attachment security – appear to use their attachment figures appropriately in some circumstances, however, so it is important that infants experience qualitatively and psychologically similar degrees of stress in the Strange Situation, otherwise their behaviour is not comparable. When the brief separations are especially stressful for some infants (as they apparently were for the Japanese infants), when the separations are not stressful (as they apparently were for the Swedish and German infants), or when the stranger is an unusually threatening event (as for the Israeli infants), the infants' experiences in the Strange Situation are psychologically different and their behaviour may thus differ from that of American infants. It may be different because there are differences in security, but it may be different for other reasons, too, so we cannot assume that the behaviour observed in the Strange Situation in another country has the same meaning as when it is observed in the United States. Stated differently, Strange Situation behaviour *may* reflect differences in security of attachment, as Ainsworth and her colleagues have argued, but it may also reflect differences in temperament, and differences in the familiarity, stressfulness, or interpretation of the procedure on the part of infants and parents. To complicate matters further, it seems likely that the relative importance of these factors will vary across cultures and probably within cultures as well. For example, temperamental factors may have a greater influence on the Strange Situation behaviour when prior experiences make the procedure less stressful, as the Grossmanns' analysis of avoidant behaviour seems to indicate.

I have focused at length on Strange Situation behaviour because these findings provide a particularly compelling example of the cultural specificity of index behaviours. We should expect cultural differences to have similar effects on the meaning of any test, score, or behaviour used to measure the impact of behaviours or practices of interest to researchers or policy-makers. Consequently, validity must be demonstrated empirically, not simply assumed.

'How?' As Opposed to 'How Much?'

Even when cross-cultural similarities and differences have been taken into account, research findings may often be of less value to policy-makers than scholars wish because researchers and policy-makers have fundamentally different agendas. Researchers are typically driven by a desire to test theoretical formulations, and thus use statistical analyses to determine whether specific constructs are associated in the predicted way. Policy-makers need to know, of course, whether a particular practice or policy has the expected effects, but they must also consider unintended consequences and the development of practical, clear, and operational definitions that are typically less nuanced than those developed by researchers. In addition, they are more apt to pose a question that researchers can seldom answer satisfactorily even when they try to do so: How powerful are the effects in the real world? This question is hard to answer because the samples studied are rarely representative and because truly randomized experiments are quite rare. The estimated power of associations in quasi-experimental studies depends in large part on the number of constructs taken into account and the sensitivity with which all are measured, and as a result they are often of limited value to policy-makers.

Consider, for example, the 'quality of child care,' which has become an umbrella phrase referring to diverse characteristics of childcare facilities that may either impede (in the case of poor-quality) or foster (in the case of high-quality) child adaptation and adjustment. By definition, care of high quality is characterized by practices that directly or indirectly promote socio-personality adjustment, cognitive development, and the ability to learn efficiently (see Lamb, 1998, for more details). Many studies have been conducted, with quality operationalized in a variety of ways. Some researchers, including most survey researchers, have focused on the *structural* characteristics of childcare settings (adult-to-child ratios, group size, age range, etc.), arguing that these characteristics reflect quality because they potentiate or impede the quality of care provided to children. Other researchers have attempted to quantify the children's actual experiences, and they have typically employed a family of measures developed by Harms and Clifford (1980, 1989; Harms, Cryer, & Clifford, 1986). Scores on such *process* measures of quality are typically correlated with scores on the structural indices, although the associations are by no means perfect. Using data from a large sample of one- to three-year-olds in the United States, for instance, the NICHD Early Child Care Research Network (2000) reported that 'positive caregiving' was more likely to be observed in small groups, with better adult-child ratios, staffed by care-providers who were better educated and experienced, had more child-centred beliefs, and provided care in safer and more stimulating environments. Such findings confirmed the prediction that process and structural measures of quality would be intercorrelated, although, as in previous studies, the magnitude of the associations was not high. Similarly, in the Cost, Quality, and Outcomes Study, observed quality was correlated with child-adult ratios, levels of teacher education and training, and group size, although the correlation between group size and observed quality was not statistically significant (Blau, 2000).

The fact that the associations between structural and process measures of quality are quite modest has important implications for both researchers and policy-makers. Structural parameters can most readily be manipulated or regulated by policy-makers striving to enhance the quality of care received by young children in out-of-home settings. If changes in regulations regarding teacher training, group size, and adult-child ratios do not bring appreciable changes in the quality of care received by children, then the impetus to implement such potentially costly innovations will surely decline.

The results of studies focused on the effects of childcare quality on children's adjustment and development may further weaken the enthusiasm of policy-makers. In these studies, too, initial excitement over the statistical significance of associations has since been tempered by evidence concerning the small magnitude of these associations. Not only, it seems, do investments in staff training and improved ratios yield small dividends with respect to the quality of care actually received by children, but changes in the quality of care have modest – and in some respects not even reliable – effects on children's manifest behaviour (see Lamb, 1998, for a review). Nevertheless, researchers have found that care of higher quality is generally associated with more desirable child outcomes than care of poorer quality. Although some researchers have failed to find the expected associations, significant associations in the opposite direction are almost never reported, supporting the conclusion that high-quality care is indeed superior to poor-quality care.

For policy-makers in particular, the small magnitude of the association between structural and process measures of quality and between indices of quality and child outcomes are of great importance. Do they imply that the constructs are minimally related, or perhaps that the measures are deficient? It is crucial to measure quality and outcomes as sensitively and reliably as possible. Unfortunately, however, researchers are typically forced to rely on brief single observations or written observer/teacher reports, and it is unreasonable to expect such measures to capture much more than gross variations among individual children or childcare centres. Stated differently, such measures may be sufficiently reliable to determine whether various constructs are significantly associated, but not sufficiently reliable to quantify adequately the magnitude of these associations. Regrettably, researchers still tend to choose their measures with statistical significance testing in mind, whereas they are increasingly asked – by their peers as well as by policy-makers – to reach conclusions about the magnitude of associations that their studies are ill designed and ill equipped to address. Those conducting applied research should be especially attentive to this issue, as the unrestrained willingness to offer inadequately qualified advice may ultimately undercut the credibility of researchers and other experts.

The better and more thoroughly researchers measure each of the factors included in their models (quality of care, quality of child outcome, social risk status, endogenous child characteristics, the child's characteristics before entering childcare, to mention but a few), the greater the proportion of variance they will be able to explain, and the better they will be able to quantify, at least in relative terms, the associations of greatest interest to them. Human behaviour is multidimensional and multidetermined, however, and the more possible influences or determinants one takes into account, the smaller will be the proportion of variance explained by any one of these frequently non-independent factors. When combined with measurement strategies that limit the explainable proportion of variance in the outcome measures, the implementation of multivariate analytic strategies thus ensures that important and highly reliable associations appear small in magnitude.

Given unlimited resources, the strength of these associations might not matter – a policy-maker eager to enhance children's well-being would want to maximize the quality of care anyway. Policy-makers do not have unlimited resources, however, and the cost-effectiveness of alternative policies must always be taken into account. In the absence of credible information from scientists, policy-makers may opt to invest in policies whose effectiveness has been established or make decisions on the basis of political considerations rather than scientific ones.

Even while sharpening the quality of research, therefore, applied researchers need to be more circumspect about the conclusions they draw. Their well-honed tendency to exaggerate results in order to promote certain polices and practices only feeds cynical scepticism about recommendations in the future. Quality of childcare is a salient and statistically significant modulator and moderator of the associations between type of care and child development, for example, but we have much to learn about the mechanisms whereby the associations are mediated and about the magnitude of the associations themselves.

Conclusion

Cross-cultural research is of enormous value to students of development, who should examine parental practices and developmental processes in multiple cultures for a variety of reasons. I would argue that an inclusive and successful science of child development is unattainable unless careful attention is paid to societies with widely divergent goals and patterns of social organization.

Furthermore, in a world marked by extraordinary degrees of inequity, leaders in better-off countries often feel impelled to share their affluence and knowledge with those whose circumstances are perilously inadequate. Unfortunately, this laudable impulse may lead to interventions that are inappropriate and have unintended consequences. By attempting to explain some of the difficulties in this chapter, I hope to foster transnational exchanges that are more likely than many of today's patronizing policies to enhance the lives and welfare of the millions of children who live in the impoverished shadow of our affluence.

I am grateful to Hillel Goelman, Barry S. Hewlett, Eli Orbach, and Ross A. Thompson for helpful comments on an earlier draft of this essay.

References

Ahnert, L. (Ed.). (1998). *Tagesbetreuung für Kinder unter 3 Jahren: Theorien und Tatsachen* [*Childcare for children under three years: Theories and facts*]. Bern, Switzerland: Hans Huber.

Ainsworth, M.D., Blehar, M.C., Waters, E., & Wall, S. (1978). *Patterns of attachment*. Hillsdale, NJ: Erlbaum.

Baumrind, D. (1972). An exploratory study of socialization effects on Black children: Some black-white comparisons. *Child Development, 43*, 261–267.

Bekman, S. (1998). Long-term effects of the Turkish home-based early enrichment program. In U.P. Gielen & A.L. Comunian, et al. (Eds.), *The family and family therapy in international perspective* (pp. 401–417). Trieste, Italy: Edizioni Lint Trieste.

Blau, D.M. (1997). The production of quality in child care centers. *Journal of Human Resources, 32*, 354–387.

Cahan, E.D. (1989). *Past caring: A history of U.S. preschool care and education for the poor, 1820–1965*. New York: National Center for Children in Poverty.

Clerkx, L.E., & van IJzendoorn, M.H. (1992). Child care in a Dutch context: On the history, current status, and evaluation of nonmaternal child care in the Netherlands. In M.E. Lamb, K.J. Sternberg, C.-P. Hwang, & A.G. Broberg (Eds.), *Child care in context: Cross-cultural perspectives* (pp. 55–79). Hillsdale, NJ: Erlbaum.

Cochran, M. (Ed.). (1993). *International handbook of child care policies and programs*. Westport, CT: Greenwood Press.

Cohen, B. (1993). The United Kingdom. In M. Cochran (Ed.), *International handbook of child care policies and programs* (pp. 515–534). Westport, CT: Greenwood Press.

Corsaro, W.A., & Emiliani, F. (1992). Child care, early education, and children's peer culture in Italy. In M.E. Lamb, K.J. Sternberg, C.P. Hwang, & A.G. Broberg (Eds.), *Child care in context: Cross-cultural perspectives* (pp. 81–115). Hillsdale, NJ: Erlbaum.

Fein, G.G., & Clarke-Stewart, K.A. (1973). *Day care in context*. New York: Wiley.

Fiske, A.P., Kitayama, S., Markus, H.R., & Nisbett, R.E. (1998). The cultural matrix of social psychology. In D.T. Gilbert et al. (Eds.), *The handbook of social psychology* (Vol. 2, 4th ed., pp. 915–981). Boston, MA: McGraw-Hill.

Giovannoni, J.M., Conklin, J., & Iiyama, P. (1978). *Child abuse and neglect: An examination from the perspective of child development knowledge*. San Francisco: R&E Associates.

Goelman, H. (1992). Day care in Canada. In M.E. Lamb, K.J. Sternberg, C.-P. Hwang, & A.G. Broberg (Eds.), *Child care in context: Cross-cultural perspectives* (pp. 223–263). Hillsdale, NJ: Erlbaum.

Goldstein, J., Freud, A., & Solnit, A. (1973). *Beyond the best interests of the child.* New York: Free Press.

Grossmann, K.E., & Grossmann, K. (1983). *Cultural and temperamental aspects of the avoidant attachment behavior patterns in infants.* Paper presented to the Society for Research in Child Development, Detroit, MI.

Grossmann, K.E., & Grossmann, K. (1987–88). Preliminary observations on Japanese infants' behavior in the Ainsworth's Strange Situation. *Research and Clinical Center for Child Development Annual Report, No. 11,* 1–12. Hokkaido University, Sapporo, Japan.

Grossmann, K.E., Grossmann, K., Huber, F., & Wartner, U. (1981). German children's behavior towards their mothers at 12 months and their fathers at 18 months in Ainsworth's Strange Situation. *International Journal of Behavioral Development, 4,* 157–181.

Grossmann, K., Grossmann, K.E., Spangler, G., Suess, G., & Unzner, L. (1985). Maternal sensitivity and newborns' orientation responses as related to quality of attachment in northern Germany. In I. Bretherton & E. Waters (Eds.), Growing points of attachment theory and research. *Monographs of the Society for Research in Child Development, 50* (1/2, Serial No. 209), 233–256.

Harms, T., & Clifford, R.M. (1980). *The early childhood environment rating scale.* New York: Teachers College Press.

Harms, T., & Clifford, R.M. (1989). *The family day care rating scale.* New York: Teachers College Press.

Harms, T., Cryer, D., & Clifford, R.M. (1986). *Infant/toddler environment rating scale.* New York: Teachers College Press.

Hess, R.D. (1970). Social class and ethnic influences upon socialization. In P.H. Mussen (Ed.), *Carmichael's manual of child psychology* (Vol. 2, 3rd ed., pp. 457–557). New York: Wiley.

Hwang, C.P., & Broberg, A.G. (1992). The historical and social context of child care in Sweden. In M.E. Lamb, K.J. Sternberg, C.P. Hwang, & A.G. Broberg (Eds.), *Child care in context: Cross-cultural perspectives* (pp. 27–54). Hillsdale, NJ: Erlbaum.

Kamerman, S.B., & Kahn, A.J., Eds. (1978). *Family policy: Government and families in fourteen countries.* New York: Columbia University Press.

Kamerman, S.B., & Kahn, A.J. (1981). *Child care, family benefits, and working parents.* New York: Columbia University Press.

Korbin, J.E. (1981). *Child abuse and neglect: Cross cultural comparisons.* Berkeley: University of California Press.

Lamb, M.E. (1998). Nonparental child care: Context, quality, correlates, and consequences. In W. Damon, I.E. Sigel, & K.A. Renninger (Eds.), *Handbook of child psychology: Child psychology in practice* (5th ed., pp. 73–133). New York: Wiley.

Lamb, M.E., Frodi, A.M., Frodi, M., & Hwang, C.P. (1982). Characteristics of maternal and paternal behavior in traditional and nontraditional Swedish families. *International Journal of Behavioral Development, 5,* 131–141.

Lamb, M.E., Sternberg, K.J., Hwang, C.P., & Broberg, A. (Eds.). (1992). *Child care in context: Cross-cultural perspectives.* Hillsdale, NJ: Erlbaum.

Lamb, M.E., Thompson, R.A., Gardner, W., & Charnov, E.L. (1985). *Infant-mother attachment.* Hillsdale, NJ: Erlbaum.

Lee, L.C. (1992). Day care in the People's Republic of China. In M.E. Lamb, K.J. Sternberg, C.P. Hwang, & A.G. Broberg (Eds.), *Child care in context: Cross-cultural perspectives* (pp. 355–392). Hillsdale, NJ: Erlbaum.

McGee, R.A., & Wolfe, D.A. (1991). Between a rock and a hard place: Where do we go from here in defining psychological maltreatment? *Development & Psychopathology, 3,* 119–124.

Melhuish, E.C., & Moss, P. (1992). Day care in the United Kingdom in histori-cal perspective. In M.E. Lamb, K.J. Sternberg, C.P. Hwang, & A.G. Broberg (Eds.), *Child care in context: Cross-cultural perspectives* (pp. 157–183). Hillsdale, NJ: Erlbaum.

Miyake, K., Chen, S.J., & Campos, J.J. (1985). Infant temperament, mother's mode of interaction, and attachment in Japan: An interim report. In I. Bretherton & E. Waters (Eds.), Growing points of attachment theory and research. *Monographs of the Society for Research in Child Development, 50* (1/2, Serial No. 209), 276–297.

Nakagawa, M., Lamb, M.E., & Miyake, K. (1987–88). Psychological experi-ences of Japanese infants in the Strange Situation. *Research and Clinical Center for Child Development Annual Report, No. 11,* 13–24. Sapporo, Japan: Hokkaido University.

National Academy of Science (1990). *Who cares for America's children?* Washing-ton, DC: National Academy Press.

New, R. (1993). Italy. In M. Cochran (Ed.), *International handbook of child care policies and programs* (pp. 291–311). Westport, CT: Greenwood Press.

O'Connor, S.M. (1995). Mothering in public: The division of organized child care in the kindergarten and day nursery, St Louis, 1886–1920. *Early Child-hood Research Quarterly, 10,* 63–80.

Olmsted, P.P. (1992). A cross-national perspective on the demand for and supply of early childhood services. In A. Booth (Ed.), *Child care in the 1990s: Trends and consequences* (pp. 26–33). Hillsdale, NJ: Erlbaum.

Olmsted, P.P., & Weikart, D.P. (1989). *How nations serve young children: Profiles of child care and education in 14 countries.* Ypsilanti, MI: The High/Scope Press.

Pence, A.R. (1993). Canada. In M. Cochran (Ed.), *International handbook of child care policies and programs* (pp. 57–81). Westport, CT: Greenwood Press.

Riseman, P. (1992). *First find yourself a good mother.* New Brunswick, NJ: Rutgers University Press.

Rosenthal, M.K. (1992). Nonparental child care in Israel: A cultural and historical perspective. In M.E. Lamb, K.J. Sternberg, C.P. Hwang, & A.G. Broberg (Eds.), *Child care in context: Cross-cultural perspectives* (pp. 305–330). Hillsdale, NJ: Erlbaum.

Rothbaum, F., Pott, M., Azuma, H., Miyake, K., & Weisz, J. (2000). The development of close relationships in Japan and the United States: Paths of symbiotic harmony and generative tension. *Child Development, 71,* 1121–1142.

Rothbaum, R., Weisz, J., Pott, M., Miyake, K., & Morelli, G. (2000). Attachment and culture: Security in the United States and Japan. *American Psychologist, 55,* 1093–1104.

Sagi, A., Lamb, M.E., & Gardner, W. (1986). Relations between Strange Situation behavior and stranger sociability among infants on Israeli kibbutzim. *Infant Behavior & Development, 9,* 271–282.

Sagi, A., Lamb, M.E., Lewkowicz, K., Shoham, R., Dvir, R., & Estes, D. (1985). Security of infant-mother, -father, and metapelet attachments among kibbutz-reared Israeli children. In I. Bretherton & E. Waters (Eds.), Growing points of attachment theory and research. *Monographs of the Society for Research in Child Development, 50* (Serial No. 209), 257–275.

Shwalb, D.W., & Chen, S.J. (1994–95). Sacred or selfish: A survey of parental images of Japanese children. *Research and Clinical Center for Child Development Annual Report, No. 18,* 33–44. Sapporo, Japan: Hokkaido University.

Shwalb, D.W., Shwalb, B.J., Sukemune, S., & Tatsumoto, S. (1992). Japanese nonmaternal child care: Past, present, and future. In M.E. Lamb, K.J. Sternberg, C.P. Hwang, & A.G. Broberg (Eds.), *Child care in context: Cross-cultural perspectives* (pp. 331–353). Hillsdale, NJ: Erlbaum.

Spedding, P. (1993). United States of America. In M. Cochran (Ed.), *International handbook of child care policies and programs* (pp. 535–557). Westport, CT: Greenwood Press.

Stevenson, M.B., & Lamb, M.E. (1979). Effects of infant sociability and the caretaking environment on infant cognitive performance. *Child Development, 50(2),* 340–349.

Stoltenberg, J. (1994). Day care centers: Quality and provision. In A.E. Borge, E. Hartmann, & S. Strom (Eds.), *Day care centers: Quality and provision* (pp. 7–11). Oslo, Norway: National Institute of Public Health.

Thompson, R.A. (1998). Early sociopersonality development. In W. Damon & N. Eisenberg (Eds.), *Handbook of child psychology: Vol. 3. Social, emotional, and personality development* (5th ed., pp. 25–104). New York: Wiley.

Thompson, R.A., & Lamb, M.E. (1982). Stranger sociability and its relationships to temperament and social experience during the second year. *Infant Behavior and Development, 5,* 277–287.

Trommsdorff, G., & Friedlmeier, W. (1993). Control and responsiveness in Japanese and German mother-infant interactions. *Early Development and Parenting, 3,* 65–78.

Van IJzendoorn, M.H., & Kroonenberg, P.M. (1988). Cross-cultural patterns of attachment: A meta-analysis of the Strange Situation. *Child Development, 59,* 147–156.

Wald, M.S. (1975). State intervention on behalf of 'neglected' children: A search for realistic standards. *Stanford Law Review, 27,* 984–1040.

Zigler, E.F., & Valentine, J. (1979). *Project Head Start.* New York: Free Press.

7

Multiple Constructions of Childhood

JAYANTHI MISTRY AND VIRGINIA DIEZ

In this chapter, we emphasize the need to view children's development from multiple lenses so that scholars, researchers, and practitioners alike can understand the variety of the human condition from a truly global perspective. We highlight the diversity of cultural constructs of childhood and child rearing to broaden our field's vision and mission of understanding and promoting the development of all children and families. We use sociocultural theory as the preferred theoretical framework to integrate the study of culture and human development and, thereby, create new lenses for understanding different developmental processes and outcomes across cultural groups. We emphasize this perspective because it highlights the culturally bound nature of our assumptions about desirable developmental outcomes and widens the range of what we deem normative processes and behaviours.

The work of Vygotsky (1978) and his colleagues (e.g., Leont'ev, 1981) laid the foundation for what is now widely known as sociohistorical or sociocultural perspectives of human development. Since then, sociocultural theorists have fundamentally reconceptualized the developmental process (Cole, 1990, 1996; Rogoff, 1990; Valsiner, 1989; Werstch, 1991, 1995). In their view, individuals construct shared meanings by using the systems of cultural symbols available to them in the context of their social interactions. Symbolically mediated experiences, in conjunction with the behavioural practices and historically accumulated ideas and meanings of particular cultural communities, give rise to diverse forms of psychological functioning (Shweder et al., 1998).

Sociocultural theorists maintain that culture and individual psychological functioning, although not reducible to each other, are mutually constitutive and cannot be understood in isolation (Cole, 1996; Miller,

1997; Rogoff, 1990). In other words, culture and behaviour cannot be separated into independent and dependent variables. Rather, behaviour shapes and is shaped by the context of the cultural activity in which it occurs and is observed. Particular modes of thinking, speaking, and behaving *arise from* and *remain integrally tied to* concrete forms of social practice (Cole, 1990; Vygotsky, 1978; Wertsch, 1985). 'Mind, cognition, memory, and so forth are understood not as attributes or properties of the individual, but as functions that may be carried out inter-mentally or intra-mentally' (Wertsch & Tulviste, 1992, p. 549). This means that rather than conceiving the individual as 'having abilities and skills,' the focus is on the 'person-acting-with-mediation-means' (Wertsch, 1991, p. 119). Such reconceptualization means that individual 'ability' or 'tendency' is not separated from the contexts in which it is used. The argument is that when the focus is on human 'actions,' we are immediately forced to account for the culturally meaningful context of the actions and therefore must look for units of analysis that do not separate culture from human functioning.

So, how is culture conceptualized and operationalized in such views of children's development? Concepts such as 'activity' (Leont'ev, 1981; Wertsch, 1985), 'cultural practices' (Miller & Goodnow, 1995), and 'situated practice' (Lave, 1990) have been used to operationalize culture. Cole (1996) offers a particularly comprehensive discussion of these concepts as he defines a 'supraindividual sociocultural entity' that is the cultural medium within which individual growth and development take place. Cole draws on both the sociohistorical school of thought and on anthropological theory to offer the definition of 'culture as a medium constituted of artifacts' (p. 31).

Artefacts refer to tools and objects that were developed by prior generations to become subsequently institutionalized and privileged in the practices and valued activities of a cultural community. Books, calculators, and computers are common examples of physical artefacts or tools of our present-day literate and technological society that mediate how we interact with our social and physical world. This is why they are called 'mediation means.' Written language, the alphabet, numeral systems, the decimal system (as a way of organizing numbers), and the calendar (organizing time into years, months, days) are examples of conceptual tools or mediation means that also regulate human functioning and behaviour.

This notion of culture as a medium constituted of historically developed artefacts, the tools of human growth, highlights the centrality of culture for understanding the processes or mechanisms of human development (Cole, 1996). As we said earlier, this leads to the underlying assumption that human functioning cannot be separated from the activities through which development takes place. It follows, therefore, that individuals do not stand alone as entities separate from their environment. Rather, individuals are seen as active agents engaged in goal-directed behaviour, carrying out actions, and using culturally valued tools and mediation means within a framework of shared cultural assumptions and expectations (Cole, 1996; Leont'ev, 1981; Tharp & Gallimore, 1988; Wertsch, 1985). The study of the interaction between individual, social, and sociohistorical or cultural phenomena becomes the study of the individual in activity (Cole, 1995, 1996; Leont'ev, 1981; Tharp & Gallimore, 1988; Wertsch, 1985, 1991).

Using activity as the unit of analysis contrasts with the independent/dependent variable approach which is prevalent in developmental psychology. In theoretical models that examine the relationship between individual and environment such as the ecological model (Bronfenbrenner, 1979, 1986), developmental contextualism (Lerner, 1991, 1996), and the lifespan approaches (Baltes, Reese, & Lipsitt, 1980; Baltes, Lindenberger, & Staudinger, 1998) culture is treated as a contextual variable. Although the focus in ecological models is on determining patterns of mutual interaction or transactions, organisms are conceptualized as separate from their environment. Lifespan psychologists (Baltes, et al., 1998) also emphasize social context, based on the central assumption that changes in the individual's social context across the lifespan interact with the individual's unique history of experiences, roles, and biology to produce a unique developmental pathway. More recently, theorizing on the dynamic relation between individual and context has been brought to a more abstract and complex level through the concepts associated with developmental systems models of human development (Dixon & Lerner, 1999; Lerner, 2002). In such models, integrative, reciprocal, and dynamic relations and interactions between variables from multiple levels of organization are assumed to constitute the core processes of developmental change (Ford & Lerner, 1992; Lerner, 1998; Thelen & Smith, 1998; Gottlieb, 1997).

Despite their increasingly sophisticated formulations of developmental processes and contexts, these theories still exhibit an underlying tendency to treat culture and context as synonymous in the field of child development. Culture is operationalized as a context variable (e.g., socio-economic status, education, ethnicity) and treated as an independent variable influencing individual behaviour. Even when investigated as a critical variable in the transactional relationship between individual and context (Sameroff, 1983) or as one of the multiple levels of organization in dynamic developmental systems models (Lerner, 1998, 2002), culture is nonetheless operationalized as separate from the individual developmental outcomes with which it interacts.

In contrast to treating culture as context, sociocultural theorists emphasize culture as meaning-making, and therefore often rely on the use of interpretive methodology to study developmental processes. Since it is assumed that culture and behaviour are essentially inseparable, psychological functioning tends to be described in terms of how the members of a cultural group understand their own behaviour and experience. The focus is on representing the meaning that behaviour has for the individual. Thus, the goal is to understand the directive force of shared meaning systems and how these meanings are constructed in given contexts (D'Andrade & Strauss, 1992; Harkness & Super, 1992). Understanding context, therefore, includes understanding the tacit social and interactional norms of the individuals existing within those settings and whose behaviours and expectations both shape and are shaped by the institutional structures of which they are a part (Harwood, Miller, & Irizarry, 1995).

So, how do we move from this conceptual discussion of the interface between culture and individual development to more explicit examples of multiple cultural constructions of childhood? We have chosen exemplars of cross-cultural research to emphasize the value of documenting alternative and multiple conceptualizations of specific aspects of intellectual and social development, such as the construction of a sense of self, parenting beliefs about ideal child outcomes, and corresponding parenting practices.

The Self through Multiple Lenses

We focus on the topic of the self because research provides a rich source of information regarding the significance of culture in development (Greenfield and Cockin, 1994; Markus & Kitayama, 1991, 1994; Shweder, 1991; Kagitcibasi, 1996b; Markus, Mullally & Kitayama, 1997). From the moment of birth, or even before, every individual is immersed in a complex cultural milieu that provides the settings, meanings, and expectations that enable the growing child to become an acceptable member of a given culture. The total immersion of the individual child in culture is clearly recognized by most scholars, irrespective of their theoretical perspective (Kagitcibasi, 1996a, 1996b; Markus et al., Miller, 1997; Shweder & Bourne, 1991; Triandis, 1989).

Reviewing literature from developmental psychology, Harter (1998) notes that the integration of research in cognitive, affective, and social domains in the past fifteen years has contributed to a more comprehensive understanding of the development of self-awareness, self-representation, and self-evaluations through normative developmental shifts and transitions. Though the developmental progression is primarily descriptive at this point, Harter (1998) underscores increasing theoretical emphasis on the role of interactions with caregivers and socialization agents in influencing normative progression, not just in creating individual differences. Although in earlier research 'caregiving styles were related to *individual differences* in child self-related behaviours, recent conceptualizations and supporting evidence point to the major role that caregiver-infant interactions play in influencing the *normative* progression of self-development' (Harter, 1998, p. 566).

Most of the theorizing and research in developmental psychology has been based on a European and American view of the self that emphasizes separateness, autonomy, individualism, and distinctness. In contrast, the cross-cultural literature provides a much richer and in-depth analysis of alternative constructions of the self that are considered appropriate and mature within different cultural communities. This cross-cultural research reveals a general consensus regarding the predominance of two major alternative views of the self. Terminology for these alternative cultural frameworks or cultural lenses varies in the research literature. These include independence-interdependence as developmental scripts (Greenfield and Cockin, 1994; Markus & Kitayama, 1994), individualistic–collectivistic orientations (Kim & Choi, 1994; Triandis, 1989), and autonomous–relational self (Kagitcibasi, 1996a, 1996b).

Based on the ideology of individualism, definitions of the self, derived from research conducted in North America, emphasize it as an independent, self-contained entity. The self is viewed as comprising a unique configuration of internal attributes (including traits, emotions, motives, values, and rights), and behaviour is primarily directed at meeting the demands of these attributes (Markus & Kitayama, 1994). The self in this perspective is seen as 'bounded, unique, singular, encapsulated, noncorporeal' (Landrine, 1992 p. 747). The autonomous self is seen as an active agent that promotes selective abstraction of information from the environment (Triandis, 1989), as stable over time and across contexts, and as using environmental resources and all relationships instrumentally in its own service. The normal, healthy, independent self is expected to be assertive, confident, and goal oriented toward self-fulfilment, enhancement, and actualization (Landrine, 1992).

In contrast to the autonomous self, the interdependent or relational self is not discrete, bound, separate, or unique. Rather, it is constituted (created and recreated) through social interactions, contexts, and relationships (Landrine, 1992). Seen from this perspective, the self is embedded in relationships and the social context and has no existence independent of them (Markus & Kitayama, 1994). In fact, 'experiencing interdependence entails seeing oneself as part of an encompassing social relationship and recognizing that one's behaviour is determined by, contingent on and, to a large extent, organized by what the actor perceives to be the thoughts, feelings, and actions of others in the relationships' (Markus and Kitayama, 1991, p. 26). Further, the boundaries of the individual self are permeable with fusion between self and others, self and social roles, and, in some African cultures (Nsamenang & Lamb, 1994) and Hindu India (Shweder & Bourne, 1991; Marriott, 1989), self and supernatural and ancestral spirits.

Along with documenting cultural variations in views of the self, cross-cultural research has also emphasized the culturally bounded nature of what is considered the appropriate goal or end point of development. Contrasting the relation between the autonomous self and society with the socially and contextually embedded Indian self, Marriott (1989) comments that in the former world view, 'individuals are seen as indivisible, integrated, self-developing units, not normally subject to disjunction or reconstitution' (p. 17). These same characteristics that denote positive features when viewed from the independence/autonomy dimension may be perceived as immodest, arrogant and aggressive when viewed from the perspective of the interdependent or relational self. 'To members of socio-centric organic cultures the concept of the autonomous individual, free to choose and mind his or her own business, must feel alien, a bizarre idea cutting the self off from the interdependent whole, dooming it to a life of isolation and loneliness' (Kakar, 1978, p. 86).

Although cross-cultural research that documents the existence of alternative conceptualizations of self has made a significant contribution to our understanding of developmental end points, it is important to remember that these multiple constructions of the self also imply multiple developmental pathways. Though much remains to be done, recent attempts in the literature to describe different developmental pathways for the appropriation of alternative conceptualizations of self and for accounting for individual differences are also emerging (Neisser & Jopling, 1997). Recent research provides some empirical support for alternative developmental pathways related to distinctions between individualistic and socio-centric concepts of self. Development of self-consistency, stability of self-concepts, and emphasis on uniqueness are important developmental milestones representing increasing maturity when the individualistic self is the culturally valued goal of development (Harter, 1998; Neisser and Jopling, 1997).

However, contrasting individualism and autonomy with the Hindu world view of socio-centricism, Marriott (1989) comments that in Hindu postulations 'persons are in various degrees nonreflexive (not necessarily consistent) in their relations' (p. 16). The emphasis here is on persons as 'composite and divisible' (what one might better call 'dividuals'), and interpersonal relations are viewed as irregular and fluid (Marriott, 1989). It follows that such a self would exhibit little stability across contexts and time, and the individual self's attributes, values, and needs emerge from or reflect the needs of the relationships and contexts (Kim & Choi, 1994; Greenfield and Cockin, 1994; Shweder & Bourne, 1991; Miller, 1997). Thus, in cultures like India, context sensitivity is the preferred formulation (Shweder & Bourne, 1991; Miller, 1997; Ramanujam, 1990) and, one might extrapolate, the preferred indicator of increasing maturity.

There is some evidence to support the notion of different developmental pathways. When asked to describe themselves in twenty statements, Japanese youths offered responses that were predominantly contextualized, in contrast to those of American youths, which emphasized personal attributes (Cousins, 1989). In a similar vein, Miller (1997) presents developmental data showing that statements reflecting context sensitivity increase with age among Indian children and adolescents, whereas statements about general dispositions of the agent increase with age among their American counterparts. Similarly, Hart and Fegley (1995) document African-American children's relatively more sophisticated self-descriptions compared to children tested in Iceland and explain the difference in terms of the cultural heterogeneity of life experiences, suggesting that children who encounter a variety of perspectives are better able to articulate their self-concepts.

A particularly coherent example of developmental pathways in which context sensitivity is the appropriate indicator of increasing maturity is offered by scholars of the Japanese sense of self (e.g., Doi, 1986; Lebra, 1976; Rosenberger, 1992; Tobin, 1992). In these descriptions of the self as 'relational' or as 'shifting in relation to situational context,' the need to make distinctions between *omote* (what is presented to the public) and *ura* (that which is hidden from pubic view), between *tatemae* (appearance) and *honne* (inner feelings), and between *uchi* (home) and *soto* (outside home) is highlighted. Tobin (1992) goes a step further in putting such depictions of the multiple or relational self into a developmental context. He suggests that while the first two years of life for a Japanese child are focused on learning *amae* (the sense of being lovable and being able to give and receive pleasure in intimate, interpersonal relationships), the years from three to six are focused on learning *kejime*, or the ability to make distinctions (Bachnik, 1992). To have an appropriately multifaceted sense of self, one must learn to make fluid and subtle distinctions, learn to step back and forth across the distinct but complementary dimensions of *omote* and *ura, tatemae* and *honne, uchi* and *soto*. The ability to shift perspectives in relation to situational contexts that need to be appropriately identified along these dimensions (Bachnik, 1992) is a crucial social skill that Tobin (1992) suggests has become a specific socializing function of Japanese pre-schools. Thus, sensitivity to context is viewed as an important developmental goal because it is an essential requirement of a mature 'relational' self.

Since development occurs in the context of the family (however broadly it is defined), we move to a focus on cultural models of parenting to provide other examples of alternative and multiple constructions of childhood. We shift our focus to parenting beliefs about ideal child outcomes and corresponding parenting practices.

Cultural Models for Parenting and Child Rearing

This is another area of research where multiple modalities have been documented through a vast number of studies of parental beliefs and care-taking practices, and their different impacts on child development (Bornstein, 1995; McGillicuddy-DeLisi & Sigel, 1995; Park & Buriel, 1998; Super & Harkness, 1986). Some researchers (Gonzalez-Ramos, Zayas, & Cohen, 1998) have found that respect, obedience, affection, honesty, and loyalty to family are highly valued characteristics in Puerto Rican families. Sinha (1995) identifies submission to authority, dependency, and respect for the hierarchical ordering of relationships as admirable qualities for Indian children. These beliefs are in contrast to the value that European-American parents place on children's independence and autonomy (New & Richman 1996; Richman et al., 1988). In fact, contrasting beliefs about independence versus interdependence, individuality versus harmony, and autonomy versus respect for authority recur in much of the research that compares the cultural beliefs and practices of European-American and Asian parents (e.g., Azuma, 1994; Rothbaum, Morelli, Pott, & Liu-Constant, 2000).

Through extensive research among the Gusii people of northeastern Africa and among urban, middle-class communities in the northeastern United States, LeVine et al. (1994) provide exceptionally valuable examples of contrasting cultural models of early childcare that are culturally coherent and adaptive within each of the contrasting communities. We describe these models at some length to illustrate the existence of equally valid alternative conceptualizations of parenting and children's development. LeVine et al. (1994) define cultural models of early childcare as the ethnographic reconstructions of the premises on which the childcare practices of a people are based. These cultural models include assumptions and beliefs about normative and desired child-rearing goals, the general strategy for attaining these goals, and the scripts for action in specific situations. LeVine et al. (1994) label the Gusii model *pediatric*, because its primary concern is with the survival, health, and physical growth of the infant, and the American model *pedagogical*, because its primary concern is with the behavioural and educational development of the infant. The adaptive and culturally coherent links between parenting goals, parenting strategies, and scripts, and children's development in each model are briefly summarized from LeVine et al. (1994, pp. 248–270).

The primary goal in the pediatric model of the Gusii is to protect infants from life-threatening illnesses and environmental hazards, a goal that is particularly adaptive in the context of high mortality rates. Gusii mothers implicitly assume that infancy is a period of great danger to the child's life, and that infants require constant protection. Therefore, they keep their infants in physical proximity as a means of providing constant protection, and they focus primarily on soothing distress and keeping infants satisfied and calm. They assume that these states indicate that the baby is well and safe from harm. In contrast, the goals of the American pedagogical model are to promote the infant's alertness, curiosity, interest in surroundings, exploration, and communication with others. Survival and health are background concerns, perhaps because they are more likely assured in the context of modern medicine and comparatively lower infant mortality rates. In LeVine et al.'s (1994) construction of the pedagogical model, the American mother sees herself as a teacher whose primary responsibility is to ensure the infant pupil's readiness for early education. Parenting strategies therefore focus on stimulation and proto-conversation aimed at facilitating engagement with the physical and social worlds.

When cultural models of childcare are so different from each other, it follows that from the perspective of each model the alternative model's goals and practices are likely to be criticized as inappropriate and ineffective. For example, LeVine et al. (1994) acknowledge that from the perspective of the American pedagogical model, Gusii infants appear to be deprived of the stimulation and emotional support offered by American mothers and viewed as essential to facilitate the emergence of social, emotional, and cognitive skills. However, from the perspective of the Gusii pediatric model, with its emphasis on physical proximity, responsive protection, and soothing, American care-taking practices appear to reflect incompetent caregiving. Practices that restrict the infants' physical contact with their mother, such as putting babies to sleep in separate beds or rooms, breastfeeding for relatively short periods of time after birth, casual responsiveness to infant crying, and lower frequencies of holding and carrying, seem harsh from the Gusii perspective.

LeVine et al.'s (1994) case study of infant care in the Gusii community goes beyond merely emphasizing the cultural relativity of childcare goals and practices. Their careful and comprehensive assessment of the consequences of the Gusii pattern of care shows alternative pathways toward normative outcomes not biased by our ethnocentric assumptions about what constitutes appropriate parenting or childcare. Even though Gusii toddlers did not experience the type of stimulation and support of cognitive and language skills common among American toddlers, the social experience of Gusii children with peer and community members after thirty months facilitated the development of capacities that were not acquired earlier:

> The Gusii case teaches us that the absence, during the first 2 to 3 years, of specific parental practices that promote cognitive, emotional, and language skills in Western contexts, does not necessarily constitute failure to provide what every child needs. Like many other peoples in Africa and elsewhere, the Gusii had socially organized ways of cultivating skill,

virtue, and personal fulfillment that were not dependent on mothers after weaning and were not concluded until long after the third year of life; they involved learning through participation in established, hierarchical structures of interaction at home and in the larger community – a kind of apprenticeship learning, once widespread in the West, that we are only beginning to understand. (LeVine et al., 1994, p. 274)

Culture-comparative research conducted by Rogoff, Mistry, Goncu, and Mosier (1993) offers yet another example of contrasting, yet culturally coherent, models of toddler-caregiver interaction. This work illustrates contrasting patterns of behaviour, each of which nonetheless reflects internal coherence between cultural context, beliefs, practices, and child behaviours. These researchers selected four cultural communities (a Mayan peasant community in Guatemala, a tribal village in India, a middle-class community in Turkey, and a middle-class community in the United States) that represented variations in the extent to which children were segregated from adult activities. Observations of caregiver-toddler interaction revealed two patterns for learning that were consistent with variations in whether children were able to observe and participate in adult activities.

In communities where children were segregated from adult activities, adults took on the responsibility for organizing children's learning by managing their motivation, by instructing them verbally, and by treating them as peers in play and conversation. By contrast, in the communities in which children had the opportunity to observe and participate in adult activities, caregivers supported their toddlers' own efforts with responsive assistance. Toddlers appeared to take responsibility for learning by observing ongoing events and beginning to enter adult activities (Rogoff et al., 1993). Learning occurred through active observation and participation. Toddlers and caregivers often maintained simultaneous attention to several ongoing activities, and were responsive to each other, often through non-verbal means. Thus, within each community there was a coherence of patterns linking cultural context in terms of the extent of segregation from adult activities, parental goals for children's development, differing assumptions about who takes responsibility for learning, and patterns of caregiver-toddler interaction.

In addition to the type of culture-comparative research illustrated by LeVine et al. (1994) and Rogoff et al. (1993), research generated within particular cultural communities sometimes allows for a rich, insightful reading of child-rearing practices that sometimes appear to be at odds with those highlighted by research on European-American families. The example that follows refers to Latinos living in the United States. In using the term 'Latino' we do not imply homogeneity among the numerous ethnic groups originating in Europe, Africa, and North, Central, and South America, or among people with very different economic and social experiences. In fact, we understand the term 'Latino' as an arbitrary label that often leads to unwarranted stereotyping and discriminatory practices. Yet, to the extent that Latino groups share Spanish as a common language, this 'mediation tool' creates opportunities for the emergence of terms whose meanings are shared across subgroups. One such term is *bien educado* (well educated). What is striking about this term is the considerably different meaning attributed to the word *educado* in Spanish and to its English literal equivalent, 'educated.'

Trumbull, Rothstein-Fisch, Greenfield, & Quiroz (2001) have used this term to help understand socialization values and practices among Latino families and school-aged children living in Southern California. Their work shows that parents in general think of educating children as a division of labour, with schools holding primary responsibility for promoting cognitive development and families for social skills. Since their efforts are complementary, parents see schools as partners working toward a common goal. Parents support teachers by discussing with their children the importance of education, supervising their homework, and reinforcing school rules. In turn, they expect teachers to personally report and address their children's 'misbehaviour' since this helps them fulfil the socializing functions, which they perceive as their most important responsibility.

Based on their implicit understanding of their own roles and responsibilities in raising their children, Latinos agree with the statement 'parents are a child's first teacher.' First, they agree that the 'teaching' (of social skills) they do at home is crucial for the success of their children; second, they like to hear that the school sees them on a par with teachers and acknowledges their contribution to their children's school success. All such agreements can easily mislead teachers and parents into believing that they share the same values about education and its importance. Yet, when one looks at the meaning of the Spanish word *educación* as opposed to the English 'education' and realizes that a more accurate translation of *buena educación* is 'good upbringing,' it becomes apparent that 'education' is not shared across cultural groups using the meaning of these two different languages.

Several researchers have documented the social skills that are perceived as desirable in a person who has *buena educación* (Harwood 1992; Harwood et al., 1995; Zayas & Solari, 1994; Zayas, Canino, & Suarez, 2000; Gonzalez-Ramos et al., 1998; Valdés, 1996). In her work with Puerto Rican families living in Puerto Rico and in New Haven, Connecticut, Robin Harwood (1992, 1995, 1996) uses the term 'proper demeanour' as roughly equivalent to *buena educación*. A person with proper demeanour is '"respetuoso" (respectful, as manifested in polite, obedient, attentive behaviour), "tranquilo" (calm, quiet behaviour), and "amable" (gentle, polite behaviour)' (1995, p. 246). Harwood (1992) makes a connection between respectfulness and *educación* that extends the meaning of respect to 'a dimension of behaviour that is perhaps best described in English as "teachable" and in Spanish as "educado"' (p. 837).

In a study of Puerto Rican mothers, Gonzalez-Ramos et al. (1998) confirm the importance of respect as an organizing construct when they rank it among the three most desirable child-rearing values for their pre-school children. The other two are 'honesty' and 'responsibility.' These authors, like Harwood (1992), also point out that parents think of *buena educación* and 'proper demeanour' not only as desirable developmental outcomes but also as tools or strategies that give children the freedom to reach desired outcomes. This is expressed nicely in the Puerto Rican proverb quoted by Zayas et al. (2000), '*No es lo mismo ser una persona educada que ser una persona "instruída"*' (It is not the same to be educated as to be learned; p. 145). The implication of this proverb is that school instruction is important, but what we need to know and do in order to succeed exceeds what we learn in school.

'Self-worth' (Zayas et al., 2000) is another way of attracting and giving respect among Puerto Ricans. This outcome/behaviour encompasses two other key values governing social relations: dignity and respect. Dignity is the belief that people are innately worthy regardless of their social status, and respect is the 'interpersonal quality that accompanies having dignity.' 'Part of displaying dignity is in the manner in which the child *presents* herself or himself' (p. 145; emphasis added). Here the word 'presents' is important because it points to the importance of proper appearance and demeanour in commanding respect from one's group.

The previous examples have several implications. In the first place, in our experience, teachers in U.S. schools report that during parent-teacher conferences, immigrant parents from Central America and the

Spanish-speaking Caribbean ask more questions about whether their children are behaving well in class than about their academic performance. Teachers express frustration with this and sometimes interpret it to mean that parents do not place enough value on literacy and other cognitive skills.

However, what parents are trying to assert is whether they are succeeding at 'educating' their children at home by asking teachers about their children's behaviour in school. This does not mean they do not value academic performance but rather that they tend to trust and defer to teachers to accomplish this other educational goal.

Another implication of the importance given to *buena educación*, 'proper demeanour,' or just *respeto* (Valdes, 1996) is that it points to 'respectfulness' as a key normative outcome sought across Latino communities. When working in the field, one is likely to encounter the word *respeto* in a variety of contexts. Often, it can be used in a narrow sense, merely as synonymous with obedience to authority. Yet, respectfulness speaks of a way of living one's life as an ethical and productive member of one's community. This outcome seems quite in line with the desire of European-Americans that their children become 'good citizens.' Yet, the pathways to attaining this outcome can create misunderstandings and even conflict with institutions that are not familiar with the ways of newer immigrant cultural communities.

In conclusion, we hope that the different perspectives and pathways to normative development presented in this chapter will increase awareness about different ways of reaching culturally desirable outcomes. We do not wish to extrapolate any of the findings mentioned here to the Canadian context. However, it would not surprise us if some of the practices described in this chapter resonate with professionals working in the field outside the United States. If so, we hope to have made a slight contribution to broaden the conception of what is viewed as 'normal' among those who are in a position to evaluate and work with children from diverse cultural backgrounds.

References

Azuma, H. (1994). Two modes of cognitive socialization in Japan and the United States. In P.M. Greenfield & R.R. Cocking (Eds.), *Cross-cultural roots of minority child development* (pp. 275–284). Hillsdale, NJ: Erlbaum.

Bachnik, J. (1992). Kejime: Defining a shifting self in multiple organizational modes. In N. Rosenberger (Ed.), *Japanese sense of self* (pp. 152–172). Cambridge: Cambridge University Press.

Baltes, P.B., Lindenberger, U., Staudinger, U.M. (1998). Life-span theory in developmental psychology. In R.L. Lerner (Ed.), *Handbook of Child Psychology: Vol. 1. Theoretical Models of Human Development* (pp. 1029–1144). New York: Wiley.

Baltes, P.B., Reese, H.W., & Lipsitt, L.P. (1980). Life-span developmental psychology. *Annual Review of Psychology, 31,* 65–110.

Bornstein, M.H. (Ed.). (1995). *Handbook of parenting* (Vol. 3). Mahwah, NJ: Erlbaum.

Bronfenbrenner, U. (1979). *The ecology of human development.* Cambridge, MA: Harvard University Press.

Bronfenbrenner, U. (1986). Ecology of the family as a context for human development. *Developmental Psychology, 22(6),* 723–742.

Cole, M. (1990). Cognitive development and formal schooling. In L. Moll (Ed.) *Vygotsky & Education.* New York: Cambridge University Press.

Cole, M. (1995). Culture and cognition development: From cross-cultural research to creating systems of cultural mediation. *Culture and Psychology, 1(1),* 25–54.

Cole, M. (1996). *Cultural psychology: A once and future discipline.* Cambridge, MA: Belknap/Harvard.

Cousins, S.D. (1989). Culture and self-perception in Japan and the United States. *Journal of Personality and Social Psychology, 56,* 124–131.

Damon, W. (Series Ed.) (1998). *Handbook of child psychology, Vols. 1–4.* New York: Wiley.

D'Andrade, R.G. (1984). Cultural meaning systems. In R.A. Shweder & R.A. LeVine (Eds.), *Culture theory: Essays on mind, self, and emotion* (pp. 88–119). New York: Cambridge University Press.

D'Andrade, R.G., & Strauss, C. (1992). *Cultural models and human motives.* Cambridge: Cambridge University Press.

Dixon, R.A., & Lerner, R.M. (1999). History and systems in developmental psychology. In M. Bornstein & M. Lamb (Eds.), *Developmental psychology: An advanced textbook* (4th ed., pp. 3–45). Mahwah, NJ: Lawrence Erlbaum.

Doi, T. (1986). *The autonomy of self.* Tokyo: Kodansha.

Eisenberg, N. (1998). Introduction. In W. Damon (Series Ed.) & N. Eisenberg (Vol. Ed.), *Handbook of child psychology: Vol. 1. Social, emotional, and personality development* (5th ed., pp. 1–24). New York: Wiley.

Ford, D.L., & Lerner, R.M. (1992). *Developmental systems theory: An integrative approach.* Newbury Park, CA: Sage.

Gallimore, R., & Goldenburg, C. (1993). Activity settings of early literacy:

Home and school factors in children's emergent literacy. In E.A. Forman, N. Minick, & C.A. Stone (Eds.), *Contexts for learning: Sociocultural dynamics in children's development* (pp. 315–335). New York: Oxford University Press.

Garcia, E. (2001). Parenting in Mexican-American families. In N.B. Webb (Ed.), *Culturally diverse parent-child and family relationships: A guide for social workers and other practitioners* (pp. 133–155). New York: Columbia University Press.

Gardiner, H.W., Mutter, J.D., & Kosmitzki, C. (1998). *Lives across cultures: Cross-Cultural Human Development.* Boston, MA: Allyn & Bacon.

Goldenberg, C., & Gallimore, R. (1995). Immigrant Latino parents' values and beliefs about their children's education: Continuities and discontinuities across cultures and generations. In P. Pintrich & M. Maehr (Eds.), *Advances in achievement motivation.* (Vol. 9, pp. 183–228). Greenwich, CT: JAI Press.

Gonzalez-Ramos, G., Zayas, L. H., & Cohen, E. V. (1998). Child-rearing values of low-income, urban Puerto Rican mothers of preschool children. *Professional Psychology – Research & Practice, 29(4)*, 377–382.

Gottlieb, G. (1997). *Synthesizing nature-nurture: Prenatal roots of instinctive behavior.* Mahwah, NJ: Erlbaum.

Greenfield, P.M, & Cocking, R.R. (1994). *Cross-cultural roots of minority child development.* Hillsdale, NJ: Erlbaum

Harkness, S., & Super, C.M. (1992). Parental ethnotheories in action. In I.E. Sigel, A.V. McGillicuddy-DeLisi, & J.J. Goodnow (Eds.), *Parental belief systems* (pp. 373–391). Hillsdale, NJ: Erlbaum.

Harkness, S., & Super, C. (1995). Culture and parenting. In M.H. Bornstein (Ed.), *Handbook of parenting* (Vol. 2, pp. 211–234). Mahwah, NJ: Erlbaum.

Harkness, S., & Super, C. M. (Eds.). (1996). *Parents' cultural belief systems: Their origins, expressions, and consequences.* New York: Guildford Press.

Hart, D., & Fegley, S. (1995). Prosocial behavior and caring in adolescence: Relations to self-understanding and social judgement. *Child Development, 66,* 1346–1359.

Harter, S. (1998). The development of self-representations. In W. Damon (Series Ed.) & N. Eisenberg (Vol. Ed.), *Handbook of child psychology: Vol. 1. Theoretical models of human development* (5th ed., pp. 553–617). New York: Wiley.

Harwood, R.L. (1992). The influence of culturally derived values on Anglo and Puerto Rican mothers perceptions of attachment behavior. *Child Development, 63,* 822–839.

Harwood, R.L., Miller, J.G., & Irizarry, N.L. (1995). *Culture and attachment: Perceptions of the child in context.* New York: Guilford Press.

Kagitcibasi, C. (1996a). *Family and human development across cultures: A view from the other side.* Mahwah, NJ: LEA.

Kagitcibasi, C. (1996b). The autonomous–relational self: A new synthesis. *European Psychologist, 1(3),* 180–186.

Kakar, S. (Ed.). (1978). *Identity and adulthood.* Delhi, India: Oxford University Press.

Kim, U., & Choi, S.H. (1994). Individualism, collectivism and child development: A Korean perspective. In P.M. Greenfield & R.R. Cocking (Eds.), *Cross-cultural roots of minority child development* (pp. 227–256). Hillsdale, NJ: Erlbaum.

Landrine, H. (1992). Clinical implications of cultural differences: The referential versus the indexical self. *Clinical Psychology Review, 12,* 401–415.

Lave, J. (1990). The culture of acquisition and the practice of understanding. In J.W. Stigler, R.A. Shweder, & G. Herdt (Eds.), *Cultural psychology* (pp. 309–327). New York: Cambridge University Press.

Lebra, T.S. (1976). *Japanese patterns of behavior.* Honolulu: University of Hawaii Press.

Leont'ev, A.N. (1981). The problem of activity in psychology. In J. V.Wertsch (Ed.), *The concept of activity in Soviet psychology* (pp. 37–71). Armonk, NY: M.E. Sharpe.

Lerner, R.M. (1991). Changing organism-context relation as the basic process of development: A developmental-contextual perspective. *Developmental Psychology, 27,* 27–32.

Lerner, R.M. (1992). Dialectics, developmental contextualism, and the further enhancement of theory about puberty and psychosocial development. *Journal of Early Adolescence, 12(4),* 366–388.

Lerner, R.M. (1996). Relative plasticity, integration, temporality, and diversity in human development: A developmental contextual perspective about theory, process, and method. *Developmental Psychology, 32,* 781–786.

Lerner, R.M. (1998). Theories of human development: Contemporary perspectives. In R.M. Lerner (Ed.), *Handbook of child psychology: Theoretical models of human development.* Vol. 1. (5th ed., pp. 1–24). New York: Wiley.

Lerner, R.M. (2002). *Concepts and theories of human development* (3rd ed.). Mahwah, NJ: Erlbaum.

Lerner, R.M., Easterbrooks, M.A., and Mistry, J. (2003). Dynamic systems across the life span: From developmental psychology to developmental science. In I.B. Weiner (Series Ed.), R.M. Lerner, M.A. Easterbrooks, & J. Mistry (Vol. Eds.), *Handbook of psychology: Vol. 6. Developmental psychology* (5th ed., pp. 1–10). New York: Wiley.

LeVine, R.A. (1973). *Culture, behavior, and personality.* Chicago: Aldine.

LeVine, R.A., Dixon, S. LeVine, S., Richman, A., Leiderman, P.H., Keefer, C., & Brazelton, T.B. (1994). *Child care and culture: Lessons from Africa.* Cambridge: Cambridge University Press.

Maasten, A. (Ed.). (1999). *Cultural processes in child development: The Minnesota symposia on child psychology* (Vol. 29). Hillsdale, NJ: Erlbaum.

Markus, H., & Kitayama, S. (1991). Culture and the self: Implications for cognition, emotion, and motivation. *Psychological Review, 98*, 224–53.

Markus, H.R., & Kitayama, S. (1994). The cultural construction of self and emotion: Implications for social behavior. In S. Kitayama & H.R. Markus (Eds.), *Emotion and culture: Empirical studies of mutual influence* (pp. 89–130). Washington, DC: American Psychological Association.

Markus, H.R., Mullally, P.R., & Kitayama, S. (1997). Self ways: Diversity in modes of cultural participation. In U. Neisser & D.A. Jopling (Eds.), *The conceptual self in context: Culture, experience, self-understanding* (pp. 13–61). Cambridge: Cambridge University Press.

Marriot, M. (1989). Constructing an Indian ethnosociology. In M. Marriott's (Ed.) *India through Hindu categories* (pp. 1–40). Newbury Park, CA: Sage.

Marsella, A.J. (1998). Toward a 'Global-Community Psychology': Meeting the needs of a changing world. *American Psychologist, 53(2)*, 1282–1291.

McCloyd, V.C. (1998). Children in poverty: Development, public policy, and practice. In W. Damon (Series Ed.) & I.E. Sigel & K.A. Renninger (Vol. Eds.), *Handbook of child psychology: Vol. 4: Child psychology in practice* (5th ed., pp. 135–210). New York: Wiley.

McGillicuddy-De Lisi, A.V., & Sigel, I.E. (1995). Parental beliefs. In M.H. Bornstein (Ed.), *Handbook of parenting* (Vol. 3, pp. 333–358). Mahwah, NJ: Erlbaum.

Miller, J.G. (1997). Theoretical issues in cultural psychology. In J.W. Berry, Y.H. Poortinga, J. Pandey, P.R. Dasen, T.S. Saraswathi, M.H. Segall, & C. Kagitcibasi (Series Eds.) & J.W. Berry, Y.H. Poortinga, & J. Pandey (Vol. Eds.) *Handbook of cross-cultural psychology: Vol. 1. Theory and method* (2nd ed., pp. 85–128). Needham Heights, MA: Allyn & Bacon.

Miller, P.J., & Goodnow, J.J. (1995). Cultural practices: Toward an integration of culture and development. In J.J. Goodnow, P.J. Miller, & F. Kessel (Eds.), *Cultural practices as contexts for development* (pp. 5–16). San Francisco: Jossey-Bass.

Neisser, U., & Jopling, D.A. (Eds.). (1997). *The conceptual self in context: Culture, experience, self-understanding* (pp. 13–61). Cambridge: Cambridge University Press.

New, R.S., & Richman, A.L. (1996). Maternal beliefs and infant care practices in Italy and the United States. In S. Harkness & C.M. Super (Eds.), *Parents' cultural belief systems: Their origins, expressions, and consequences* (pp. 385–404). New York: Guildford Press.

Nsamenang, B.A., & Lamb, M.E. (1994). Socialization of Nso children in the Bamenda Grassfields of Northwest Cameroon. In P.M. Greenfield & R.R.

Cocking (Eds.), *Cross-cultural roots of minority child development* (pp. 133–146). Hillsdale, NJ: Erlbaum.

Park, R.D., and Buriel, R. (1998). Socialization in the family: Ethnic and ecological perspectives. In W. Damon (Series Ed.) & N. Eisenberg (Vol. Ed.), *Handbook of child psychology: Vol. 1. Social, emotional, and personality development* (5th ed., pp. 1–24). New York: Wiley.

Ramanujam, A.K. (1990). Is there an Indian way of thinking? An informal essay. In M. Marriot (Ed.), *India through Hindu categories* (pp. 41–58). Newbury Park, CA: Sage.

Richman, A.L., LeVine, R.A., New, R.S., Howrigan, G.A., Welles-Nystrom, B., & LeVine, S.E. (1988). Maternal behavior to infants in five cultures. In R.A. LeVine & P.M. Miller et al. (Eds.), *Parental behavior in diverse societies: New directions for child development* (Vol. 40, pp. 81–97). San Francisco: Jossey-Bass.

Rogoff, B. (1990). *Apprenticeship in thinking*. New York: Oxford University Press.

Rogoff, B., Mistry, J., Goncu, A., & Mosier, C. (1993). *Guided participation in cultural activity by toddlers and caregivers*. Monographs of the Society for Research for Child Development. (Vol. 58). Chicago: University of Chicago Press.

Rosenberger, N. (1992). *Japanese sense of self*. Cambridge: Cambridge University Press.

Rothbaum, F., Morelli, G., Pott, M., & Liu-Constant, Y. (2000). Immigrant-Chinese and Euro-American parents' physical closeness with young children: Themes of family relatedness. *Journal of Family Psychology, 14(3)*, 334–348.

Sameroff, A.J. (1983). Developmental systems: Contexts and evolution. In W. Kessen (Ed.), *Handbook of child psychology: Vol. 1. History, theory, and methods* (5th ed., pp. 237–294). New York: Wiley.

Shweder, R.A. (1991). *Thinking through cultures: Expeditions in cultural psychology*. Cambridge, MA: Harvard University Press.

Shweder, R.A. (1995). Cultural psychology: What is it? *The culture and psychology reader* (pp. 41–86). New York: New York University Press.

Shweder, R.A., & Bourne, E.J. (1991). Does the concept of the person vary cross-culturally? In R.A. Shweder (Ed.), *Thinking through cultures: Expeditions in cultural psychology* (pp. 113–155). Cambridge, MA: Harvard University Press.

Shweder, R.A., Goodnow, J., Hatano, G., LeVine, R.A., Markus, H., & Miller, P. (1998). In R.L. Lerner (Ed.), *Handbook of child psychology: Vol. 1. Theoretical models of human development* (pp. 865–938). New York: Wiley.

Shweder, R.A., & Miller, J.G. (1991). The social construction of the person:

How is it possible? In R.A. Shweder (Ed.), *Thinking through culture: Expeditions in cultural psychology* (pp. 156–185). Cambridge, MA: Harvard University Press.

Sinha, S.R. (1995). Child-rearing practices relevant for the growth of dependency and competence in children. In J. Valsiner (Ed.), *Comparative-cultural and constructivist perspectives: Child development within culturally structured environments* (Vol. 3, pp. 105–137). Norwood, NJ: Ablex.

Super, C.M., & Harkness, S. (1986). The developmental niche: A conceptualization at the interface of child and culture. *International Journal of Behavioral Development, 9*, 545–569.

Tharp, R., & Gallimore, R. (1988). *Rousing minds to lifeTeaching, learning, and schooling in social context*. Cambridge.: Cambridge University Press.

Thelen, E., & Smith, L.B. (1998). Dynamic systems theories. In W. Damon (Series Ed.) & R.M. Lerner (Vol. Ed.), *Handbook of child psychology: Vol. 1. Theoretical models of human development* (5th ed., pp. 563–633). New York: Wiley.

Tobin, J. (1992). Japanese preschools and the pedagogy of selfhood. In N. Rosenberger (Ed.), *Japanese sense of self*. Cambridge: Cambridge University Press. (pp. 21–39).

Triandis, H.C. (1980). Introduction to handbook of cross-cultural psychology. In H.C. Triandis & W.W. Lambert (Eds.), *Handbook of cross-cultural psychology, Vol. 1* (pp. 1–14). Boston: Allyn & Bacon.

Triandis, H.C. (1989). The self and social behavior in differing cultural contexts. *Psychological Review, 96(3)*, 506–520.

Trumbull, E., Rothstein-Fisch, C., Greenfield, P.M., Quiroz, B. (2001). *Bridging cultures between home and school: A guide for teachers*. Hillsdale, NJ: Erlbaum.

Valdés, G. (1996). *Con respecto*. New York: Teachers College Press.

Valsiner, J. (1989). *Human development and culture*. Toronto: Lexington.

Vygotsky, L.S. (1978). *Mind in society: The development of higher psychological processes*. Cambridge, MA: Harvard University Press.

Wertsch, J.V. (1985). *Culture, communication, and cognition: Vygotskian perspectives*. New York: Cambridge University Press.

Wertsch, J. (1991). *Voices of the mind*. Cambridge, MA: Harvard University Press.

Wertsch, J. (1995). Introduction. In J.V. Werstch, P. del Rio, & A. Alvarez (Eds.), *Sociocultural studies of the mind*. New York: Cambridge University Press.

Wertsch, J.V., & Tulviste, P. (1992). L.S. Vygotsky and contemporary developmental psychology. *Developmental Psychology 28(4)*, pp. 548–557.

Wozniak, R.H., & Fischer, K.W. (1993). *Development in context: Acting and thinking in specific environments*. Hillsdale, NJ: Erlbaum.

Zayas, L.H., Canino, I., & Suarez, Z.E. (2001). Parenting in mainland Puerto Rican families. In N.B. Webb (Ed.). *Culturally diverse parent-child and family relationships: A guide for social workers and other practitioners* (pp. 133–155). New York: Columbia University Press.

Zayas, L.H., & Solari, F. (1994). Early childhood socialization in Hispanic families: Context, culture and practice implications. *Professional Psychology: Research and Practice* 25, (3), 200–206.

8

Spirituality and Children:
Paying Attention to Experience

DANIEL SCOTT

This volume includes chapters that explore the ways in which children are made invisible or are diminished by adult-oriented theories that treat them as property, as incomplete, or as being only in preparation for 'real' (that is, adult) life (see chapters 4 & 10). Spirituality in children is, unfortunately, not an exception to either invisibility or to an adult-focused orientation. Until recently, the spiritual life experiences of children were seldom acknowledged or explored. The dominant Euro-Western cultural assumptions about spirituality are typified by comments in Ronald Goldman's (1964) influential *Religious Thinking from Childhood to Adolescence*. It is clear to him that as 'the mystics, who claim to have direct sensations of the divine, are exceptions ... extremely rare cases, rarer in adolescence and unknown in childhood' (p. 14), children do not have, or are not capable of having, mystical experiences. This assumption not only reflects but also informs much of recent Euro-Western cultural understanding. In dismissing mystical experience, Goldman has contributed to two confusions about spiritual experiences: first, that they are always or only religious experiences; and second, that children are unlikely to have any such experiences. Experiences that are declared non-existent necessarily fall outside of our consideration of children's lives.

I will argue a different case in this chapter in an attempt to encourage a view of children's lives that includes spirituality and spiritual experience, and I will try to do so in a way that is not dependent on an assumption of religious experience. For me, there are two central questions in viewing children as spiritual: Is it possible to identify any inherent spiritual sensibility, awareness, or experience in children's lives? And is it possible to develop an image of the child as spiritual that is not determined by images of the child as religious?

The confusion of religious and spiritual experience is being altered by shifting perspectives in the contemporary context. For instance, the United Nations Convention on the Rights of the Child (UNCRC: 1991) recognizes that spirituality and religion are not identical. They are identified and dealt with under separate articles in the UNCRC. Article 27 recognizes 'the right of every child to a standard of living adequate for the child's physical, mental, spiritual, moral and social development' (p. 14), while Article 17 underlines an 'access to information and material from a diversity of national and international sources, especially those aimed at the promotion of his or her social, spiritual and moral well-being and physical and mental health' (p. 8). Article 32 claims children have the right 'to be protected from economic exploitation' (p. 16) or any work that is hazardous or may interfere with their health or their development, including their spiritual development. Spirituality is seen in these articles as part of human development.

Religion is protected in a different set of articles, and the implications are significant. Article 14 notes 'the right of the child to freedom of thought, conscience and religion' (p. 7), and, in subsection 3, the 'freedom to manifest one's religion or beliefs' is only limited by the need to protect the freedoms and rights of others, both developments of the general statement of Article 2. Article 12 protects the right of children to 'express' their 'own views' in all matters affecting them (p. 6). Article 29(d) encourages 'a spirit of understanding, peace, tolerance, equality of sexes, and friendship among all peoples, ethnic, national and religious groups and persons of indigenous origin' (p. 15), and Article 30 clarifies minority 'ethnic, religious or linguistic' rights so that any member of those minorities can 'enjoy his or her own culture, to profess and practice his or her own religion, or to use his or her own language' (p. 16). Religion is a matter of mind, belief, and practice. It is identified as an aspect of cultural expression and is associated with minority rights and human equality.

This is clearly a different conceptualization from that of spirituality as a developmental process. The Convention does not elaborate on the distinction between spirituality and religion, but the two sets of articles acknowledge them as separate concerns. The challenge remains to elaborate an understanding of spirituality as a process of development.

The word *spirituality* itself, formerly a term to describe specific religious approaches or disciplines,[1] has come to have a range of meanings and is now invoked in a variety of settings. Attention to spirituality has become a theme in the media and is being explored in writing, in film, in television and in the self-development workshop field. With a few exceptions, the focus is on adult life and experience. Themes range widely from angelic visitations, after-life experience, shamanic practices, health and healing, prayer and meditation, to religious renewal and the exploration of old and new religious practices. Spirituality takes on many meanings in this melange of ideas and perspectives. My concern is with the way children live and experience the spiritual in this cultural context with its unstable, unsettled meanings and shifting perspectives on spirituality. In what follows, I suggest a perspective on spirituality that draws on research and literature in the field that views children's lives as including and experiencing the spiritual.

In the first section, I will look briefly at the interplay of religion and spirituality in the Euro-Western tradition, exploring the importance of teasing apart the two in order to see children and their spiritual experience as arising within their own existence, while they remain within the context of their culture. It must be acknowledged that the invisibility of spirituality is not common to all cultures. In some cultures, the spiritual is included in their very epistemological framework (Calliou, 1995), while in others where religion plays a strong communal role, assumptions around the significance of spiritual life for all, including children, continue to operate. However, religion is not the only source of spiritual experience. There are children and families whose context does not include religious institutions or connections and yet they experience and express spirituality.

In the second section, I will explore some contemporary views of children's spirituality, offering an interpretive lens that acknowledges a spiritual capacity and ability in their lives. I will draw on a selection of the images of children's spirituality that arise in examples from the work of Robinson (1983) and Coles (1990) and a consideration of the theory of relational consciousness from the work of Hay and Nye (1998).

In the third section, I will offer examples of the kinds of spiritual experiences that children are having as reported by them either at first hand or in retrospective reflections. Children, I argue, may be having spiritual experiences without the awareness or knowledge of adults. Adults who report their own childhood spiritual experiences often comment that they were silenced or ignored when they tried to relate them (Robinson, 1983). If we insist on viewing children as immune to or outside of spiritual life, it will not be possible for us to assist them in telling, interpreting, and integrating these experiences into their understanding of the world (Scott, 2001). Paying attention to the occluded and silenced narratives of spiritual experience is a necessary part of opening our understanding to children as spiritual.

In the final section, I will argue that the spiritual lives of children are worthy of thought and research. Children have a right to develop and nurture their own spiritual lives. Adults must therefore be willing to take a realistic approach to children's spiritual needs. This includes an understanding that what matters to adults, what they are willing to value, and what is worthy of their energy, resources, and attention will be determined by the spiritual and moral experiences of life that they have already had as children. If these experiences are ignored, rendered invisible, or treated as unacceptable, there will be consequences in the way these children take up their lives as adults.

Considering Culture and Locating the Lens

In distinguishing the religious life of children from their spiritual development, the UNCRC supports a view of children different from the traditional one in Euro-Western culture, where spirituality is considered an exclusive concern of the religious and a matter for religion. In that tradition, children are spiritual only if they are engaged in religion or the religious life. It is now possible to imagine a spiritual child who may not express or experience his or her spirituality in a religious way. Separating religion and spirituality is theoretically tidy but remains problematic for how children are actually viewed in practice. In the educational settings where children spend much of their lives, the tension between religion and spirituality as frames of reference are evident. Education serves as a useful place to begin an exploration.

Education is always rooted in a context, and there is little cultural common ground between various jurisdictions that manage the issue of spirituality quite differently. The confusion of religion and spirituality persists in practice in most areas of North America, where public religious expression has been restricted by regulation or legislation as part of assuring freedom of expression and freedom from forced religious observance. The dominant attitude is informed by the American doctrine of the separation of church and state (Carter, 1993), with the result that any initiative to include spirituality is resisted as a religious intrusion. However, there have been attempts by educators in North America to begin to address spirituality in its own terms.

Led by educators including Heubner (Hillis, 1999) and Palmer (1983, 1998), a discourse is developing on the inclusion of spirituality in education. Pinar, Reynolds, Slattery, and Taubman (1995) write of understanding education as a theological text. Moffett (1994) looks for 'spiritual awakening' in the classroom and the need to establish a metaphysics for spirituality. However, political tension around religion continues to skew the discussion, and the debate often returns to 'God in the classroom' (Sweet, 1997), focusing on religious political issues. The Canadian approach has tended to follow the American example and has not drawn, in any significant way, on the very different approaches that exist in Europe. The debate in the United Kingdom offers a fascinating look at the issue.

Because the 1944 School Act in the United Kingdom mandates religious education (RE) as part of the required school curriculum, educators in the United Kingdom have struggled to formulate a way to accommodate RE in a society that has evolved from an assumed cultural homogeneity to multiculturalism in a few years. It was not possible to teach RE as a faith-based practice, that is, through instruction in religion, as society was secularized, and the existing religious context had been pluralized. The United Kingdom was no longer a 'Christian' society but one in which a variety of religious faiths and secular beliefs were present. The result was a vigorous discourse on spirituality as an educational approach that would meet the demand for a public, secular education that was seen as religiously neutral, yet allow a discussion of values and traditions representing interfaith and non-faith perspectives in the United Kingdom (see, for example, Hay, 1982; Grimmitt, 1987; Best, 1996; Erricker, Erricker, Sullivan, Ota, & Fletcher, 1997; Erricker, Ota, & Erricker, 2001). The concern for RE approaches has also spurred a body of educational research in the area of spirituality and children as well as academic journals like the *International Journal of Children's Spirituality* and the *Journal of Beliefs and Values Studies in Religion and Education*.

The dilemma in education, reflecting the re-surfacing of spirituality in popular culture, is paralleled in other academic disciplines where writers have attempted to clarify the place of spirituality in human experience and culture (Torrance, 1994; Evans, 1993; Kovel, 1991). Ó Murchú (1998) argues that spirituality predates and comprises religious experience. Even the dominant cultural sector of business has begun to consider the role of spirituality. Spirituality has become a theme in leadership (Owen, 1987; Bolman & Deal, 1995; Moxley, 2000) and is seen as an aspect of individual development, as well as an essential element in forming working teams, in managing organizations, and in building collegiality and energy for working contexts.

How has this cultural movement played out in the lives of children, and what are the implications for them? Let me turn to some of the discussions in the United Kingdom to trace the debate. Hay (1998) traces the Euro-Western diminishment of spirituality as he explores ideas from Western psychology and philosophy. Hay (2000) asserts his research found that 'children are embarrassed by their own spiritual awareness, particularly by the time they reach the age of ten ... There is evidence here of the ongoing construction of a taboo on the expression or recognition of the spiritual dimension of human existence. My previous research has shown that once adult life is reached this prohibition is extremely widespread' (p. 39).

Hay identifies a social reality in his experience of spirituality in the United Kingdom. However, this is but one cultural form, and it is important to acknowledge its limitations. There are other understandings of children and their lives. For example, in personal conversations with Aboriginal people of two very different communities (one from the Amazon valley and one from the Pacific Northwest) I was assured that in their cultures the first seven to ten years of a child's life are seen as the time for the development of a spiritual voice and awareness. It is considered normal for spirituality to fade into the background at around eight to ten years of age, as the development of the body and physical voice takes precedence.[2] In Aboriginal understanding, the spiritual voice has been nurtured and is already in place to be a resource for and part of other developmental processes. Hay's (2000) comments can be seen, then, as a concern for the missing formation of spirituality in children's lives in contemporary Euro-Western culture and the consequence of its potential long-term absence in their development.

Children's spiritual lives have not been a major focus of the developmental literature in Euro-Western contexts. Hay & Nye (1998) indicate uneasiness 'about the adequacy of developmental theory to give an account of [childhood spirituality]' (p. 50). This unconcern persists. The Association for Child and Youth Care Practice has produced 'Competencies for Professional Child and Youth Work Practitioners' (Mattingly & Stuart, 2001), listing competencies for child- and youth-care licensing criteria. The list includes 'spiritual development' as part of the foundational knowledge for a child- and youth-care worker in the area of applied human development. However, what this might entail is not described. During the time when the document was being circulated for comments, one of the appendices suggested issues for discussion. The first question was 'How do we meet spiritual needs?' (p. 28). There is an evident awareness to include spiritual development, but little certainty about how to do so.

There have been some attempts to understand spirituality by imitating stage theories to explain religious development. Fowler's (1980) work on faith development, clearly based on cognitive development, is an example. I see his work as an attempt to create a model for religious development that fits a cultural understanding based on rationality and stage theory. One danger that Hay and Nye (1998) note is that the process of 'dissolving religion into reason' implies that childhood spirituality is 'nothing more than a form of immaturity or inadequacy' (p. 51). This approach continues the confusion of religion and spirituality, making the development of religious faith the marker of spiritual formation.

The contemporary Euro-Western mainstream view of children's spirituality is problematic in another way. There has been a romanticized notion that children are innocent and pure, that they have a kind of natural, naive spirituality, an idea that Higonnet (Erricker, 2001) claims originated with the Romantics. The dominant Christian tradition has supported this notion by often depicting a romanticized Jesus surrounded by children who gaze at him with admiring eyes. These images are based on Jesus' advice to his disciples to 'Suffer the little children to come unto me' and the notion that adults have to become like children to be part of the promised spiritual realm (Matthew 18 or Luke 18: 15–17). Erricker (2001) points out this idea exists in tension with another perspective from the same tradition in which the child is impure from birth (born in sin) and needs instruction and discipline to be purified. Erricker insists that 'this form of representation is damaging' because 'it ignores the potential of the young person and the relational possibilities that are present once the ideas of representation and instruction are removed' (p. 83).

Children, viewed through this polarity in which they are both naive and soiled, remain simultaneously spiritual and non-spiritual. Because of that mixed message, children are not acknowledged as innately spiritual but rather are considered incomplete or less-than-adult. Their spirituality is non-existent until they have experienced a religious awakening or had appropriate discipline and education to correct their corrupted souls and origins. Childhood spirituality is not acknowledged as something that might arise from children's existing experience and awareness but rather must be added to their lives through religious practice focused on belief, creed, and understanding.

Teasing Apart Religion and Spirituality

In teasing apart spirituality and religion, the goal is to give room to think of children as spiritual, regardless of cultural context. In a cross-cultural, multiperspective world, an understanding of the potential range and diversity of spiritual experience is needed. A child may be viewed as either spiritual or religious, on both spiritual and religious, or religious and not spiritual; but if spirituality is a natural part of human development and a right, a child should not be seen as neither religious nor spiritual. All children possess some spirituality.

Coles (1990) describes his struggle to understand a troubled young Roman Catholic girl during the early years of his psychiatric practice. After consultations with colleagues, he stopped resisting her religious self-presentation and entered into a dialogue with her about her beliefs and experiences: 'Most important, she let me know her religious life was far more many-sided than I had been prepared to admit – and that there was a personal, *spiritual* life in her that was by no means to be equated with her *religious* life' (p. 14).

Hay and Nye (1998) make a similar point when they take Catholic theologian Karl Rahner's claim that 'It is possible to talk about God without being spiritual' and add the reverse: 'It is also possible to be spiritual without talking about God.' They conclude:

> That knowledge *about* religion and the ability to use religious language is not the whole story when we are thinking about spirituality. It is important not to get caught into the assumption that spirituality can only be recognized in the use of a specialized religious language. I have spoken about the difficulty with almost all research on children's spiritual life, up to the very recent past, in that it has been focused on God-talk rather than spirituality. I have also presented a notion of spirituality as something biologically built into the human species, an holistic awareness of reality which is potentially to be found in every human being. (p. 57)

Both Hay and Nye (1998) and Coles (1990) are working to find a view of children that brings their spirituality into focus in a particular way. However, confusion continues to cloud thinking about spirituality and religion and whether they are separate domains. I think it is necessary to tease them apart to clarify the primacy of children's experience of the spiritual. In many cases, where the familial or social context includes religious practice, this will be a temporary delineation. McLaughlin

(2001), an English educator, has distinguished between spiritual experiences that are 'tethered to religion' and those that are 'untethered to
religion.' This distinction foregrounds the nature of spiritual experience
that is not bound to or contained by religious forms. It acknowledges
that spirituality is a common human quality and religions are particular
cultural and historical expressions of communal spiritual life. The image of the spiritual experience being tethered to religion reflects the
continuing central role that religion plays as the definer of spiritual
realities. My hope is that children's spirituality can be acknowledged on
its own terms as part of understanding spiritual development.

Because of the extensive cultural influence of the major religions,
there is an assumption in Euro-Western contexts that religion has always been part of culture. Ó Murchú (1998) argues that, historically,
religion has followed rather than preceded spirituality, and that spirituality is part of the long-range experience of humanity with religions
developing at specific times, arising out of already existing spiritual
practices and sensibilities. He provides a time line stretching back into
prehistory which suggests that the acknowledgment of mystery and the
experience of transcendence are of primary importance. The expression
of communal spiritual life in a regulated or structured form is a later
development and constitutes what we know as religion. Although
Berman (2000) offers religion as an expression of vertical relations developing in human society in response to changes in population, settlement patterns, and food production and distribution, he still sees
spirituality as preceding religion. Berman suggests early nomadic
cultures had a spirituality based on horizontal relationships. Spirituality infused all of life and was not above or outside daily events. The
move to a vertical-ascent model of religious practice, locating a transcendent divine beyond the earth mediated through a priestly class,
was part of a cultural shift to hierarchies in social life and governance.
Spirituality is not absent from human history but is differently formed
and understood.

The spirituality proposed by Ó Murchú (1998) and Berman (2000)
may serve as a model for a view of children as spiritual, one that allows
spirituality in their lives whether or not it has structured forms and
defining beliefs and practices. If spirituality is prior in time historically
to religion, might it also be prior in experience in children's lives to
instruction or enculturation? And if children are inherently spiritual,
what care or nurturing might their spiritual lives require?

I have argued elsewhere (Scott, 1993) that to approach physical development the way spiritual development has been managed would be unacceptable. Children are physical beings and have physical needs and abilities. Education is constructed accordingly. This, however, was not always true for women or girls. During most of the last century, women were not considered as physical as men in abilities or needs, and they struggled to gain access to public space, adequate resources, and recognition for physical activity and competitive sports. Cultural assumptions determine the use of resources and the provision of cultural space for enacting beliefs about the nature of human character and experience. Spirituality needs to be reconsidered in children's development and in meeting their needs. Let us turn now to the kinds of spiritual experiences children are already having.

Images of Children's Spirituality

Adults live with the assumption that they are the arbiters of children's experiences. It is difficult to acknowledge that children can and do have experiences that adults do not have, are not having, or may not have had. To identify experiences as spiritual and then suggest that children may have these experiences without adult intervention or management is problematic in two ways. First, it implies that some adults have a limited range of perceptions and that children may have experiences that are outside of adult awareness. Children may be attuned to the phenomenal world in a way that adults around them are not and may, therefore, have insights or difficulties unavailable to them.

Second, there is the challenge of identifying the sorts of experiences that might be spiritual for children. An initial step is an acknowledgment that many humans have experiences that they themselves identify as spiritual. These include moments of sensed transcendence in which there is a blurring of the borders of the self and a sense of unity or oneness with life; sightings of angelic figures, meetings with deceased relatives, or knowledge of events out of or across time that may come in dreams or in visionary experiences; moments of great calm and a sense of wonder or awe at life. They might also include moments of terror in the face of threatening and dark forces. For some people, these experiences arise in moments of struggle with meaning in the midst of difficulty and loss. Do children have these kinds of experiences? How might they express them? What kind of influence do these experiences have on their lives?

In the contemporary literature exploring the spiritual lives of children, there are a number of images used to express what can be remarkably difficult to pin down. Unfortunately, there is not a clear set of distinct experiences or agreed interpretations of them that can be identified as spiritual. Distinguishing religious and spiritual experiences has been part of that difficulty, and a cultural tradition that has excluded spiritual development from its understanding of human formation has also compounded the difficulty. Among the images or metaphors that can help us to understand children's spirituality are those that lead to a helpful picture of the child as pilgrim and the child as visionary.

The Child as Pilgrim

Robert Coles (1990), who interviewed children of religious (Protestant and Catholic, Jewish and Muslim) and non-religious (including Aboriginal children and atheists) families in several different national settings to explore their spirituality, concludes with the image of the child as a pilgrim. He draws on narratives he has collected and sets them in the context of a series of conversations with Dorothy Day, co-founder of the Catholic Worker movement, who describes her childhood questions when she was troubled by the injustice of having enough to eat and discovering that there were children who did not:

> I think my pilgrimage began when I was a child, when I was seven or eight ... I have a memory and to me it's the start of my spiritual journey. I'm sitting with my mother, and she's telling me about some trouble in the world, about children like me who don't have enough food – they're dying. I'm eating a doughnut, I think. I ask my mother why other children don't have doughnuts and I do ... Anyway I remember her face – she was troubled. Maybe she was trying to decide what to tell her troublesome daughter! Most of all I remember trying to decide what it meant – me eating a doughnut, and lots of children with no food at all. Finally I must have decided to solve the world's problem of hunger on my own. (Coles, 1990, pp. 326–327)

These questions and conclusions recurred in Day's life as she grew up and developed her vocation. Coles (1990) sees traces of this troubled and inquiring voice in other children and names this as part of the core of their spiritual lives. Children notice and try to make sense of the world by drawing on the resources of their own context: their family, their community, and their religious life. As Coles and other researchers

(Hay 1998; Bosacki & Ota, 2000) note, children use the language of their own context to do this work. The matter of making sense of the world often comes in moments of reflection in response to awareness of the world. Coles (1990) is drawn to these young men and women who ask hard questions and who pursue their understanding of the world and 'God' as they have been taught. They include Natalie, a Hopi girl whose visions of unity are powerful; Ginny, a working-class girl who sees her life task of living better and caring for others as a step forward in social progress; Asif, a young Pakistani Muslim who is living in England and struggling with the inconsistencies of two cultures and two ways of life as he strives to be faithful to Islam; Eric, a boy with no religious family tradition who grapples with the death of his cousin Ned; or Margarita, a young, impoverished Brazilian girl whose mother is dying of tuberculosis and who critiques the local priest and rages about the injustice of life in her favela. All these individuals illustrate the power of the quest for understanding in children in their mid-childhood and early adolescent years. These children use the forms and language of their context and culture (including religious culture) to express their struggles, to make sense of their circumstances, even as they attempt criticism and resist those structures, offering insightful questions and commentary.

The image of a pilgrim is linked to many spiritual traditions and implies that there are issues of justice, goodness, and morality in seeking and questioning. As these young people work to find a way that has some meaning and integrity for them, they are drawing on a range of abilities. What makes these experiences spiritual? Can they be understood developmentally without a spiritual component? Children use other developing skills, including cognitive and social abilities, to consider their world and its implications. They have an ability to absorb and integrate the values being offered by their context and then use the same values to question and critique it. As they do so, they are caught up in relational questions and connections beyond themselves. How do they take up hope in the face of their difficulties? What inspires their visions of unity or their longing for justice or a better world? How do they integrate their experiences of difficulty and their aspirations for life? I suggest that the process of integration and the beyond-the-self quality of their questions and insights are expressions of spirituality. They are pilgrims. As Torrance (1994) points out, the quest has qualities that are rooted in biology, language, psychology, and religion, and this integrative movement outward into life is spiritual. Evans (1993) views the seeking quality of human nature in terms of energy that he also identifies as spiritual.

The Child as Visionary

A second glimpse into children's spirituality arises in the work of Robinson (1983), based on the research of the Religious Experience Unit at Manchester College, Oxford. Robinson does not rely on children's immediate accounts of events, but offers adults' reports of childhood experiences that they identified as spiritual or religious. He includes a number of accounts from adults who as children had visionary experiences of mystery and wonder marked by reports of a felt sense of being at one with the universe, while simultaneously having a strong sense of their own uniqueness and their place in the vastness of life. For some, the enduring quality of these visions has informed the rest of their lives: 'I think I have been simply trying, in adult life, to grow towards the vision of childhood, and to comprehend more fully the significance of the light that was so interwoven into those early years. The original impact of light was so powerful that my inner world still reverberates with it' (F. 45, p. 52).[3]

Altered perceptions of light or intense light-based experiences are also recurring themes in spiritual and mystical traditions and are frequently understood as revelatory encounters. It is difficult to ascertain what children experience and how such visionary moments can be understood. The image of the child as visionary implies a degree of insight and connection beyond the self and underscores the claims that these experiences are reported to have had long-lasting impact:

> But for the brief seconds (when I was about eleven) while it lasted I had known that in some strange way I, the essential 'me,' was a part of the trees, of the sunshine, and the river, that we all belonged to a great unity. I was left filled with exhilaration and exultation of spirit. This is one of the most memorable experiences of my life. (F. 40, p. 37)

> The most profound experience of my life came to me when I was very young – between four and five years old ... In that moment I knew that I had my own special place, as had all the other things, animate and so-called inanimate, and that we were all part of the universal tissue which was both fragile yet immensely strong, and utterly good and beneficient. This vision has never left me.' (F. 57, p. 32)

Coles (1990) includes a detailed report of the Hopi girl Natalie's vision of unity and harmony that is poetic and imaginative, a vision he describes as 'one in which edges and corners give way to a final round-ness that would pull us all together in a celebratory union that surely resembles the more prophetic moments of both our Old and New Testament' (p. 156). Natalie goes beyond a vision of her own people to embrace and include all peoples in a circle dance. She draws strongly on the images and metaphors of her own cultural context but seems able to see further using familiar language. Robinson (1983) also adds examples of children expressing visionary experiences in the context, language, and images of their families' religious practices.

Visionary moments of awe and wonder may also be darker and difficult. There are troubling moments, particularly through misunder-standing of words or sayings, that produce visions of loss and hopeless-ness. However, there are also first encounters with death that include a wide range of childhood responses from fear – 'I had a terrible horror of death that I couldn't mention to anyone' (F. 56, p. 124) – through frustration with adult attitudes – 'There were no words to explain that it was not overtiredness, it was the unutterable black emptiness of every-thing and everywhere' (F. 47, p. 125) – to a sense of the naturalness of death – 'It was as if I instinctively felt only the wonder and unity of life and that death is merely part of the natural cycle' (F. 44, p. 128). Even in the face of death, Robinson's correspondents reported a childhood knowl-edge that saw death as 'a great teacher and friend' (F. 60, p. 129) and 'surrounded by mystery and wonder' (F. 16, p. 129).

Many of Robinson's (1983) correspondents insist on the lasting influ-ence of early spiritual or religious experiences in their lives. They also report that the spiritual experiences they had as children were outside of adult awareness and understanding. Their attempts to report these events were dismissed or met with disbelief. Adults neither played a significant role in the events nor influenced the children's interpretation of them. The reported experiences seem to have provided them with a degree of resilience in meeting and enduring difficulty: 'All my life, in times of great pain or distress or failure, I have been able to look back and remember, quite sure that the present agony was not the whole picture and that my understanding of it was limited as were the ants in comparison to their part in the world I knew' (F. 55, P. 13).

For both the child-pilgrim and the child-visionary, there is a sense they are independent agents. They are meeting and taking up life through their own interpretive responses, trying to make sense of the world and what they see as happening in it by drawing on personal resources based on their experiences. Life is happening; they are caught up in contexts and experiences and work to process them. What is fascinating for me is the power these experiences seem to have in shaping their way of engaging the world. Dorothy Day has a childhood question about hunger and justice, and it remains in her life, shaping her way of life and her vocation. Several of Robinson's (1983) correspondents name their experiences of wonder as touchstones of meaning and purpose for the rest of their lives. The intensity of these early life experiences gives them durability and potency, affecting life choices and perspective. Neither Coles (1990) nor Robinson (1983) provide an interpretive frame for these experiences. They are offering evidence that certain experiences and understandings are operative in children's lives.

Relational Consciousness

Hay and Nye (1998) attempt to develop an interpretive framework for children's spiritual lives based on face-to-face interviews. They suggest that children have a series of natural sensitivities that attune them to the spiritual dimension from life's earliest stages. They have named this collection of sensitivities 'relational consciousness' (p. 120). Children, they claim, have a distinct relational consciousness of themselves in relation to the world, to other people, to their own selves, and to God or the Divine. In their view of children, relational consciousness is informed by three sensitivities: awareness-sensing, mystery-sensing, and value-sensing.

Children's awareness-sensing includes being aware of and present in the here-and-now of immediate experience, and it is further enhanced by their capacity for tuning in to experience and by their ability to be lost in the flow of experience. Consequently, children have the capacity to transcend themselves and enter into a moment or series of experiences without distraction, caught up in the event that may lead to a sense of oneness beyond the self. Children experience the here-and-now with a felt-sense, which means their experiences are body based, not detached or abstracted – a form of holistic awareness. Hay and Nye (1998) claim that children are naturally spiritual through this way of relating to the world and are open to spiritual experiences beyond themselves in parallel to the goals of disciplined spiritual and mystic life advocated in religious and spiritual traditions.

In addition, Hay and Nye (1998) maintain that children have a capacity for mystery-sensing. The ability to be present makes every moment rich in imagination and possibility. Life is not already explained but is experienced as fresh and 'therefore mysterious' (p. 69). This leads to an intense interest in and persistent inquiry about, the nature of things and the workings of the world. It is not clear what makes this capacity spiritual. Being fascinated with the workings of life is part of developing thinking and inquiring skills. A lived sense of mystery can contribute significantly to the formation of imagination and curiosity. Children's minds are capable of flights of imagination and engagement, testing the world for its processes (Gopnik, Meltzoff, & Kuhl, 1999). Levine (1999) argues that children have the ability to function simultaneously in both concrete and imaginative modes of thinking, which opens them to the potential of spiritual experience. Their spiritual experience is both linked to the transcendent and rooted in their daily life events.

Jane Goodall's (1990) fascination, at the age of five, with the mystery of how a hen lays an egg is part of her developing a passion for the study of living things in their own context. The mystery-sensing capacity in children may give them perceptions beyond the expected. Children who see angels or other figures or who are told things by voices or through visions may possess a heightened awareness that needs to be respected. These kinds of childhood experiences have not been carefully studied. What is their role in development? What support might children need to interpret and integrate such experiences into their lives?

The third identified sensitivity is that of value-sensing. Hay and Nye (1998) believe children are capable of an astonishing range of emotions and feelings, from terror to delight, and from despair to hope. Children can be immediately emotionally responsive to what is happening around them. Their emotional, psychological, spiritual, and sometimes physical survival depends on them being able to read their context and understand its implications. They learn to discern what matters in their context and how to respond to it. Their sensitivity to context provides an ability to sense what is valued both implicitly and explicitly by the adults in their lives. Again, it is not clear how this particular sensitivity is spiritual rather than emotional or social, nor is it clear how a child who is not able to read social and emotional contexts accurately might be considered spiritual.

Hay and Nye (1998) state that children have a sense of ultimate goodness that is part of their capacity for to delight and despair. I would argue that children are pragmatic and may know what is valued in their context and respond to what they see as being of higher value. They may have a sensitivity to ultimate goodness, but meaning and values are contextual. I think that their value-sensing capacity is itself a significant factor in understanding their relational attunement and is not dependent on any ultimate awareness. It may well be that Hay and Nye are noting a number of sensitivities in children that are linked to a range of developmental factors and are not exclusively spiritual. Children may well be expressing some of their sensitivities in religious or spiritual language. It may be that both the visionary and searching nature of their experience includes a developing spiritual sensitivity and awareness that works in conjunction with developing emotional, social, and cognitive skills.

Some children may have moments of meaning-sensing – transcendent moments of unity or oneness – that take them out of or beyond the limits of their context and provide them with a sense of meaning that has a life-long sustaining potential. Not all children have the same ability or capacity in any area of development. How might this be a factor in spiritual development? The loss of personal boundaries in a sensation of oneness and connection with the world or life is an experience that is frequently self-identified as spiritual. Robinson's (1983) sample includes a number of children between the ages of four and seven and one report of a child less than a year old who were aware of being at one with life. Not all children have these experiences, but recent studies of adults (Hawker, 2000) would indicate that a larger percentage of adults than we expect report these kinds of experiences in their life histories.

Let me turn now to further explore some experiences that children and younger adolescents report that further indicate what spiritual experience and perception might be for them.

Children's Spiritual Experiences: Power and Impact

Gathering accounts of spiritual experiences is not without difficulty. In identifying their experiences as spiritual, both children and adults are already thinking within contexts that provide a frame of reference for these experiences. One challenge in the Euro-Western context is the suppression of such stories by cultural mechanisms and attitudes. Children as young as nine or ten express their reluctance to tell their stories of religious experience, as Hay and Nye (1998) note: 'For others it was apparent that embarrassment was at the root of their reluctance. They were cautious of straying for too long beyond the acceptable confines of secular discourse. Some children admitted that they were afraid of being laughed at or thought stupid or even mad, not only by their peer group but also within their families (including "religious" families), if they talked about the personal sense of the religious in their lives' (p. 105).

Hay and Nye (1998) are concerned 'to respect children's reticence (perhaps evident in a disinclination to engage consciously in spiritually expressive discourse at all) as potentially spiritually informed, rather than as indicative of an absence of spiritual awareness' (p. 106). Children may be inhibiting their expression of spirituality in response to cultural signals that communicate an intolerance of their spiritual awareness and experience.

Hay (2000) argues that the work of rethinking spiritual education in Euro-Western culture consists in deconstructing the alienation that leads to the silencing of spiritual experience. Repressed stories can have a significant impact on lives in ways that are not always positive. Spiritual stories may remain active in children's lives, lingering just below the surface, more occluded than repressed. Children may not be able to speak them, but the stories may be consciously (or unconsciously) active in their lives, influencing their choices and direction.

It is my contention that a critical aspect of this work (Scott, 2001) is to acknowledge spirituality as part of human life and children's experience, and to create space for telling stories of spiritual experiences. Among the many reasons for story-telling is a need to make sense of out-of-the-ordinary experiences through accounts of them. It is not possible to successfully integrate or sort these kinds of experiences if they remain silenced. Important access to these experiences as resources for decision-making is potentially being lost in children's lives. These untold or unexpressed stories may offer assistance in forming meaning and values, in developing a sense of being connected to life, and in making life, and vocational choices. They may also give us insights into children's problems and their ways of dealing with them.

Coles (1990) demonstrates his own growing awareness of this possibility in his work with children. He admits to learning to pay attention to children's spiritual yearnings and insights in order to better understand how they see the world and make sense of their difficulties in it: 'Instead of seeing Connie's religious and spiritual life as evidence of a disturbed mind, we [Coles and Dr Abraham Fineman] tried to let that life be our guide and teacher; and, too, we began to understand how her spiritual life had kept the child together psychologically' (p. 19).

To understand spirituality as a resource for the child and for those who take care of children is to remain open to children's experiences and their interpretations of them, and to respect the insights and strength they gain from them. Coles (1990) tells the story of a North Carolina girl of eight named Laurie who was being bused to school as part of a desegregation program and had to walk a gauntlet of screaming antagonists into the school. She tells Coles that in the midst of such a walk 'I was all alone and those people were screaming and suddenly I saw God smiling, and I smiled. A woman ... was standing there [near the school door], and she shouted at me, "Hey, you little nigger, what you smiling at?" I looked right at her face and I said "At God." Then she looked up at the sky, and then she looked at me, and she didn't call me any more names' (pp. 19–20).

Coles (1990) points out that this child 'was convinced that God had suddenly intervened in the world's reality' even as he worried about 'the psychology that was at work in her.' Her religious experience had altered her world. It is not easy to understand how she 'knew exactly how and when to invoke God' (p. 20), and her ability raises as many questions as it explains. What is evident is that in moments of difficulty children find comfort and support in experiences that take them beyond themselves, and they express these experiences in spiritual and/ or religious language. It is not sufficient to dismiss these experiences as fanciful or as illusion. Children are being affected by these experiences; they are part of their way of managing and understanding life. It is my contention that we can help children by acknowledging these kinds of experiences and their impact. However, it is not only in the midst of difficulty that children have beyond-themselves experiences. There is a potentially wide range of possible spiritual sensitivity and experience in children's lives. Some children may be quite adept and perceptive spiritually, able to integrate and manage both good and bad spiritual experience. Others may have less capacity for such integrative work and need support or encouragement to draw on personal spiritual resources. Still others may have little spiritual sensitivity and need more extensive support or care.

For some children, experiences of awe and wonder may begin at an early age and provide a defining orientation that becomes a long-term life focus. In a report to me, a woman (Joyce) claimed a childhood experience, at the age of three, in which her seven-year-old brother 'invited' her to 'see a surprise' that shaped her life-long understanding of the world. At midnight he woke her and showed her

> the full moon low in the southern sky. I have never seen the moon, did not really know it exists – now I am astonished by its utter beauty and glittering light. My brother tells me that the moon is a big ball out in space, just as the sun is ... He tells me that we are on the world, called the Earth, and that Earth is also a big ball in the sky! I remember this, with wonder, all my life. So beautiful, these balls. I feel connected with these three balls: this is a feeling inside me. I don't speak of this to my parents, it is my own story (and picture), shared in some way with my brother. (Vancouver, BC, 1999)

This first-time experience of awe is not necessarily remarkable, but Joyce viewed it as central to her understanding of the world. Her relational consciousness was shaped by this experience as were her sense of self and purpose. During her early adolescence, the Cold War threatened world safety. She relates her response:

> somewhere between sleeping and walking, I dream that I can see the whole of the world – that our Earth is a whole, a beautiful whole sphere, 'a beautiful ball,' as I delighted to think of it as a young child. The insights fills me: To refuse to talk to people, not to want to know anything about them, to only want to fight them, is insane. I fully wake up, saying, 'The more they are like us, the more we want to know about them; the less they are like us, the less we want to know about them. This is insane!'

She attempts to discover when her high-school curriculum will study these countries and peoples and is rebuffed by her teacher. 'I am indignant that only a part of our world is valued. In talking with myself about this, I repeatedly use the word "insane" about the way ignorance about others seems to be valued. I say to myself, "I will learn Chinese."'

Her childhood vision persists into adulthood, where she translates her passion into career choices and political action. Joyce's early experience informs her life choices and interests, providing her with an affirming and strengthening vision of what is right and what must be done. She is able to integrate her developing cognitive and social awareness with her visionary experience. But questions arise: Do all children who have visionary experiences have the ability to turn them to positive effect and influence? What about children who have dark or threatening visionary experiences? What life choices will they produce? It is not clear what aspects of spiritual experiences in children's lives need attention or intervention. Nor is it obvious how to identify which children might require more support to integrate them. Joyce turned her visionary experience, as did Dorothy Day, into a vocational focus.

Issues of identity may also arise in events that are understood and expressed as spiritual. Merle, a successful writer and artist, wrote me a story of her tomboy childhood (age nine or ten) when she fell from an ivy-covered wall she was climbing and was winded:

> I soon realized that there was no breath within, either coming or going. Lost in that ageless interlude of not knowing what might happen next, I was totally disoriented. But within and without that solitude of waiting came a directive which was extremely clear and extremely simple. I remember focusing on my hands as other objects faded to the periphery. Insistently, like a chant from a very present but silent 'voice' came the question 'Who am I?,' over and over and over again. Staring into the palms of my hands, the intonation was persistent, endlessly looping over and over the same three words. (Victoria, BC, 2000)

Merle identifies her experience as spiritual, yet it focuses on a question about identity. The 'voice' she heard raises 'an underlying question of life.' What does that mean for her? Why does she frame it as spiritual, and why has it retained its potency for her? Other artists have spoken to me of childhood visions of light that shape their vocation of writing or painting. There seem to be numinous experiences that shape the life journey of some people. What 'voice' has Merle heard? Her own? An 'Other's' that transmits to her?

Spirituality, Loss, and Pain

A confrontation with death is often a source of spiritual insights and experiences for children. Children are aware of and sensitive to death and its presence in life. They wonder about its threat in their lives and express a range of reactions to it:

> Before the age of six, I was in terror of eternity, that endless floating around and around in space. Death became a nightmare. A child once quoted to me at that time 'world without end.' I was shaken to the core and had no one to help me. (Robinson, 1983, F. 65, p. 117)

I must have been five when my mother felt she should enlighten me about death ... 'I want to talk to you about Mr. _____ ,' she said. After some time I tumbled to what she was trying to get over and said, relieved, 'Oh, you mean he's dead.' Shocked, mother said: 'Oh, darling, you do know about death?' 'Of course' (scornfully), 'everything dies sometimes' or words to that effect. (F. 64, p. 127)

Experiences of loss may lead children to questions of identity, meaning, and value. It is possible to consider these issues developmentally, as well as the emotional, cognitive and social implications arising from a child's developmental stage. There is not much understanding about how a child's spiritual development comes into play in meeting loss. What contributes to one child's fear and another's down-to-earth sensibility? How do children make sense of their own lives in the face of mortality? What are the implications for children who report knowledge of the death of a loved one before it happens or are visited in dreams or visionary experiences by deceased friends or family members? These experiences may or may not be healthy and helpful for children. A spiritual interpretation of them might lead to a better understanding of children who are experiencing loss and grief.

Pain in children's lives comes in many other forms. Gwen reports (to me) being taken on a school trip to the shrine at Sainte-Anne-de-Beaupré in Quebec. Her family situation was 'bitter and feudal.' There was physical violence, alcoholism, and a family life of 'walking on eggshells' in fear of the next outburst: 'As I walked into the church I was prepared to be skeptical. Miracles and healings were not a part of my vocabulary, and religious instruction played no role in my life. Nothing in my 12 years could have prepared me for what I saw.'

What she sees is an array of 'medical paraphernalia' hanging on the walls: 'crutches, eye-glasses, braces, wheelchairs, casts and canes of every size, colour and description.' She notes the beauty of the small church, the pews, stained glass windows, and flowers, but she and her friends are drawn to an alcove where there is

a larger-than-life size carved wooden statue of the Madonna. She was quite beautiful ... My best friends and I went and kneeled down and leaned on the little railing that surrounded her. I recall noticing that she could have used a new coat of paint, as her's was rather chipped and fading ... As I kneeled there I remember feeling rather disoriented. I was not a devout child. What happened next perplexed me for many years. I was suddenly overcome. There is no other way to describe it. I remember with incredible brightness and clarity every sensation of my body as I could focus on nothing but the Madonna. All the rest of the kids and adults in that little church just faded away. I felt as if there was only me and the Madonna there, and that she was speaking directly to me, through me, touching me with light. I was in the presence of something divine. I had the most overwhelming sense of being mothered, protected and cradled by something safe and forgiving, and energy so much larger than myself. I had so much pain inside me and I finally felt permission to let it go. I started to cry. Right there, in front of my girlfriends and 12-year-old boys I cried, but that didn't matter to me. I don't know how long I knelt there for. I remember my best friend B. helping me up and digging around for Kleenex in her purse. We walked outside and sat in the little garden. Strangely, no one else seemed to have noticed me. No one ever said anything, not even the boys, some of whom would never have missed such an opportunity for harassment. (Victoria, BC, 1998)

Gwen's story – self-described as spiritual – is rich with complex psychological and emotional implications. She obviously needed care and support and found, in this unexpected encounter, a way to begin to externalize her difficulties, to have them expressed and, at least emotionally, released. She reports that she did try to speak to her mother about it, but her mother 'didn't understand.' Gwen moved on with her life:

As children we could not share our fear and terror with anyone ... My mother was dealing with this in the only way she knew, which was to intercept the punches intended for us, as well as taking those directed at her ... I knew that I could not share my pain with my friends, as we had been trained well to keep the 'family secret.' It was here, in a village, a country away from my home, that I finally broke down and revealed all the pain inside me to an old, faded, chipped wooden statue.

In this mystical encounter, Gwen finds an acceptance and compassion that energizes her with 'an energy so much larger than myself.' The energy arises outside of her and comes to her. Her transcendent encounter meets her human needs. It is not a complete solution, but it is a moment of insight and relief in the midst of difficulty.

Children's spiritual experiences offer them strength and perspective. The experiences may also provide those who care for them with opportunities for engagement and understanding. An ability to be aware, to sense, to perceive mystery, and to seek values and meaning in relations with oneself, with others, and with the Other may be markers in a child's experience of spiritual sensitivity. It may be necessary for educators and caregivers to support such sensitivity by acknowledging its potential and attending to its impact on children's lives.

Reviewing Spirituality: Summing Up

If, as the UNCRC suggests, children have a right to develop and nurture their own spiritual lives, then there needs to be a realistic and grounded approach to spiritual development that respects and is held in tension with existing developmental understanding. Like other areas of development – emotional, social, physical, cognitive – spiritual development will be expressed in different children in varying ways depending on a child's life experience. Currently, spiritual development lacks a strong theoretical basis. This is work that can only be accomplished when spirituality is seen as possible in children's lives and acknowledged as part of their life formation.

I believe care must be taken to respect that the UNCRC also promotes the child's right to religious experience. It is important, however, not to conflate or confuse religion and spirituality. Religion is rooted in social and cultural traditions and includes processes of training or education particular to cultural milieus. I am suggesting that children have a normative life process that includes spiritual development and sensitivity, and that is not dependent on training or education, nor on religious context. Spirituality may be shaped by religion and expressed by children in a religious vocabulary even when they do not have religious instruction in their lives. There is not an acknowledged vocabulary of spirituality for children to draw on to describe their experiences. The religious vocabulary is available and often, because religious tradition has acknowledged the spiritual, provides concepts and language that express some of what has been felt or known.

I have tried to give examples of some of the kinds of experiences that people designate as spiritual and also to suggest that models to help us understand spiritual development and experience are beginning to be formed. Hay and Nye's (1998) relational consciousness is one theory in an early stage of formation, but it has limitations and is clearly culturally embedded. The challenge remains to formulate an understanding of human development with an integrated spiritual component. If children living within a cultural epistemology that included spirituality were to be asked to articulate their spiritual knowledge, perhaps they would provide insight into the process of spiritual development and its normative expression to guide our further explorations.

Where spirituality has not been assumed as an aspect of human life, there are issues to be addressed. The first will be finding ways to overcome the silencing of spiritual experience. As Hay and Nye (1998) have pointed out, the devaluing of spiritual perception has impeded children's willingness to give voice to their experiences.

Many of the adult correspondents who reported spiritual experiences to me in writing or in person – as well as in accounts in the literature (Hawker, 2000; Hay, 1998; Robinson, 1983) – added, after telling their stories, that they had never told that story to anyone before. Many had kept their experiences secret (like Joyce), or failed in attempts to tell their parents or other adults, or were dismissed, ignored, or misunderstood (like Gwen). Whether this is a deliberate form of being silenced or whether it is because there has never been either a safe site in which to tell these stories or a willing listener to hear is not as important to me as the persistent absence of the telling. This silencing, begun in childhood, persists into adult life.

Perhaps there are some parallels between the repression of spiritual narratives and the silence that surrounded children's stories of sexual abuse for so many years. Adults were not able to hear children's stories of sexual abuse because they assumed that children could not have such knowledge and certainly did not have such experiences. Children, lacking a clear articulation and vocabulary for their experience of sexual abuse, could not be heard in spite of their attempts. The first step in reversing this process was the belief of some adults in the children's accounts. Adults had to make this shift. Adults had to acknowledge that, indeed, some children had these experiences and needed not only to speak of them but to have care around them.

Perhaps spirituality now needs a similar shift in perception so that childhood experiences can be heard and processed. What significance do these untold stories have? How might silencing affect children's perceptions of the world and, more importantly, their view of themselves? What role might the experiences carried in these stories have in shaping life choices? Are children's spiritual experiences important in forming what matters to them, what they are willing to value and what is worthy of their energies, resources, and attentions as they become adults?

I am not suggesting that ignoring spiritual experience is abusive, but the silence may be causing children to doubt their own experiences, question their own perceptions, and repress or ignore any knowledge that has arisen from those experiences. I am also concerned that in some cases children may have had troubling experiences that require more than affirmation and support. Children may be frightened or wounded, or have difficult questions that come from their experiences and need care or healing.

If, in becoming adults, children have already learned that the spiritual is restricted territory, what are the implications? Are they being taught that there is no possibility of Other or mystery? Or that wonder is to be ignored? Are there aspects of their lives that are being, or might be, impaired by the occlusion of spirituality? If spiritual experience is part of developing perception, awareness, or imagination, it may have a significant role to play in sensitizing children to otherness and to creativity. There are other implications arising out of belief in their own experiences. What happens to a child whose visionary experience is dismissed or ignored? What are the consequences for confidence and belief in self? If that part of a life story is not true or believable, what parts are? Must children hide some of their experiences in order to be acceptable?

For children who see their lives as journeys of pilgrimage or who have a sense of vocation or purpose through a visionary experience, there is a danger that a dismissal of their perception could deter or destroy a life focus. If Dorothy Day's mother had told her to stop being so concerned or to stop asking about hunger that she could not change, would she have persisted? Would Jane Goodall have studied animals if her family had punished her for hiding in the hen house to observe the production of an egg?

These are not simple questions. Children do not live in isolation. To see children as spiritual will require adults to see themselves as spiritual and to be willing to attend to their own spiritual formation and life journey. Children are unlikely to develop the personal freedom necessary to explore spirituality without adults who are similarly engaged. If children are sensitive, they will learn that what is hidden or denied must be hidden and denied. If silencing is valued, they will be silent.

Adults need to be willing to share their pilgrimage, to be willing and able to listen, notice, and respond openly to children's attempts to express spiritual insights or experience, resisting any silencing or alienation of spirituality. To respect the UNCRC and its call for spiritual development as a right of a child means that those involved in the study and care of children will have to explore in research and express theoretically and practically the nature of spiritual formation and development in children and adolescents.

Notes

1 A religious person might follow a particular spiritual tradition that would include a specific style of prayer, or meditation and other disciplines, as well as a set of core beliefs or theology; hence, Benedictine spirituality or Franciscan spirituality or any one particular Zen discipline.
2 There are some parallels in the work of Rudolf Steiner, which underpins the Waldorf school movement. Moffett (1994) explores Steiner's views in some detail.
3 Robinson follows all citations with the gender and age of the contributor, which I include followed by the page number.

References

Berman, M. (2000). *Wandering God: A study in nomadic spirituality*. Albany: State University of New York Press.

Best, R. (Ed.). (1996). *Education, spirituality and the whole child*. London: Cassell.

Bolman, L.G., & Deal, T.E. (1995). *Leading with soul: An uncommon journey of spirit*. San Francisco: Jossey-Bass.

Bosacki, S., & Ota, C. (2000). Preadolescents' voices: A consideration of British and Canadian children's reflections on religion, spirituality and their sense of self. *International Journal of Children's Spirituality, 5(2)*, 203–220.

Calliou, S. (1995). Peacekeeping actions at home: A medicine wheel model for a peacekeeping pedagogy. In M. Battiste & J. Barman (Eds.), *First Nations education in Canada: The circle unfolds* (pp. 47–72). Vancouver: UBC Press.

Carter, S.L. (1993). *The culture of disbelief: How American law and politics trivialize religious devotion*. New York: BasicBooks.

Coles, R. (1990). *The spiritual life of children*. Boston: Houghton Mifflin.

Erricker, C. (2001). Living in a post-punk papacy: Religion and education in a modernist world. *International Journal of Children's Spirituality, 22(1)*, 73–85.

Erricker, C., Erricker, J., Sullivan, D., Ota, C., & Fletcher, M. (1997). *The education of the whole child*. London: Cassell.

Erricker, J., Ota, C., & Erricker C. (Eds.). (2001). *Spiritual education: Cultural, religious and social differences*. Brighton: Sussex Academic Press.

Evans, D. (1993). *Spirituality and human nature*. Albany: State University of New York Press.

Fowler, J. (1980). *Stages of faith*. New York: Harper & Row.

Goldman, R. (1964). *Religious thinking from childhood to adolescence*. London: Routledge & Kegan Paul.

Goodall, J. (1990). *Jane Goodall: My life with the chimpanzees*. Washington, DC: National Geographic Society.

Gopnik, A., Meltzoff, A. N., & Kuhl, P. K. (1999). *The scientist in the crib: Minds, brains, and how children learn*. New York: William Morrow.

Grimmitt, M. (1987). *Religious education and human development: The relationship between studying religions and personal and social and moral education*. Great Wakering, UK: McCrimmon.

Hadot, P. (1995). *Philosophy as a way of life: Spiritual exercises from Socrates to Foucault*. Oxford: Blackwell.

Hawker, P. (2000). *Secret affairs of the soul: Ordinary people's extraordinary experiences of the sacred*. Kelowna, BC: Northstone.

Hay, D. (1982). *Exploring inner space. Scientists and religious experience*. Harmondsworth, UK: Penguin.

Hay, D. (2000). Spirituality versus individualism: Why we should nurture our relational consciousness. *International Journal of Children's Spirituality, (1)*, 37–48.

Hay, D., & Nye, R. (1998). *The spirit of the child*. London: Fount Paperbacks, HarperCollins.

Hillis, V. (Ed.). (1999). *The lure of the transcendent: Collected essays by Dwayne E. Huebner*. Mahwah, NJ: Erlbaum.

Kovel, J. (1991). *History and spirit: An inquiry into the philosophy of liberation*. Boston: Beacon Press.

Levine, S. (1999). Children's cognition as the foundation of spirituality. *International Journal of Children's Spirituality, 4(2)*, 121–140.

Mattingly, M.A., with Stuart, C. (2001). Competencies for professional child and youth work practitioners. http://www.acycp.org, North American Certification Project.

McLaughlin, T.H. (2001). A spiritual dimension to sex education? *International Journal of Children's Spirituality, 6(2)*, 223–232.

Moffett, J. (1994). *The universal schoolhouse: Spiritual awakening through education*. San Francisco: Jossey-Bass.

Moxley, R.S. (2000). *Leadership and spirit: Breathing new vitality and energy into individuals an organizations*. San Francisco: Jossey-Bass and the Center for Creative Leadership.

Ó Murchú, D. (1998). *Reclaiming spirituality*. New York: Crossroad.

Owen, H. (1987). *Spirit: Transformation and development in organizations*. Potomac, MD: Abbott.

Palmer, P.J. (1983). *To know as we are known: A spirituality of education*. New York: Harper & Row.

Palmer, P.J. (1998). *The courage to teach: Exploring the inner landscape of a teacher's life*. San Francisco: Jossey-Bass.

Pinar, W.F., Reynolds, W.M., Slattery, P., & Taubman, P.M. (1995). *Understanding curriculum: An introduction to the study of historical and contemporary curriculum discourses*. New York: Peter Lang.

Robinson, E. (1983). *The original vision: A study of the religious experience of childhood*. New York: Seabury Press.

Scott, D.G. (1993). In and between: Poetry self other language movement. *Curriculum and Instruction*. Victoria, BC: University of Victoria.

Scott, D.G. (2001). Storytelling, voice and qualitative research: Spirituality as a site of ambiguity and difficulty. *Spiritual education: cultural, religious and social differences*. Brighton, UK: Sussex Academic Press.

Sweet, L. (1997). *God in the classroom*. Toronto: McClelland and Stewart.

Torrance, R.M. (1994). *The spiritual quest: Transcendence in myth, religion, and science*. Berkeley: University of California Press.

United Nations Convention on the Rights of the Child. (1991). Ottawa, Ministry of Supply and Services Canada: 28.

9

The Child as Agent in Family Life

LEON KUCZYNSKI AND SUSAN LOLLIS

There is increasing recognition within the social sciences that children have been viewed through narrow and restrictive lenses. Research questions regarding children and the categories and contexts used to describe them have mostly reflected the experiences and agendas of adults, rather than those of children as actors and agents in their own right. In developmental psychology, the lenses of development and socialization focused upon children as incomplete or unfinished products in the process of becoming adults and acquiring adult competencies, knowledge, and culture (Hogan, Etz, & Tudge, 1999; Mayall, 1994; James & Prout, 1990). In sociology, children have been all but ignored except as they affect the roles, relationships, and concerns of adults (Shehan & Seccombe, 1996). Neglected has been the lens of children as 'being' – the lived experiences of children in their everyday lives, family dynamics, and relationships as understood by children from their own perspective.

Central to the project of re-visioning of the roles and behaviours of children in disciplines such as developmental psychology, behavioural genetics, and the sociology of childhood is the idea that children are actors and agents in family life. Developmental psychology's perspective on children's agency has been shaped by the study of parent-child interaction, where it was learned that children, from the first days of life, actively engage parents in social interactions and shape the nature of the environments in which their parents raise them (Grusec & Goodnow, 1994). Behavioural genetics has contributed new conceptualizations of the way in which children actively manifest gene-environment interactions (Rowe, 1994; Scarr, 1992, 1993). The sociology of childhood, a new field, is centred on the idea that children are active social agents who influence the structures and processes around them and whose relationships and cultures should be studied for their own sake independent of adult agendas (Corsaro, 1997; Morrow, 2003).

All of these disciplinary perspectives share a common interest in developing an alternative to the passive conception of the child that developed under the conceptual framework of socialization theory. The focus of traditional perspectives on socialization was on the intergenerational transmission of values, knowledge, and other products of adult culture. Socialization within the family was regarded as a unidirectional process of influence in which parents moulded and shaped their children's development (Hartup, 1978). Hidden in the language and concepts of socialization theory was an unstated assumption about agency. Parents were considered to be the active agents in the socialization process, and research was concerned with the dimensions and characteristics of parental behaviour, such as parental attitudes and discipline strategies (Baumrind, 1971), that were presumed to constitute parents' activities as socializers of their children. Children were considered to be the passive recipients and products of parental socialization efforts, and research on children focused on variables such as compliance, internalization, personality, achievement, and other characteristics that were presumed to constitute the outcomes of parental socialization. The very language of socialization research made it difficult to conceive of the child as being active in any meaningful way. For example, words and phrases such as 'teaching,' 'disciplining,' 'nurturing,' 'guiding,' 'monitoring, ' child rearing,' 'child management,' and even the term 'parenting' all assert that the parent is the agent in parent-child relations. The same words seem unnatural or have no counterparts when applied to children's actions toward parents. In contrast, terms exclusively applied to children, such as 'compliance,' 'submission,' 'obedience,' 'learning,' or, more negatively, 'noncompliance,' 'disobedience,' 'misbehaviour,' and 'transgression' all assert that the proper role for well-developing, competent children is passive conformity to parental demands and expectations.

Critiques of this view of socialization both as a process of cultural transmission and as a family process are not new. The perspective was unrealistically optimistic about the conformity of individuals to social demands and promoted a model of society that was deterministic, uniform, and unchanging (Wrong, 1961). Additionally, it underestimated the active and innovative capacities of children in interpreting and modifying the ideas of the previous generation (Sapir, 1934). Essentially, traditional socialization theories provided a simplistic perspective on very complex processes and overlooked the importance of children in the process of socialization, in family life, and in society.

Although the idea of the child as having an active role in socialization has been evolving for several decades, there is renewed vigour in theorizing children's agency. We have been drawing together ideas from psychology, sociology, and behavioural genetics to develop a comprehensive framework in which to study the child as an agent in family life. The purpose of this chapter is to unpack the concept of children's agency, first, by reviewing the conceptual tools available in the social sciences for understanding human agency, and second, by showing our efforts to use these tools to form a new lens for perceiving how young children act as agents in their everyday interactions with parents.

Elsewhere, we have reviewed research and theoretical literature that places the study of children's agency in a larger conceptual framework that we have called a 'bilateral model of parent-child relations' (Kuczynski, 2003; Kuczynski & Lollis, 2002; Lollis & Kuczynski, 1997). The bilateral model considers how phenomena such as the bidirectional influence in the family, the agency of parent and child, and the dynamics of power asymmetries in parent-child relations must be understood in the distinctive intimate, enduring, and interdependent context of the parent-child relationship. The model also asserts that the context of parent-child relationships themselves must be understood in the context of culture (Kuczynski, 2003; Trommsdorff & Kornadt, 2003). This is important because cultures differ in their norms regarding the kinds of power relations and levels of intimacy that are appropriate for parent-child relationships.

In the model of children's agency that we will be presenting, the goal is to identify the dimensions of agency that can be considered as universal or human characteristics. However, we recognize that the form in which these dimensions are expressed will depend on the specific cultural context of parent-child relationships. Our research is designed to understand how children act as agents in the context of parent-child relationships in North American culture. In the North American context, there has been considerable social change in norms regarding parent-child relationships throughout the twentieth century. Notably, Alwin (1996) has found a dramatic decrease in strict obedience as a child-rearing goal and an increase in preference for children to be independent and to express their autonomy in the parent-child relationship. In addition, there have been changes in fathers' involvement in the child-rearing process and, more generally, in parents' valuing of and enjoyment of close parent-child relationships for their own sake (Hoffman, 1988). We would argue that the context of parent-child relationships in contemporary Western culture affords children considerable scope both to express their agency and to have such expressions accepted by their parents.

The Concept of Agency

At the heart of the bilateral framework for studying relationships is the assumption that children and their parents are equally agents (Kuczynski, 2003; Kuczynski & Lollis, 2002). This is a difficult idea to understand given the power difference between parents and children and the role and responsibilities of parents as socializing agents. However, the concept of equal agency can be understood if one first appreciates our separation of the concept of agency from the concept of power. We assume the main categories of agency as universal givens; all individuals cannot help but be agents. However, individuals differ in the extent to which their practice of agency is supported by resources or power. Parents, especially when their children are young, are equipped with more individual and cultural resources than their children. Parents have a greater capacity for both coercion and reward, and more expertise in forming and acting on long-term goals for their children. Nevertheless, we believe that no matter how great the difference in power between parents and children or what differences in maturity, the agency of children can be understood using the same categories as the agency of parents.

In the broadest terms, agency is used to describe an individual in an active role rather than a passive one, in the role of actor rather than reactor. Many different ideas have been associated with the concept of agency, including self, autonomy, intentionality, creativity, and initiative. The social sciences have been unsystematic in the analysis of agency, each discipline or theory emphasizing one aspect and ignoring others. In addition, most concepts of agency were originally developed with adult actors in mind. However, our review of the interdisciplinary literature indicated to us that despite differences in language, similar important ideas have emerged concerning the concept of agency. These are the ideas of *autonomy*, a motivational aspect of agency; *construction*, a cognitive aspect of agency; and *action*, a behavioural aspect of agency. Separate literatures have grown up around these components in isolation. Although we will describe them separately for the purposes of analysis, the components are interconnected in children's expressions of self in everyday life.

Autonomy

The aspect of agency we call autonomy refers to an individual's conception and expression of self in interpersonal relations. We distinguish two aspects of autonomy that have been considered by the research literature, self-determination and self-preservation.

Self-determination refers to a human motive to achieve personal control over interactions with the environment (White, 1959; Skinner, 1995). The attainment of a sense of personal control over environmental outcomes has long been considered important for enhancing an individual's feelings of competence and well-being. In contrast, individuals feel helpless or incompetent when they are not able to influence their social and physical environments (Seligman, 1975). From the first weeks of life, infants have been found to respond more positively when their actions on the physical or social environment get a contingent response and more negatively when they do not get a response. This phenomenon has had a powerful effect on developmental psychology and has been fundamental to the analyses of the impact of responsive and nonresponsive parenting on children's attachment, their concept of self, and their cognitive outcomes.

Children's preference for personal mastery of the environment has also been studied in the context of different theories of intrinsic motivation, such as the attribution theory of socialization (Lepper, 1983) and, most recently, self-determination theory (Grolnick, Deci, & Ryan, 1997). These theories seek to understand how parents may engage internal sources of motivation for valued behaviour in children, such as achievement or moral values, and how they can avoid undermining intrinsic motivation by excessive external control. In summary, individuals of all ages prefer to have personal control over outcomes: they seek out environments that respond to their initiations, they thrive when they get a response, and they may experience helplessness or dissatisfaction when the environment is unresponsive to their efforts.

Self-preservation is another aspect of autonomy that is assumed to be universal and is also not dependent on the age of the individual. Self-preservation refers to a motive to preserve the self from excessive control by others. For instance, psychological reactance (Brehm, 1981) refers to the motive to restore self-perceived behavioural freedoms that have been threatened or eliminated. The stronger the external threat or pressure to comply, the stronger the reactance motivation. Reactance may be masked by a person's overt compliance while the threat is present. However, the individual may act to restore his or her freedom when it is safe to do so.

In psychotherapy and behaviour therapy the same phenomenon of autonomy preservation has been studied as a practical problem that diminishes the effectiveness of psychotherapy and behaviour-therapy interventions. The concepts of client resistance (Wade, 1997) and counter control (Davidson, 1973) suggest that therapeutic interventions may fail because clients engage in acts of autonomy protection. In other words, they actively or passively resist doing what their high-powered therapists think is best for them.

The idea of resistance as reflecting a self-preservation motive can also be found in classic analyses of toddler negativism in developmental psychology (Wenar, 1982). There is evidence that by the second year of life, when toddlers become more and more able to comply because of maturation in cognitive and self-regulatory skills (Kopp, 1982), they also become less and less willing to comply. During this time children are thought to develop a sense of independent self and a motive to resist threats to their autonomy. This apparent motivational change is manifested by a period of negativism or increased active resistance to parental requests and commands. Early research on toddler negativism suggested that the frequency of overt acts of defiance peaks at age two and wanes by early school age. However, we have argued (Kuczynski & Kochanska, 1990) that once they appear, resistance and other forms of autonomy assertion remain a continuing theme in parent-child relations. Negativism appears to disappear because children develop social skills that enable them to express their autonomy publicly in subtle, socially acceptable ways. Consistent with the autonomy-development hypothesis, several studies have found that passive non-compliance becomes replaced by more active forms of resistance during the second and third years of life (Kuczynski, Kochanska, Radke-Yarrow, & Gurinius Brown, 1987) and from the toddler period to age five (Kuczynski & Kochanska, 1990). Other research (McQuillen, 1986) indicates that the strategic quality of children's non-compliance continues to develop into adolescence. Evidence of the cross-cultural generality of children's expression of autonomy through resistance to adult demands and restrictions has been found in research with South African children (Reynolds, 1991) and children in rural Bolivia (Punch, 2002).

The motive of self-preservation can also seem to disappear by going underground, especially in circumstances when direct expression would be dangerous or maladaptive. Sociologists, in particular, have explored concealed or symbolic forms of autonomy expression. Examples include Erving Goffman's (1961) concept of secondary adjustment and James Scott's (1990) concept of everyday resistance to oppression.

In his classic work, *Asylums*, Goffman (1961) described how inmates of institutions such as mental hospitals, prisons, and concentration camps preserve their definition of themselves by resisting, evading, or negating the total control of authorities. Goffman introduced the concept of primary adjustment and secondary adjustment to organizations in order to describe actions that are done in the service of preservation of the self. Primary adjustment refers to an individual's complete conformity or willing identification with the wishes of the organization. Secondary adjustment refers to efforts on the part of a member of an organization to employ unauthorized means or to obtain unauthorized ends in an attempt to get around the organization's assumptions as to what the member should do and should be. The concept of secondary adjustment considers a whole array of activities, some proscribed, some not strictly forbidden, which express the attitude that the individual remains his or her own self despite being under the control of another. Sometimes a person expresses overt non-compliance, or defiance. More often, individuals covertly mock the authority or communicate that compliance is non-voluntary or carried out purely to meet self-serving ends. Other examples include complying in the most minimal way possible, evading unwanted duties, pilfering office or cleaning supplies, and showing rigidly stereotyped and obviously insincere signs of deference and respect. Secondary adjustments are interesting because they highlight the difference between public conformity and private opposition to authority. A person may publicly comply with an authority but privately signal independence and perhaps rejection of the authority's goals.

An interesting aspect of Goffman's treatment of secondary adjustments is that most of the acts of autonomy expression that individuals make are contained. They are incorporated as 'small acts of living' (Goffman, 1961, p. 181) into everyday contexts without disrupting the day-to-day functioning of the institution. In other words, the individual goes along with the general definition of the situation, but in small ways refuses to allow that definition to fix the boundaries of his or her behaviour (Ingram, 1986). Institutional authorities, for their part, are sometimes aware that this is going on and, depending on circumstances, may turn a blind eye to the existence of secondary adjustments in order to prevent more serious acts of rebellion.

The concept of secondary adjustments is relevant to the study of children's agency in the family because it provides a framework for studying an unacknowledged, yet prevalent, aspect of everyday family life that has been missing from traditional socialization research. The idea that contained secondary adjustments are implicitly tolerated by institutions is analogous to parental acceptance of some forms of autonomy expression within the parent-child relationship. Children's expressions of autonomy and parents' reactions to them do not occur in isolation, but in the context of an interdependent relationship in which each must accommodate to the needs and goals of the other. A quote from Mark Twain's essay 'Advice to Little Girls' illustrates this discussion of secondary adjustment: 'If your mother tells you to do a thing, it is wrong to reply that you won't. It is better and more becoming to intimate that you will do as she bids you, and then afterward act quietly in the manner according to the dictates of your best judgment.'

Corsaro (1997) describes incidents of secondary adjustments in the context of nursery school. He observed that children often evaded adult rules by collaborating with peers in secondary adjustments that enabled them to gain a certain amount of control over their lives. For example, in response to a standing rule prohibiting children from bringing toys from home, a popular practice developed whereby children continued to bring toys but concealed them and exchanged them in secret. The response of the teachers to these actions of self-preservation on the part of the children was to tolerate this as a 'contained' secondary adjustment. Teachers were amused at the creativity of the children and, at the same time, recognized that this particular expression of autonomy did not threaten the larger goals of the prohibition that they established.

Another sociological treatment of the motive of self-preservation comes from research on autonomy expression in populations where there are huge and oppressive discrepancies in power. Scott (1990), in his *Domination and the Arts of Resistance*, considered relations between peasants and landowners in Third World countries, populations under totalitarianism, and slaves and slave owners in America. We do not wish to imply that relations between parents and children are analogous to those between slaves and slave owners, particularly since it is sometimes debatable as to which would be which; however, the larger point that Scott makes concerns the human condition. Whenever people are blatantly controlled or abused, humiliated or exploited, they resist. When there is gross power imbalance, direct opposition or rebellion could be unwise or dangerous. Instead, the powerless adapt to their situation, make a performance of compliance and deference in face-to-face encounters with their oppressors, but covertly express their resistance in prudent, concealed, and creative ways. To illustrate this, Scott quoted an Ethiopian proverb that indicates both the ubiquitous nature of the self-preservation motive even among the most powerless and the hidden forms that its expression takes: 'When the great lord passes the wise peasant bows deeply and silently farts' (Scott, 1990, p. v).

We think it is important to study the nature of these acts of resistance in children. Although there is a difference in some forms of power between children and parents in normal families, such power is not necessarily oppressive or arbitrary. However, a more direct analogy between the relations in the populations studied by Scott and parent-child relations can be found in families where authoritarian power structures prevail and also in families where there has been physical and sexual child abuse. It is remarkable that there is little literature or theory on children's agency in these situations. Indeed, researchers may have considered it inappropriate to regard abused children as agents for fear that such research might invite blaming or laying responsibility for avoiding abuse on the victim. However, we believe that the study of children's agency needs to include oppressed children. According to Alanen (1990), 'it is methodologically wrong for researchers to consider children as passive objects or victims no matter how much children appear to be victims in their real-life situations' (p. 20). Currently there are only a few case studies, such as David Pelzer's (1995) autobiographical *A Child Called 'It'* and qualitative investigations by clinical researchers (Kelly, 1988; Kitzinger, 1990; Wade, 1997), that describe how children act as agents even in families where physical or sexual child abuse is occurring. These studies suggest that children do not passively submit to their victimization but attempt to pre-empt, evade, resist, or decrease the physical and psychological impact of sexual assault, or exact retribution by a large array of creative behavioural and cognitive strategies. Moreover, Kitzinger (1990) describes how children not only act individually in these circumstances, but also form alliances with siblings or other persons in their resistance to adult violence. The study of children's agency even in the face of an extreme power imbalance enables researchers to see children's agency as an exemplar of a fully human phenomenon that must be accommodated in our theories.

Construction

The dimension of agency we call construction emphasizes the capacity of children to create new meanings from their interactions with their environments. This differs from the concept of intergenerational transmission in traditional socialization theories. The socialization metaphor of transmission suggests that ideas and values are transmitted without change from the older generation and passively received by the younger generation (Strauss, 1992). The idea that children actively interpret information in their environment, including the information provided by parents, can be found in the writings of many developmental psychologists such as Piaget (1965) and Kohlberg (1969) and is a central tenet of symbolic interactionism (Mead, 1934). There are many examples of studies that have investigated children's own understanding of phenomena such as parental divorce and relationships within the family (Hogan et al., 1999). Such studies indicate that children inherently make their own sense of their experiences in the family. Recently, however, conceptions of the construction process, inspired by Vygotsky, are increasingly being applied to understanding the cognitive aspect of children's agency. According to Vygotsky, children make use of information available in the culture in the attempt to solve everyday problems. However, this process of using cultural knowledge is not passive because children must interpret that information in terms of their own current understanding and adapt that knowledge to fit the tasks at hand. This process allows children to participate actively in the culture and create new meanings that they introduce back into the culture.

Within psychology, Lawrence and Valsiner (1993) amplify this idea of cognitive construction in their concepts of internalization and externalization. In their view, internalization refers to the cognitive processing that takes place as children attempt to understand the social environment in terms of their personal experiences and ways of knowing. Externalization refers to the further processing that takes place as children manifest or act upon what they know. 'The latter relation takes the form of externalization of one's "personal culture" – organization of one's environment and external appearance in ways that fit the person's internalized psychological "needs." The externalization of the person's (previously) internalized psychological processes reintroduces the products of internalization into the sphere of social transaction' (Lawrence & Valsiner, 1993, p. 288). Thus, innovative construction occurs at two levels. Messages, values, and other information emanating from parents or the culture at large undergo a process of interpretation and transformation as they are internalized and a process of interpretation and transformation as they are externalized. This conception of the cognitive constructive process is especially useful for understanding socialization as a process of continual innovation involving transactions and reconstructions between the parent, the child, and society and contributing to changes in each over time (Kuczynski, Marshall, & Schell, 1997).

Sociologist Corsaro (1997) has developed a similar idea of the constructive process in his conception of interpretive reproduction. According to Corsaro, interpretive reproduction involves a process of appropriation, reinvention, and reproduction. By appropriation, Corsaro means that children use elements of adult culture for their own purposes and needs: 'The term interpretive captures the innovative and creative aspects of children's participation in society' (Corsaro, 1997, p. 18). Children, like adults, are constrained by society's rules and scripts. However, children have a great deal of leeway to interpret or challenge cultural prescriptions. Children, therefore, play a very active role in the process of socialization. Children do not just repeat old patterns, as intergenerational transmission models would predict; they also invent new possibilities for thought and action and introduce novelty and change into society.

Like Lawrence and Valsiner (1993), Corsaro (1997) stresses the creative dimensions of agency. However, he places particular emphasis on peers in the process of construction. Children do not always act as agents alone; they often collaborate with peers and siblings in a peer culture that operates alongside the adult culture of their parents and other authorities. The peer culture is important because it is a separate source of cultural knowledge and practices that eventually also become translated into knowledge and skills necessary in the adult world (Rubin, Bukowski, & Parker, 1998). Moreover, in the peer culture, children collaborate in the process of reworking adult knowledge, thus adding an additional process of innovation. Lastly, as was discussed earlier, the peer group provides an under-life that operates alongside, and in reaction to, the rules imposed by parents and teachers and that impinge on children's autonomy. It is within this under-life that children also collectively find creative ways to mock authority, evade, judge, or challenge adult rules, and collectively gain a measure of control over their own lives.

Action

The idea of agency as action emphasizes the behavioural aspects of agency. A large body of research has documented the massive impact that infants and children have on the lives of parents, not all of which can be attributed to the agency of children. Many important influences of children on parents are inadvertent consequence of simply being present in the parents' environment. For example, during the first two years of life the presence of children in the parents' environment has been found to affect their health, structure of daily activities, employment and finances, marital satisfaction, social interactions, community interactions, personality, attitudes, values and beliefs, life plans, and feelings of control over their lives (Ambert, 2001). Moreover, in the process of rearing their children, parents experience many challenges, emotional experiences and opportunities for problem solving that also indirectly cause changes in their personality, attitudes, and values (Frankel, 1991; Palkovitz, 1996). Centrally relevant to the study of children's agency is observational research by developmental psychologists on parent-child interaction demonstrating how children actively influence parents during social interactions. Two categories of research on children's actions on parents are children's temperament and children's strategic action.

TEMPERAMENT

Temperament refers to the child's early personality, which is generally accepted as reflecting an interaction between the child's biological inheritance and his or her environment. Historically, the study of children's temperament was important in illustrating the capacity of children to influence and shape the parents' behaviour and therefore the child's own environment. This was often conceptualized as children being agents of their own socialization (Bell, 1968; Bell & Chapman, 1986; Bell & Harper, 1977).

Early research on the effects of children's temperament on parents described temperament in terms of global traits such as social responsiveness, dependence, and difficult temperament (Sanson & Rothbart, 1995). From the point of view of a theory of agency, this research could

be considered ambiguous because a category such as difficult temperament implies a relatively indirect form of influence or leaves unclear
the precise nature of the child's behaviour that influenced the parent.
The concept of temperament, for example, conveys the idea of the child
as having a global, diffuse, and inadvertent effect on the family environment that makes it possible to overlook the direct agency of the
child.

However, behavioural geneticists have recently begun to talk in a
more active way about the influence of children on their environment,
through their genotype. The child's inherited genotype is thought to
determine not only how environments are experienced by the child,
but also which environments the child will seek for himself or herself
(Scarr, 1993; Rowe, 1994). In this way, the genotype acts through the
child to create an environment for itself. According to Scarr, there are
three ways that a child's genotype works to influence and select
the environment (Scarr & McCartney, 1983). First, the genotype can
'passively' reside in an environment provided by genetically similar
parents who create a rearing environment that is correlated with the
genotype of the child. Second, the genotype can 'evoke' responses
from the parents that may be either rewarding or punitive. Third, the
genotype can influence a child's 'selective' attention to aspects of the
environment which are compatible with the child's talents, interests,
and personality and actively interprets the environment in unique ways.
Conceptualized in this way, a fine-grained analysis of the behaviour of
a child of a given temperament may reveal that each child's expression of agency has a unique, biologically influenced style with characteristic patterns of action, individual patterns of construction, and
unique concerns and intensities regarding autonomy expression and
protection.

STRATEGIC ACTION

Studies of parent-child interaction have also contributed to the understanding of children's agency. The child's direct activity is easier to
perceive in research that describes the specific behaviours and strategies that children use to influence parents during social interactions.

In early studies of adult-infant interactions, infants were described as
influencing their mothers by means of non-verbal 'cues and bids.' They
signal their needs and emotional states through emotional cues such as
cries and facial expressions (Lewis & Feinman, 1991; Lewis & Rosenblum,
1974; Ross & Lollis, 1987; Stern, 1977). They also initiate interactions

and provide differential feedback, rewarding and punishing mothers' attempts at care or communication. Rheingold (1969) illustrated how a presumably helpless infant takes an active and powerful role from birth in shaping the lives of parents in a mutual process of socialization. Infants, by the powerful feedback of their rewarding smiles and aversive cries, teach ordinary women and men to become mothers and fathers: 'The infant modulates, tempers, regulates, and refines the caretaker's activities. He produces delicate shades and nuances in these operations to suit his own needs of the moment. By such responses as fretting, sounds of impatience or satisfaction, by facial expressions of pleasure, contentment, or alertness he produces elaborations here and dampening there' (Rheingold, 1969; p. 785).

Particularly compelling evidence for the agency of the child is found during situations of parent-child conflict and parental discipline, which in the older socialization literature constituted the prototype of unidirectional influence where parents clearly seemed to have the upper hand. Studies of children's interactive behaviours during episodes of parental discipline and control have illustrated not only how children actively modify the strategies parents direct towards them, but also how children actively resist and negotiate the nature of parental demands.

At the most indirect level, an important determinant of parental strategies is the nature of the child's misbehaviour (e.g., Grusec & Kuczynski, 1980; Lollis, Ross, & Tate, 1992; Grusec & Goodnow, 1994). Some transgressions predictably elicit strategies of power assertion, such as punishment or force, and some transgressions predictably elicit psychological forms of control, such as reasoning or guilt induction. To an important extent, children's choice of transgression influences parents' choice of discipline or control strategy.

Children's interactive behaviours have also been viewed as intentional strategies that they employ to influence parents. Patterson's research on coercive processes in families of clinic-referred aggressive children describes the active role that children take in controlling the outcomes of parent-child conflict (Patterson, 1982; Patterson, Reid, & Dishion, 1992). Analyses of social interactions among family members in the home indicate how pre-adolescent children contribute to the initiation and escalation of aggressive patterns of parent-child interaction. Children initiate coercive interactions and contribute to the escalation of irritable coercive interactions by using unpleasant coercive behaviours as social strategies to get what they want from their parents. Moreover, conduct-disordered children become quite effective in exercising their coercive skills and frequently sidetrack and evade effective disciplinary responses by the parent and intimidate parents to avoid confronting bad behaviour altogether.

Research with normative, well-functioning families also illustrates the daily use of strategic action by children in their everyday interactions with parents (e.g., Crockenberg & Littman, 1990; Eisenberg, 1992; Kuczynski & Kochanska, 1990; Kuczynski et al., 1987; Perlman & Ross, 1997). Thus, children issue commands and suggestions to parents with expectations of parental compliance. They actively resist intrusions on their autonomy. They use reasoning, question parental actions, and negotiate compromises with their parents.

A series of qualitative interview studies indicates that children are aware of their ability to influence parents and can verbalize the strategic nature of their actions. For example, in a recent study (Hildebrandt & Kuczynski, 1998), nine- to twelve-year-old children were asked about their ability to influence their own mother, their friend's mother, or an unfamiliar mother in various situations. Children expressed greater confidence that they would be successful in influencing their own mothers than mothers who were not their own. Children's explanations of their enhanced sense of agency in their interactions with their own mothers included an implicit understanding of the unique relationship they have with their mothers and how the relationship context can be worked to their advantage. For example, in contrast to unrelated mothers, children could base their attempts at influence on an intimate knowledge of their mothers' personality, on knowledge of their mothers' reactions in similar past situations, and on expectations of entitlements stemming from the relationship. Children report that they more often rely on direct, assertive strategies with their own mothers (Hildebrandt & Kuczynski, 1998). One girl in grade 4 outlined the following deliberate campaign of pestering: 'I'd ask my mom if we could watch T.V. and I'd keep asking her and asking her and asking her, but if she ... kept on saying "no" after I say it a thousand times or something, I'd stop.'

In another study, mothers and fathers of school age children described a variety of strategies and capacities of their children when explaining why they had complied with their children's demands to change an aspect of their behaviour (Ta, Kuczynski, Bernardini, & Harach, 1999). Examples included direct assertion (91 per cent), negotiation (72 per cent), and expertise (58 per cent). The following quotations illustrate that parents attribute both legitimacy and expertise to their children's actions: 'In [older son's] case, it is his ability to make an effective argument, to bring in the right hooks. In [younger son's] case, it's the ability that he has to make me forget what it was that I was against; you know it's his ability to reroute the whole thing, to take me on another way' (mother of ten- and eight- year-old boys).

Parents also acknowledged the psychological sophistication of their children's influence strategies: 'She is very good at emotional blackmail. She's a child which will, when something is not given, or denied to her, she can turn it around. She can look very upset, cry, she turns it around like "that means you don't like me." It's the pure emotional blackmail, she's very good at that. She's very good at working your conscience' (mother of a ten-year-old girl).

Children appear to be aware of the benefits of 'psychological' forms of discipline with parents. An early study (Parke, Sebastian, Collmer, and Sawin, 1974, cited in Parke, 1974) described the strategic quality of the children's responses to the reprimands of adults. After viewing a videotape of a child being reprimanded for deliberately knocking a book off a peer's desk, children as young as age four years had well-defined expectations about how adults would react to different responses (reparation, pleading, ignoring, defying) to the reprimand. Children predicted that they could elicit more positive reactions from the adult if they made reparative gestures than if they reacted with defiance.

Although there is much still to be discovered about children's strategic and planned actions within family life, it is already possible to describe children's behavioural agency using categories that are identical to those used to describe parents.

Agency in the Context of the Parent-Child Relationship

We would like to return to a point made earlier that the child's agency, influence, and power in family life must be understood in the special context of the parent-child relationship. In the developmental literature, the parent-child relationship is increasingly being considered an essential micro-context that both constrains and supports children's development and action (Reiss, Collins, & Berscheid, 2000).

Extrapolating from general theories on close relationships (Hinde, 1979; Kelly, et al., 1983; Maccoby & Martin, 1983) to parent-child relationships, we (Lollis & Kuczynski, 1997) argued that the parent-child relationship contributes distinctive dynamics to the patterns of influence, agency, and power that children experience in their interactions with parents. The long-term nature of the parent-child relationship contributes expectancies formed from the past history of the relationship and anticipations of the future course of the relationship, both of which influence the way that parents and children interact in the present. Moreover, parents and children are both thought to participate in this interdependent, intimate relationship where the parents' needs and goals are intertwined with the children's needs and goals.

Essentially, a relational perspective considers that interactions between persons who have a close, enduring relationship follow different dynamics from interactions between adults and children who are unfamiliar with each other (Dawber & Kuczynski, 1999). The close relationship context both facilitates and constrains the agency of the relationship partners and makes possible distinctive interactional dynamics including a high degree of mutual influence, a considerable amount of both cooperation and conflict, and patterns of extraordinary power and vulnerability.

Learning to See Agency in Children's Responses to Parental Control

In our current research we are exploring the implications of an enhanced perspective on children's agency for the way children are perceived and described in research on parent-child interactions. We think of our work as 'learning to see agency' in children because the unilateral socialization model is so culturally ingrained that the ordinary language of parenting has not allowed us to 'see' the agency of children. We are reminded of a story told by Lawrence Blair (1975) in his book *Rhythms of Vision*:

> When Magellan's expedition first landed at Tierra del Fuego, the Fuegans, who for centuries had been isolated with their canoe culture, were unable to see the ships that were anchored in the bay. [The ships] were so far beyond their experience that, despite their bulk, the horizon continued unbroken: the ships were invisible. This was learned on later expeditions to the area when the Fuegans described how, according to one account, the shaman had first brought to the villagers' attention that the strangers had arrived in something, something which although outside their experience could be seen if one looked carefully. We ask how could they not see the ships – they were so obvious, so 'real' – yet others ask how we cannot see things just as obviously real. (p. 30)

The traditional perspective on children's obedience was imbued with a double standard regarding the perception of behaviour. Even when parents and children performed the objectively identical behaviour such as conforming to or resisting another's request, these behaviours were perceived as responsiveness or sensitivity when performed by the parent and compliance when performed by the child; as competent assertion or agency by the parent and non-compliance, defiance, misbehaviour, wilfulness, in short, deviance by the child.

Compliance with, or obedience to, a parent's request or command was conceptualized in a manner consistent with unidirectional parent-to-child determinism. Typical operationalizatons of this concept defined compliance as a match between the child's behaviour and the parent's request occurring within six to fifteen seconds after the request (Kuczynski & Hildebrandt, 1997). Immediate compliance was considered to be a form of child competence; non-compliance was considered to be coercive or incompetent behaviour. Early research conducted from this perspective focused on how parents used discipline strategies that ensured that conflicts ended with children's compliance with the parents' wishes. However, once researchers started observing naturally occurring parent-child interactions, empirical findings emerged which were not consistent with the traditional view of compliance. First, children in natural settings were much less controlled and parents were much less controlling than the traditional perspectives suggested. Moreover, conflict appeared to be a normative, mutually tolerated feature of parent-child relationships.

Research on non-compliance indicated that children in non-clinic families do no comply with 20 per cent to 40 per cent of parental commands (Kuczynski et al., 1987). Incidents of verbal conflict, such as disagreements about parental assertions of fact, are even higher. Parent-child verbal conflict was studied by Eisenberg (1992) at age four and by Vuchinch (1987) at adolescence. At both ages, 60 per cent of parent-child verbal disagreements were found to end in a stand-off or mutual non-compliance. As the researchers noted, parents don't seem to enforce compliance as much as earlier theories about parental control seem to suggest.

Parallel to the conflict literature was research documenting the extraordinary degree of mutual cooperation involved in early parent-child interactions. Researchers such as Maccoby and Martin (1983) and Fogel (1993) used terms such as co-regulation to indicate the close co-ordination between parent and child that is involved in the performance of compliant behaviour. The idea of co-regulation suggested that early compliance is a process of mutual cooperation and not merely a process of the child's submission to the control strategies of the parent. Other researchers (Rheingold, Cook, & Kolowitz, 1987; Kochanska & Aksan, 1995) found that a large proportion of early compliance was carried out with enthusiasm and willingness – a willingness that appears to be voluntarily given and not coerced by parents.

In summary, research on parent-child relations during the past couple of decades has produced a picture of mutual conflict and cooperation that does not fit well with either the external or the internal control perspectives on children's conformity. To accommodate these kinds of findings, we have been in the process of formulating a relational perspective on children's conformity which incorporates the enhanced perspective on children's agency mentioned earlier and an emphasis on the interdependent parent-child relationship context within which children's expression of agency takes its special form.

We propose that the expression of agency in the form of negotiation, conflict, and resistance is as much a property of well-functioning close relationships as cooperation. Even when children do comply with their parents' wishes we assume that they do so on their own terms and, whenever possible, interject their own creative transformation of the parent's requests. We reason that during a history of interaction, parents and children evolve shared understandings of what will pass for compliance in their relationship. It is only on rare occasions that the shared understanding approximates the exact, immediate submission that is implied by 'compliance within fifteen seconds.' More often, what parents accept as compliance and what children understand compliance to be is closer to the ideas of accommodation and negotiation. Competent children do not comply immediately or rigidly with parental requests (Matas, Arend, & Sroufe, 1978). Instead, we suggest that socially competent children manifest a cooperative, co-regulated, but non-exact form of conformity that is consistent with the idea of 'accommodation.' Accommodation, seen as an expression of autonomy within the boundaries of a relationship, conveys the expectation of a cooperative response, but also that the form of the cooperative response will be chosen by the recipient rather than by the sender of a request. Thus, an accommodating response by children may acknowledge that the parent has been heard, that children will attempt to coordinate their own plans with the parent's wishes, or that children are willing to positively negotiate an alternative course of action. For example, an accommodating response may take the following form: 'Yeah, right! I'll see what I can do.'

Similarly, the construct of 'negotiation' conveys the distinctive standards of non-compliance within relationships. Some requests by parents are not met with compliance or even accommodation. Sometimes the child may unilaterally resist or defy the parent. Most children learn that they must express their autonomy within the constraints of an interdependent relationship. In other words, children are agents in a close relationship with other agents, including parents, whose choices clash with their own. The development of negotiation strategies can be regarded as the development of skills of co-regulation of autonomy during conflict.

Early work on this topic performed during the 1980s involved conceptualizing children's non-compliance as reflecting both the development of autonomy and the development of social skills for expressing autonomy. In one study, resistant behaviours were coded on the basis of the directness and aversiveness of the strategy from the parent's point of view (Kuczynski et al., 1987; Kuczynski & Kochanska, 1990). Using these criteria, strategies such as passive non-compliance (unassertively ignoring the parent) and direct defiance (temper tantrums, destructiveness, whining) were considered to be relatively unskilful, whereas simple refusals and negotiation (asking the parent to justify their request, providing an explanation, proposing compromises) were considered to be relatively more skilful. A longitudinal study of children from age two until age five years (Kuczynski and Kochanska 1990) found that unskilful forms of non-compliance decreased in frequency with age whereas socially skilful forms of resistance increased.

The general picture is that children do not become increasingly compliant with age, as a model of successful socialization might lead one to expect. Rather, children become increasingly assertive and skilful in expressing resistance and in coordinating parent and child viewpoints in a relationship context.

In our most recent research on bidirectional influences in the parent-child relationship (Lollis & Kuczynski, 1997), we are going beyond these early beginnings in order to explore children's agency in their non-compliance with their parents. Following our perspective on agency as expressed in the close relationship, we are especially interested in discovering how very young children assert themselves, resist control, interject their own definitions of co-operation, and engage in creative strategic action. Based on previous reports that compliance at ages two to five make up about 75 per cent of children's responses to control (Kuczynski & Kochanska, 1990), we are particularly exploring how much of this compliance takes the form of accommodation and negotiation, rather than a strict match between the wishes of the parent and the child's behaviour. We are also integrating Goffman's (1961) concept of secondary adjustment into our work to explore how children communicate their resistance in the face of parental power and also how much of this expression of autonomy ordinary parents accept or tolerate.

An innovative feature of our research design is that we observe parents interacting simultaneously with two of their children; in contrast, almost all of the existing information on parental control has considered control and compliance in interactions with only one child. Thus, we expect to observe the collaborative element of sibling alliance, highlighted by Corsaro (1997), in children's display of agency. Having a sibling present is a real-world element that permits the observation of collective forms of alliance making, cooperation, resistance, and evasion that have seldom been described in the literature. Now that we are learning to see agency in such a sensitive way, we are beginning to wonder how much 'compliance within fifteen seconds' really exists in family life. We predict that by looking at children's behaviour in this way, the proportion of compliance implied by traditional unilateral definitions will shrink considerably.

Data used for this search were part of a larger study on socialization in the family (Ross, Filyer, Lollis, Perlman, & Martin, 1994). Forty English-speaking Canadian families were recruited from birth announcements in the local newspaper of a medium-sized city within southwestern Ontario. At the beginning of the study, each family consisted of two parents and two children, all living together, with the gender of the older and gender of the younger children balanced in order to include an equal number of all possible brother/sister combinations. There were two time periods of data collection in the larger study; Time 1 when the children were 2 and 4 years of age, and Time 2 when the children were 4 and 6 years of age. Our present work focuses on Time 2. In Time 2, the older children were between 5.4 and 7.0 years of age (M = 6.3 years) and the younger children were between 3.8 and 4.8 years of age (M = 4.4 years). During Time 2, one of the original forty families was unable to be observed as they had moved away, ten families had a new baby added to their number, and in four of the families the parents were either in the process of separation or had divorced.

To collect the data, observers went into the homes of the thirty-nine families and recorded six ninety-minute observation sessions per home. In order to record the families in the most common constellations, the families were observed with both parents and children present half of the time (Family sessions) and only the mother and children present in the other half of the sessions (Mother sessions). During the sessions, the observers dictated a descriptive account of the children's interactions as well as all the parental behaviour that pertained to the actions of the children. On a second channel of a stereo tape recorder, observers recorded all of the actual dialogue that occurred within the session. Observers did not participate in the interactions that took place between family members. In order for the observation to proceed, parents and children had to be in either the same or adjacent rooms.

The audiotapes were transcribed into a coded record that included all dialogue and the type of actions that family members directed towards one another. Initially the data were coded for sequences of contiguous interaction based on a common theme (i.e., conflict interactions, pretence, games, contingent interactions).

Because we are in the initial stages of this research, we would like to give readers some idea of the diversity of children's agency in their responses to parental requests. In the coding system for children's responses to parental requests shown in Table 9.1 we integrated Goffman's (1961) concepts of primary and secondary adjustment described earlier to categorize two general orientations, cooperative and uncooperative, that children may express in the capacity of agents. Within this general framework, the coding system describes children's responses in terms of more discreet responses to the request. Three categories highlight children's expression of agency within compliance (compliance, accommodation, and cooperative negotiation) and six categories highlight children's expression of agency within non-compliance (uncooperative negotiation, unwilling or minimal compliance, passive non-compliance, simple refusal, defiance, and covert resistance). Although we do not expect to be able to assess covert resistance in the present observational data set, we include it because of its conceptual importance in Goffman's (1961) concepts of secondary adjustment and Scott's (1990) concept of everyday resistance to oppression. A goal in our future research program is to develop research methods that will enable us to observe incidents of covert resistance in schoolage children.

Table 9.1: Children's Agency – Coding Categories

Primary Adjustment Compliance	Cooperates with request with signs of enthusiasm, positive affect, or expressions conveying mutual interest
Accommodation	Non-exact cooperation with spirit of request incorporating creative elements that are not in parent's request
Cooperative negotiation	Attitude is cooperative; bargaining, proposing alternatives, or asking for explanations or clarification of request
Secondary Adjustment Uncooperative negotiation	Attitude is uncooperative; bargaining, persuading, questioning, with aim of changing request so as to do less than initially required
Unwilling/minimal compliance	Complies minimally (showing covert, unassertive non-acceptance) or complies with overt show of contrary attitude or protest (whining, anger, sullenness)
Passive non-compliance	Non-compliance by ignoring (usually marked by continuing in an activity that has been prohibited) or 'playing dumb'
Simple refusal	Refusal to comply through simple statement or direct assertion (e.g., 'no' or 'I don't want to')
Defiance	Non-compliance with signs of anger or other displays of negative affect. Deliberate show of persistence or dismissal of request.
Covert resistance	Resistance, mocking of parental authority, non-compliance occurring in absence of parents or outside of parents' line of sight, in company of siblings or peers

What follows are several mother-child interactions that have been coded. We present them here as illustrations of children's agency during interactions between parents and children.

Transcript 1: Compliance

We begin with the notion of Willing Compliance. In this interaction the mother makes a request of her child, Tom, age 6. Tom complies immediately, without challenging what his mother is requesting. The request that is complied with remains unchanged by the child.

Jane to Mother: (Setting the table for dinner) Mom, I'm going to
  have a spoon, are you?
Mother to Jane: No, thanks.
Jane to Tom: Tom?
Tom to Jane: Yes.
Jane to Tom: O.K.
Mother to Tom: Try again.
Tom to Jane: Please. And a fork, too.
Coded as Willing Compliance

Jane to Tom: Yes, that's what we have.

The transcripts that follow differ from the previous transcript in that
the request made by the parent is either changed by the child or the
request is not followed. In transcripts 2 and 3, the parent makes a
request and the child finds a creative way to respond, thus displaying
his or her agency, or the child modifies the parent's initial request
through negotiation.

Transcript 2: Accommodation

The following transcript is an example of Accommodation in which
Mary, age 4, finds a creative way to respond to her mother's request.

Mother to both children: O.K., tidy up a little bit.
Laura (age 6) to Mary: Mary, we're gonna ... Come on.
Mary to Mother: I don't know where to start.
Mother to Mary: Yeah, that's a big problem.
Why don't you start with the blocks?
Mary to Mother: Mom ... I can do this with my eyes closed.
(She tries to clean up with her eyes shut)
Coded as Accommodation

Transcript 3: Cooperative Negotiation

The following is an example of Cooperative Negotiation in which
David, age 6, displays agency through the use of positive negotiation
strategies – strategies that lead his mother to change her initial request
so that David obtains his wish that his mother stay to play a game with
him.

Mother to both: You and Beth play, Mom finish up her work?
David to Mother: Please can you stay. Beth won't play it right.
Coded as Cooperative Negotiation

Mother to Beth: Will you play nicely with David?
Beth to Mother: (Shakes her head.)
Mother to Beth: What!
David to Mother: Mom, Beth doesn't want to play.
Beth to both: (Vocalization)
Mom to Beth: Beth, you play with David while Mom finishes her
    work.
David to both: Or I'll play all by myself.
Mother to David: You're gonna play all by yourself?
David to both: But I certainly need someone to play with.
Coded as Cooperative Negotiation

Beth to David:I have to do the points [of the game].
David to both: One more game with just me, Mom.
Coded as Cooperative Negotiation

Mother to David: Beth's gonna do your points. She's gonna watch
    you play. How's that?
David to Mother: Well, I still want you to play just one more game,
    please Mom.
Coded as Cooperative Negotiation

Mom to David: (Plays with David for one more game.)

Transcript 4: Uncooperative Negotiation

In the following transcript, Simon, age 6, uses Uncooperative Negotiation. Simon's display of agency results in the initial request made by
Simon's mother being modified so it is suitable to both the child and the
parent. Once the request is redefined, Simon complies with the 'spirit'
of the initial request.

(Simon previously asked Mom to look for the scissors. Mom finds
    the scissors and gives them to Simon. Simon is in the living
    room).
Mother to Simon: Come to the kitchen to cut.

Simon to Mother: Why?
Mother to Simon: It makes life easier if we stay in the kitchen.
Simon to Mother: I want to stay in here.
Coded as Uncooperative Negotiation

Mother to Simon: I'd like you to do it in the kitchen at the table.
Simon to Mother: Why?
Mother to Simon: Because I asked you to.
Simon to Mother: I won't do it at the table.
Coded as Uncooperative Negotiation

Mother to Simon: You can do it on the floor then.
Simon to Mother: (Moves into the kitchen)

Transcript 5: Defiance

In this last example, a sibling alliance in non-compliance is displayed. The mother's request is not complied with by either of the two children in the family. The children work in tandem and the alliance that is formed between them seems too strong for the parent. In the end, the parent 'complies' with the children.

Mother to Tyler (age 6): Tyler, come into the kitchen to have your juice.
Tyler to Mother: I'll wait in the living room.
Coded as Simple Refusal

Mother to Tyler: You are not going to drink it in the living room.
Shelley (age 4) to Tyler: (Picks up two cups in the kitchen. Takes cups to the living room.)
Coded as Defiance Alliance

Mother to both children: (Initially does not respond ... and then says) Be careful not to spill the juice in the living room.

Conclusion

It is increasingly recognized that the study of the child reflects social constructions of a particular time and culture that are unacknowledged and taken for granted. The passive child of socialization theory is one such social construction that has had important ramifications for how the child has been perceived and the kinds of research questions that have been asked. Because the lens of socialization theory has been so limiting in its perspective on the child, attempts are underway to construct a new lens that reveals the child as an agent in family life. Such a project of reconstructing the child is a massive undertaking with important theoretical, methodological, and political challenges. In our most recent work in this area we have found that the interdisciplinary literature on childhood and human agency has been useful in helping us to re-vision the child; the different points of view have helped us to break established patterns of thought that have developed within our own discipline of developmental psychology. The interdisciplinary literature has been especially valuable in alerting us to categories of children's agency that were obscured by early socialization perspectives concerned solely with a limited perspective of parents as disciplinarians and teachers of their children. The lens on children's agency that we have constructed highlights three components of human agency: incorporating autonomy motivation, innovating construction, and strategic action. We believe that this enhanced perspective on children's agency will reveal with greater clarity children's contributions to dynamics of influence and power in the unique context of the parent-child relationship and in family life.

References

Alanen, L. (1990). Growing up in the modern family: Rethinking socialization of the family and childhood. In N. Mandell (Ed.), *Sociological studies of child development* (3rd ed., pp. 13–28). Greenwich, CT: JAI Press.

Alwin, D.F. (1996). Parental socialization in historical perspective. In C.D. Ryff & M.M. Seltzer (Eds.), *The parental experience in midlife*, (pp. 105–167). Chicago: University of Chicago Press.

Ambert, A. (2001). *The effect of children on parents*. Binghamton, NY: Haworth Press.

Baumrind, D. (1971). Current patterns of parental authority. *Developmental Psychology Monograph, 4* (1, Pt. 2).

Bell, R.Q. (1968). A reinterpretation of the direction of effects in studies of socialization. *Psychological Review, 75*, 81–95.

Bell, R.Q., & Chapman, M. (1986). Child effects in studies using experimental or brief longitudinal approaches to socialization. *Developmental Psychology,* *22,* 595–603.

Bell, R.Q., & Harper, L.V. (1977). *Child effects on adults.* Hillsdale, NJ: Erlbaum

Blair, L. (1975). *Rhythms of vision: The changing patterns of belief.* London: Croom Helm.

Brehm, S.S. (1981). Oppositional behavior in children: A reactance theory approach. In S.S. Brehm, S.M. Kassin, & F.K. Gibbons (Eds.), *Developmental social psychology: Theory and research* (pp. 96–121). New York: Oxford University Press.

Corsaro, W.A. (1997). *The sociology of childhood.* Thousand Oaks, CA: Pine Forge Press.

Crockenberg, S., & Litman, C. (1990). Autonomy as competence in 2-year-olds: Maternal correlates of child defiance, compliance, and self-assertion. *Developmental Psychology, 26,* 961–971.

Davidson, G.C. (1973). Counter-control in behavior modification. In L.A. Hamerlynck, L. Handy, & E.J. Mash (Eds.), *Behavior change: methodology and practice* (pp. 153–167). Champaign, IL: Research Press.

Dawber, T., & Kuczynski, L. (1999). The question of owness: Influence of relationship context on parental socialization strategies. *Journal of Social and Personal Relationships, 16,* 475–493.

Eisenberg, A.R. (1992). Conflicts between mothers and their young children. *Merrill-Palmer Quarterly, 38,* 21–43.

Fogel, A. (1993). *Developing through relationships: Origins of communication, self, and culture.* Chicago: University of Chicago Press.

Frankel, J. (1991). On being reared by your children: State of the art as reflected in the literature. *Free Inquiry in Creative Sociology, 19,* 193–200.

Goffman, E. (1961). *Asylums.* New York: Anchor Books.

Grolnick, W.S., Deci, E.L, & Ryan, R.M. (1997). Internationalization within the family: The self-determination theory perspective. In J.E. Grusec & L. Kuczynski (Eds.), *Parenting and children's internalization of values: A handbook of contemporary theory* (pp. 135–161). New York: Wiley.

Grusec, J.E. & Goodnow, J.J. (1994). Impact of parental discipline methods on the child's internalization of values: A reconceptualization of current points of view. *Developmental Psychology, 30,* 4–19.

Grusec, J.E., & Kuczynski, L. (1980). Direction of effect in socialization: A comparison of parent vs. child's behavior as determinants of disciplinary technique. *Developmental Psychology, 16,* 1–9.

Hartup, W.W. (1978). Perspectives on child and family interaction: Past, present and future. In R.M. Lerner & G.B. Spanier (Eds.), *Child influences on marital and family interaction: A life-span perspective* (pp. 23–45). New York: Academic Press.

Hildebrandt, N. & Kuczynski, L. (1998). Children's sense of agency within parent-child and other-child relationships. Paper presented at the 10th Biennial Conference of Child Development, University of Waterloo, Waterloo, Ontario, 9 May 1998.

Hinde, R.A. (1979). *Towards understanding relationships.* London: Academic Press.

Hoffman, L.W. (1988). Cross-cultural differences in child rearing goals. In R.A. LeVine, P.M. Miller, & M.M. West (Eds.), *Parental behavior in diverse societies* (pp. 99–122). San Francisco: Jossey Bass.

Hogan, D.M., Etz, K.E., & Tudge, J.R.H. (1999). Reconsidering the role of children in family research. In C. Shehan (Ed.), *Through the eyes of the child: revisioning children as active agents of family life* (pp. 93–108). Stamford, CT: JAI Press.

Ingram, L.C. (1986). In the crawlspace of the organization. *Human Relations,* 39, 467–486.

James, A., & Prout, A. (1990). Introduction. In A. James & A. Prout (Eds.), *Constructing and reconstructing issues in the sociological study of childhood* (pp. 1–6). London: Falmer Press.

Kelly, H.H., Berscheid, E., Christensen, A., Harvey, J.H., Huston, T.L., Levinger, G., McClintock, E., Peplau, L.A., & Peterson, D. R. (1983). Analysing close relationships. In H. Kelly, E. Berscheid, A. Christensen, J. Harvey, T. Huston, G. Levinger, E. McClintock, L. Peplau, & D. Peterson (Eds.), *Close relationships* (pp. 20–67). New York: Freeman.

Kelly, L. (1988). *Surviving sexual violence.* Minneapolis: University of Minneapolis Press.

Kitzinger, J. (1990). Who are you kidding? Children, power, and the struggle against sexual abuse. In J. Allison & A. Prout (Eds.), *Constructing and reconstructing childhood: Contemporary issues in the sociological study of childhood* (pp. 157–183). London: Falmer Press.

Kochanska, G., & Aksan, N. (1995). Mother-child mutually positive effect, the quality of child compliance to requests and prohibitions, and maternal control as correlates of early internalization. *Child Development,* 66, 236–254.

Kohlberg, L. (1969). Stage and sequence: The cognitive-developmental approach to socialization. In D.A. Goslin (Ed.), *Handbook of socialization theory and research* (pp. 347–480). Chicago: Rand McNally.

Kopp, C.B. (1982). Antecedents of self-regulation: A developmental perspective. *Developmental Psychology, 18,* 199–214.

Kuczynski, L. (2003). Beyond bidirectionality: bilateral conceptual frameworks for studying dynamics in parent-child relations. In L. Kuczynski (Ed.), *Handbook of dynamics in parent-child relations* (pp. 3–24). Thousand Oaks, CA: Sage.

Kuczynski L., & Lollis, S. (2002). Four foundations for a dynamic model of parenting. In J.R.M. Gerris (Ed.), *Dynamics of parenting: International perspectives on nature and sources of parenting* (pp. 445–462). Leuven, Belgium: Garant.

Kuczynski, L., & Hildebrandt, N. (1997). Models of conformity and resistance in socialization theory. In J.E. Grusec & L. Kuczynski (Eds.), *Parenting and the internalization of values: A handbook of contemporary theory* (pp. 227–256). New York: Wiley.

Kuczynski, L., & Kochanska, G. (1990). Development of children's noncompliance strategies from toddlerhood to age 5. *Developmental Psychology, 26,* 398–408.

Kuczynski, L., Kochanska, G., Radke-Yarrow, M., & Gurinius Brown, O. (1987). A developmental interpretation of young children's noncompliance. *Developmental Psychology, 20,* 799–806.

Kuczynski, L., Marshall, S., & Schell, K. (1997). Value socialization in a bidirectional context. In J.E. Grusec & L. Kuczynski (Eds.), *Parenting and the internalization of values: A handbook of contemporary theory* (pp. 23–50). Toronto: John Wiley & Sons.

Lawrence, J., & Valsiner, J. (1993). Conceptual roots of internalization: From transmission to transformation. *Human Development, 36,* 150–167.

Lepper, M. (1983). Social control processes, attributions of motivation, and the internalization of social values. In E.T. Higgins, D.N. Ruble, & W.W. Hartup (Eds.), *Social cognition and social development: A sociological perspective* (pp. 294–330). Cambridge: Cambridge University Press.

Lewis, M., & Feinman, S. (1991). *Social influences and socialization in infancy.* New York: Plenum.

Lewis, M., & Rosenblum, L.A. (1974). *The effect of the infant on its caregiver.* Wiley: New York.

Lollis, S., & Kuczynski, L. (1997). Beyond one hand clapping: Seeing bidirectionality in parent-child relations. *Journal of Social and Personal Relationships, 14,* 441–461.

Lollis, S.P., Ross, H.S., & Tate, E. (1992). Parents' regulation of their children's peer interaction: Direct influences. In R.D. Parke & G.W. Ladd (Eds.), *Family-peer relationships: Modes of linkage* (pp. 255–281). Hillsdale, NJ: Erlbaum.

Maccoby, E.E., & Martin, J.A. (1983). Socialization in the context of the family:

Parent-child interaction. In E.M. Hetherington (Ed.), P.H. Mussen (Series Ed.), *Handbook of child psychology: Vol. 4. Socialization, personality, and social development* (pp. 1–101). New York: Wiley.

Matas, L., Arend, R., & Sroufe, L. (1978). Continuity of adaptation in the second year: The relationship between quality of attachment and later competence. *Child Development, 49,* 547–556.

Mayall, B. (1994). Introduction. In B. Mayall (Ed.), *Children's childhoods: Observed and experienced* (pp. 1–12). Washington, DC: Falmer Press.

McQuillen, J.S. (1986). The development of listener-adapted compliance-resisting strategies. *Human Communication Research, 12,* 359–375.

Mead, G.H. (1934). *Mind, self and society.* Chicago: University of Chicago Press.

Morrow, V. (2003). Perspectives on children's agency within families. A view from the sociology of childhood. In L. Kuczynski (Ed.), *Handbook of dynamics in parent-child relations* (pp. 109–129). Thousand Oaks, CA: Sage Publications.

Palkovitz, R. (1996). Parenting as a generator of adult development: Conceptual issues and implications. *Journal of Social and Personal Relationships, 13,* 571–592.

Parke, R.D. (1974). Rules, roles and resistance to deviation in children: Explorations in punishment, discipline, and self-control. In A. Pick (Ed.), *Minnesota symposia on child psychology* (Vol. 8). Minneapolis: University of Minnesota Press.

Patterson, G.R. (1982). *Coercive family process.* Eugene, OR: Castalia

Patterson, G., Reid, J., & Dishion, T. (1992). *Antisocial boys: Vol. 4. A social interactional approach.* Eugene, OR: Castalia.

Pelzer, D. (1995). *A child called it.* Dearfield Beach, FL: Health Communications.

Perlman, M., & Ross, H.S. (1997). Who's the boss? Parents' failed attempts to influence the outcomes of conflicts between their children. *Journal of Social and Personal Relationships, 14,* 463–480.

Piaget, J. (1965). *The moral judgment of the child.* (M. Gabain, Trans.) New York: Free Press. (Original work published 1932)

Punch, S. (2001). Negotiating autonomy: Childhoods in rural Bolivia. In L. Alanen and B. Mayall (Eds.), *Conceptualizing child-adult relations* (pp. 23–36). London: Routledge-Farmer.

Reiss, H.T., Collins, W.A., & Berscheid, E. (2000). The relationship context of human behavior and development. *Psychological Bulletin, 126,* 844–872.

Reynolds, P. (1991). *Dance civet cat: Child labour in the Zambezi Valley.* Athens: Ohio University Press.

Rheingold, H.L. (1969). The social and socializing infant. In D.A. Goslin (Ed.),

Handbook of socialization theory and research (pp. 779–790). Chicago: Rand McNally.

Rheingold, H.L., Cook, K.V., & Kolowitz, V. (1987). Commands activate the behavior and pleasure of 2-year-old children. *Developmental Psychology, 23,* 146–151.

Ross, H.S., Filyer, R.E., Lollis, S.P., Perlman, M., & Martin, J.L. (1994). Administering justice in the family. *Journal of Family Psychology, 8,* 254–273.

Ross, H.S., & Lollis, S.P. (1987). Communication within infant social games. *Developmental Psychology, 23,* 241–248.

Rowe, D. (1994). *The limits of family influence: Genes, experience, and behavior.* New York: Guilford Press.

Rubin, K.H., Bukowski, W., & Parker, J.G. (1998). Peer interactions, relationships, and groups. In W. Damon (Series Ed.) & N. Eisenberg (Vol. Ed.), *Handbook of child psychology: Vol. 3. Social, Emotional, and Personality Development* (pp. 619–700). New York: John Wiley and Sons.

Sanson, A., & Rothbart, M.K. (1995). Child temperament and parenting. In M.H. Bornstein (Ed.), *Handbook of parenting: Vol. 4. Applied and practical parenting* (pp. 299–323). Mahwah, NJ: Erlbaum.

Sapir, E. (1934). The emergence of the concept of personality in a study of cultures. *Journal of Social Psychology, 5,* 408–415.

Scarr, S. (1992). Developmental theories for the 1990s: Developmental and individual differences. *Child Development, 63,* 1–19.

Scarr, S. (1993). Biological and cultural diversity. The legacy of Darwin for development. *Child Development, 64,* 1333–1353.

Scarr, S., & McCartney, K. (1983). How people make their own environments: A theory of genotype-environment effects. *Child Development, 54,* 424–435.

Scott, J.C. (1990). *Domination and the arts of resistance.* New Haven, CT: Yale University Press.

Seligman, M.P.E. (1975). *Helplessness: On depression, development and death.* San Francisco: Freeman.

Shehan, C.L., & Seccombe, C. (1996). The changing circumstances of children's lives. *Journal of Family Issues, 17(4),* 435–444.

Skinner, E.A. (1995). *Perceived control, motivation, and coping.* Thousand Oaks, CA: Sage.

Stern, D. (1977). *The first relationship.* Cambridge, MA: Harvard University Press.

Strauss, C. (1992). Models and motives. In R.G. D'Andrade & C. Strauss (Eds.), *Human motives and cultural models* (pp. 1–20). New York: Cambridge University Press.

Ta, L., Kuczynski, L., Bernardini, S.C., & Harach, L. (1999, April). *Parents' perceptions of children's influence in the context of the parent-child relationship.* Paper presented at the Society for Research in Child Development, Albuquerque, New Mexico.

Trommsdorff, G., & Kornadt H.-J. (2003). Parent-child relations in cross-cultural perspective. In L. Kuczynski (Ed.), *Handbook of dynamics in parent-child relations* (pp. 271–306). London: Sage.

Twain, Mark. (1865). Advice for little girls. <http://www.readbookonline.net/readOnLine/659/>.

Vuchinich, S. (1987). Starting and stopping spontaneous family conflicts. *Journal of Marriage in the Family, 49,* 591–601.

Wade, A. (1997). Small acts of living: Everyday acts of resistance to violence and other forms of oppression. *Contemporary Family Therapy, 19,* 23–39.

Wenar, C. (1982). On negativism. *Human Development, 25,* 1–23.

White, R.W. (1959). Motivation reconsidered. The concept of competence. *Psychological Review, 66,* 297–333.

Wrong, D.H. (1961). The oversocialized conception of man in modern sociology. *American Sociological Review, 26,* 183–193.

10

Childhood's Ends

JOHN WILLINSKY

In thinking about what we might want from childhood – that we would feel compelled to subject children through this project to multiple lenses and images, dispersed across time, space, and disciplines – the contributors to this book do a wonderful job of addressing different ways of knowing and using *childhood* as a means not only of understanding the very young, but ourselves in the largest sense. My original part in this project of composing a composite image of childhood was to work with the literary landscape set out by Naomi Sokoloff in these books through her reading of two novels. Her reading of the principal child-character in these works of literature demonstrates, for this book as a whole, how much representations of children and childhood have to say about lives that extend well beyond that seemingly magical time.

One advantage of Naomi Sokoloff's chapter is that it deals directly with a fictional world of childhood, with adult make-believe about the age of make-believe. Although she wisely advises caution over making claims about children using the lens of literature as a guide, we are all at a remove from this experience, all working in the realm of childhood represented out of adult interests. With literature, at least, there is no epistemological dilemma over the adequacy of the warrants we possess in claiming to possess this or that knowledge of children. Yet if literature is bound by claims of the imagination rather than claims to reality, it serves as all the more a caution for how we are led, by such feats of representation, to act on the world. This was, after all, the lesson that was to be drawn from the hapless misadventures of Don Quixote, the all-too-errant knight tilting at the windmills of his bookish imagination. Given that power of representation, the multiple focal points found in this book might be seen as enabling readers to check the reflection of their own interests against the disciplinary perspectives and concerns represented here. That literature wears its fallibility on its sleeve (or dust jacket) only means that literary study has much to teach us about what we would ask of the different forms of knowledge in this academic institution, in their tireless effort to make greater sense of the world we inhabit.

How are we to take seriously a source of understanding that has famously proclaimed its 'poetic faith' in 'the willing suspension of disbelief,' to use Coleridge's formulation? Literature's very art is to confound scientific demands for veracity and validity. The ability to replicate an experiment is not at issue, except in that mythopoeic structural sense which Northrop Frye (1957) made his life's work of literacy analysis. The literary work's reliability claim is, as a rule, posthumously awarded. Literature has no stake in a cumulative effect, in the sense of building up or piecing together knowledge, nor does it labour at constructing a stable platform of methodology from which to stand and observe phenomena, a point that Sokoloff makes apparent by drawing on Robert Alter's celebration of literature's 'unpredictability' and the 'quicksilver mobility of its uses of perspective.'

It might seem, then, that literature's approach to a knowledge of the child is thoroughly post-epistemological, as literature's great philosopher friend Richard Rorty might have it. It is not so much antifoundational, in an aggressive post-structural sense, as afoundational. It is not so much about a world that can uncover in its workings as it is a world made by hand. Or as Northrop Frye offered (long before the science wars over constructivism and realism): 'Literature belongs to the world that man constructs, not the world he sees' (1963, p. 8). We have only to extend that literary concept in thinking about childhood, I am suggesting, to appreciate how what we see is so much a matter of what we construct.

This sense of a world put together, which includes a world of childhood, and which is worthy of study for just how it is put together, might be directed at Foucault's conundrum, if I can call it that. His study of the human sciences led him to posit humankind as an object of knowledge of relatively recent concern. He dared, in fact, to consider at the conclusion of *The Order of Things: An Archaeology of the Human Sciences* that 'man [and thus the child] is an invention of recent date. And one perhaps nearing its end' (1970, p. 387). The possibility of understanding our own invention, which lies within this otherwise dour projection, is all about seeing more clearly how we have been constructed, in Frye's

sense, and how we might imagine it otherwise. It is about the importance of focusing on what we have made of ourselves through this
assemblage of images, lenses, and disciplines, in the terms of this book.
The aim is not to avoid mistaking what we observe for a fixed human
nature that we must somehow realize. What is at issue is not the nature
of the child born free but, rather, the values by which we are bound, and
our responsibilities for realizing values such as respect and equality
among children and adults.

Such critical reflections on the nature of knowledge, then, are not
meant to undermine what we can make of the world. They are, in fact,
intended to increase the possibilities of working with that made world,
in order to see that a primary responsibility of knowing, in the human
sciences, is to improve the world for, among others, those whom we
designate children (see, e.g., the chapters by Hansen, Lamb, and Mistry
& Diez in this volume). This increased sense of responsibility for the
human condition seems especially critical in the face of, for example,
the rising presence of an 'evolutionary psychology' that would ground
a knowledge of humanity in a Darwinian calculus of survival (Badcock
2000). Literature points to a knowing that makes no pretence to being
grounded in an original nature (or sin) to which we need yield.

Having come to this point on literature's place in learning about
childhood, I wonder if we could do more to consider what literature has
to teach us about the disciplines that would study the true nature of
child – even as literature is not a discipline itself but, like the child, is an
object of intense disciplined study. One critical lesson here is found in
Solokoff's point that the actual writing of literature is rare enough for
even the most prodigious of child prodigies, who have otherwise been
known to possess great musical and artistic gifts. Yet literature is the
first of the arts that is directed at childhood, whether through family
story-telling or the proverbial bedtime story (so often taken today as a
reading-readiness exercise).

The child's early immersion in literature's ways of knowing, especially children's stories and literature, may explain why literature provides such a fine lens for studying the nature of childhood. The very
sensibility and awareness children have of themselves as *children* is
bound to be shaped by this immersion. The story provides a framework
for the child's sense-making. It provides a means of reflecting on, as
well as judging, just how the world works, which the helter-skelter
activity of the day may not otherwise afford. This is only to say that
among the disciplines concerned with the child, literature works di-

rectly on the child's understanding of the world. And yet, the human sciences are not so far behind. A discipline such as developmental psychology asserts a less direct influence as popularizations of its findings pervade child-rearing practices by parents and teachers in ways that also inform the sense that the child makes of the world.

What does this early and direct exposure to literature mean for the child? Well, it gives truth to the Wildeism that life imitates art. Storytelling gives a narrative shape to our so-called lives from an early age, as children make up stories about themselves, their toys, and those about them. As we try to look at childhood through the lens of literature, we are in the grips of the same instinct for story and sense. We are seeing a reflection of ourselves in the lens, even as we are looking through it at a childhood that we did not experience. The lens is a device for projection as well as viewing.

This point is made by Solokoff, as she cautions us that the children's voices that we listen to so intently in literature 'often tell us a great deal more about adult concerns that are projected onto children than about children themselves.' Yet, rather than take this as entirely about literature's failing, consider, instead, the degree to which Solokoff's sense of projected concerns is true of the other lenses presented in this volume – psychological (Lamb; Kuczynski & Lollis), physiological (Hansen), historical (Benzaquén), spiritual (Scott), cultural (Mistry & Diez), or legal (McGillivray) – that we would use to catch sight of childhood. It is easy to see that most of what we study about children is driven by adult concerns with the health, education, and safety of children, with the focus on establishing the normative and appropriate behaviours that reassure us of having acted responsibly on their, and our own, behalf. What we can learn from literature, no less than from research, is truly *about* the child in the sense that it affects children's experiences, and the stories they hear as well as shaping the structuring of their days. Yet that is because so much of childhood is itself a projection of historically and culturally contingent adult concerns, beginning with the very concept of a distinct, multifaceted stage of life known as *childhood*.

It is tempting to imagine that children speak and think in ways that are unmediated and untouched by adults and their concerns, and that well-designed research experiments (or exceptionally sensitive and retentive fiction writers) are able to put us in touch with these voices and ideas. We might, then, know and act on the 'truth of the child,' which will enable us, in turn, to avoid the miseducation, if not the misshaping, of the child. If this sounds familiar, it may be because it is what inspired Jean-Jacques Rousseau to publish, in 1762, his fictional course of study for Émile. Rousseau hoped to prevent Émile's natural disposition from being corrupted and disfigured by adult opinion: 'It is, then, to these original dispositions [of the child] that everything must be related' (1979, p. 39). To the contrary, I am suggesting, there is no original disposition, no way of speaking or thinking, that exists apart from 'the hands of man,' as Rousseau puts it, in his book's opening sentence, in which 'everything degenerates' (p. 37).

The danger is not so much an author appropriating the child's voice through a work of literature, although I appreciate Solokoff's caution in this regard. Rather, the danger is in assuming, with any work of literary or scholarly inquiry, that the child harbours an original, untouched voice, an otherwise unheard but articulate sense of the world, which exists apart from the language and words that we know and use. The danger is in forgetting that we are studying what we have already made of childhood, as a site of caring, learning, development, and socialization. The lens at issue here is childhood itself. We project what we want of ourselves through childhood, and the various lenses applied in this book to childhood come together to sharpen the projected image. Paying attention to the lens is as good a way as we have of understanding what we want of children, of the ends that they serve in the world that we construct.

This is why it is to literature's advantage that it makes such an art and craft out of a writer's ability to mediate a child's words and thoughts, as Sokoloff describes it. She demonstrates the advantages of this mediation in her skilful reading of Momik in David Grossman's *See Under: Love* and Aviya in Gila Almagor's *The Summer of Aviya*. Those projections of children, Solokoff makes apparent, have everything to do with casting greater light on the poignancy of our own situation, in simply sucking on a piece of bread at dinner or wearing a yogurt moustache. What these authors describe is not the sense or meaning that a child has made of life, but the sense and meaning that we can make of childhood as a way of understanding our own lives.

This does suggest, I realize, that the child is used by literature in a way that seems totally contrary to the other disciplines that are about the child *qua* child. Yet I am also arguing here that these literary projections actually do capture aspects of the child, insofar as children have nowhere else to live but within the landscapes of prevailing literary and disciplined projections (while those projections can differ radically between cultures and across ages). There is hardly any other way of living. There is no form of life for a child (or for us) apart from those projections, with those few exceptions that we often frame as mental illness, which understandably trouble us deeply.

It is not just that children's voices are always already shaped by the language they inhabit; if this were not the case, then we would not be able to understand these children's voices. Or, as Ludwig Wittgenstein says – with his typical aphoristic twist – 'if a lion could talk, we could not understand him' (1958, p. 223). He is referring, I would hold (with as much certainty as I can muster around this king of the philosophical beasts), to how a shared form of life is critical to comprehension, and the children we study are critical to the form of our own lives. For if children tried to speak to us from this other place, from this uncorrupted nature, then we would not understand them (think of the incomprehensibility of wild and feral children, in trying to understand how they lived and in how little they end up telling us of it). And yet, sometimes they do speak in incomprehensible ways and sometimes we do not understand them. But rarely do they do so in literature.

Between the covers of a book, children tend to make eminent sense. Their very innocence becomes the source of our insight, as Solokoff makes wonderfully apparent with Momik and Aviya. The clarity and coherence of their projected thoughts would seem to represent what a lens does best: it brings a diffuse world into focus. That we use childhood to bring focus to our own lives is not so much a bad or deceptive thing. It is a reminder that literature, no less than our other intellectual efforts, contributes to the very sense and sensibility of the world that we construct. It is a reminder that we have always to study the lens that we would fabricate, to take critical note of our methods, as they form a source of clarity not otherwise available to us.

This will help us to appreciate the earnestness with which we seek to use childhood, as Rousseau imagined we could, to recover the uncorrupted qualities of (human) nature, 'as it leaves the hands of the Author of things,' that is, when 'everything is good' (1979, p. 37). It will help us to interpret the remarkable scientific precision we would apply to measure the learning, deviation, and achievements of the child. If each of these lenses, whether literary or scholarly, is a projectionist's device, a way of bringing what we've made of the world into focus, then we can bring this or that element into greater focus, larger than life, with an eye to reforming it as best we can against its subtle injustices and unconscionable cruelties, especially as they are visited on children.

The most notable example of how literature has been able to do just that is in the sometimes chilling fiction of childhood that Charles Dickens spun, working as he did, in part, with the Parliamentary Blue Books, which contained testimony on the nineteenth-century horrors of child labour and crime (Benzaquén; McGillivray). Here was literature working, pen in hand, with parliamentary commissions, an emergent social science, and journalism, to address the unconscionable state of childhood. Solokoff approaches the same point with her reflections on David Grossman's ability to bring issues of the Holocaust to the forefront of Israeli awareness. It is not that literature is somehow compelled to join in crusades against social injustice, especially in Dickens's melodramatic fashion, even when it comes to protecting children. Rather, it simply has to refuse to turn away from those cruelties and injustices; it has to find its stories within the landscapes that are not otherwise told or represented.

I also recognize that even as I would place literature at the head of these disciplines, it is more often set off from the academic concerns considered in this volume on images of childhood. The distance imagined between these two cultures, literary and scientific, is nowhere better represented than in William Wordsworth's childhood projections. In 'The Prelude, Or Growth of a Poet's Mind,' Wordsworth holds up a childhood that must be protected against an incipient science of education. He was not happy with the prospect that 'mighty workmen of our later age ... who have the skill / To manage books, make them act / On infant minds.' These mighty workman are declared the enemies of childhood and imagination, and thus the growth of the poet's mind. They are 'sages who in their prescience would control / All accidents' (1971, V, ll. 347–56). Against such ordering, Wordsworth counters by pointing to 'the unreasoning progress of the world,' while extolling the value of 'our most unfruitful hours' (ll. 359, 363). This fourteen-book verse study of the child-poet makes a strong case for the unfettered development of the imagination against the controlled demands of book managers.

Yet even as Wordsworth claims imagination to be the true intellectual capital of the poetic and literary soul, literature need not be seen as so removed from the disciplines that would focus on the child. I cannot help feeling that Wordsworth gets the point of crossover between the poet and the scholar exactly right when he holds, in the Preface of *Lyrical Ballads*, that 'the Poet binds together by passion and knowledge the vast empire of human society' (1927, p. 182). Certainly, in the study of childhood we are surely past imagining that there is a knowing that exists apart from our feeling for children. Consider the issue of whether children should spend a good portion of their hours in, to use Wordsworth's term, unfruitful activity (through free and imaginative play) or fruitful activities (focused on pre-school readiness). Scholars may line up on both sides of the question, but they are matched in their passion for improving the lives of children as reflected in measures that sound thoroughly unpoetic, such as the child's school achievement, sociability markers, employment record, or lifetime earnings. What we would understand of childhood is no less mediated by the nature of the genre in which scholars would construct this knowledge, controlled experimental laboratory design or school-yard participant-observation, be archival research or free verse.

The voices of children in literature, as in any disciplined look at childhood, are about what is lost and found in each of us. They are about how we have it in us to make the world anew, first through the imagination, and then through a passion and knowledge that we often invest in children and childhood, as we never tire of treating them as the source of a better future. To ask what we want from children is to ask after the desire to know what sense can be made of our own lives, not as given but as imagined. And this positive and necessary sense of the world, as first imagined, and then tested and pursued in its consequences, is what establishes the value of turning these many lenses onto the child.

References

Badcock, C.R. (2000). *Evolutionary psychology: A critical introduction*. Cambridge: Polity.

Foucault, M. (1970). *Order of things: An archeology of the human sciences*. New York: Vintage.

Frye, N. (1957). *Anatomy of criticism: Four essays*. Princeton, NJ: Princeton University Press.

Frye, N. (1963). *The educated imagination*. Toronto: Canadian Broadcasting Corporation.

Rousseau, J.-J. (1979). *Émile, or on education* (A. Bloom, Trans.). New York: Basic Books.

Wordsworth, W. (1971). *The prelude* (J.C. Maxwell, Ed.). New Haven, CT: Yale University Press. (Original published in 1850)

Wordsworth, W. (1927). Observations prefixed to the second edition of *Lyrical Ballads*. In *The prelude to poetry: The English poets in defence and praise of their own art* (pp. 168–198). London: Dent. (Original published in 1800)

Wittgenstein, L. (1958). *Philosophical investigations* (G.E.M. Anscombe, Trans.). London: Macmillan. (Original published in 1953)

Contributors

ADRIANA S. BENZAQUÉN, History Department, Mount Saint Vincent University

VIRGINIA DIEZ, Eliot-Pearson Department of Child Development, Tufts University

HILLEL GOELMAN, Human Early Learning Partnership, University of British Columbia

MARCI J. HANSON, Department of Special Education, San Francisco State University

SUSAN HERRINGTON, School of Landscape Architecture, University of British Columbia

LEON KUCZYNSKI, Department of Family Relations and Applied Nutrition, University of Guelph

MICHAEL E. LAMB, Developmental Psychology, Cambridge University

SUSAN LOLLIS, Department of Family Relations and Applied Nutrition, University of Guelph

SHEILA K. MARSHALL, School of Social Work and Family Studies, University of British Columbia

ANNE MCGILLIVRAY, Faculty of Law, University of Manitoba

JAYANTHI MISTRY, Eliot-Pearson Department of Child Development, Tufts University

SALLY ROSS, Community and Regional Planning Consultant, Vancouver, BC

DANIEL SCOTT, School of Child and Youth Care, University of Victoria

NAOMI SOKOLOFF, Department of Near Eastern Languages and Civilization, University of Washington

JOHN WILLINSKY, Department of Language and Literacy Education, University of British Columbia